PRAISE FOR THE KING AND DR. NICK

Dr. George Nichopoulos is one of the kindest men I know. He is a good man, and I'm glad to call him my friend. He has seen me through some tough times and I believe he helped save my life. Not many have the love and compassion Dr. Nick has for people. I am proud to say Dr. Nick is one of my best friends. God bless you, Dr. Nick.

> — Entertainer Jerry Lee Lewis, Rock and Roll Hall of Fame Inductee

Leave aside what you've previously read and this much-needed book will unbend your mind. It'll fill in many gaps regarding an incredibly close friendship and finally tell the truth about how it all ended. To produce a mighty book you must have a mighty story, and there is none more so than this.

> — Andrew Hearn, editor and publisher, *Essential Elvis UK* magazine

A remarkable first person account of the toll of fame on an American icon. It reminds us of the humanity, generosity of spirit, humor and enormous talent of the King of rock 'n' roll. You won't be able to put it down.

> — Michael Rose, producer of *Elvis: Return to Tupelo*

After reading this book, in my opinion you will discover that Nick (Dr.) was more than a "personal physician" to EP. He was a mentor, a confidante, and a friend. He really cared about the man—inside and out!

> — Joe Guercio, music director (Elvis Presley)

The King and Dr. Nick is an exciting, powerful and important memoir, revealing a sweeter, stronger Elvis than we have seen before. Finally, after 40 years of relative silence, the man at the center of it all delivers a rich and poignant story—easily outdistancing the scores of "tell alls" that have come before. When he focuses on the entertainer's drug use, Elvis' doctor also sweeps away the thick cobwebs surrounding Presley's death—thereby producing an intimate and clear picture of the final hours that have so mystified and fascinated the world. In many ways, this is THE insider account.

> — Peter Harry Brown and Pat H. Broeske, authors of *Down at the End of Lonely Street: the Life and Death of Elvis Presley*

The King and Dr. Nick: What Really Happened to Elvis and Me is a compelling memoir by Dr. George Nichopoulos, physician to the King of Rock 'n' Roll. This heartfelt account of Dr. Nick's personal and professional relationship with Elvis has something to offer everyone. For fans, new information comes to light regarding Elvis's struggle with an array of health problems. For biographers and journalists, a fuller story of his death and the controversy over the autopsy is revealed. For scholars, each new personal account from someone in Elvis's inner circle reworks and expands the Presley mythology.

Dr. Nick's account adds another piece to the puzzle—one missing for too long— regarding the events surrounding Elvis's death and the path that led him there. With each year that passes, it becomes crucial to collect the memories, points of view, and recollections of all those who were close to Elvis for the record. While their experiences with Elvis continue to comfort, inspire, and even haunt them on a personal level, Elvis is part of our history now—and their experiences belong to the ages.

> — Susan Doll, author of *Elvis for
> Dummies*; *Elvis: American Idol*;
> and *Understanding Elvis*

History needs villains, and so Dr. Nick has been cast in the popular Elvis Presley story. His own version of events, not surprisingly, differs from the prevailing narrative. In the days before addiction was public fare, before the creation of the Betty Ford Center and other celebrity retreats, the medical doctor was counselor, confidante, and gatekeeper. From the call that brought Dr. Nichopoulos into Elvis's world to the wreckage that his world became in the wake of his patient's death, it's a narrative that can't be anticipated. Tragedy looms large, but so does hope.

> — Robert Gordon, author of *It Came
> From Memphis*; director of *Respect
> Yourself: The Stax Records Story*

We as a culture love to dissect our heroes, but are loathe to resuscitate our villains. To shine today's understanding upon yesterday's dilemmas, to shed new light on past wrongs, to complicate good and evil with vulnerability, innocence and hope for a future not yet certain—this is why Dr. Nick's memoir was written and why it must be read.

> — Tara McAdams, author of *The
> Elvis Handbook*

THE KING AND DR. NICK

What Really Happened to Elvis and Me

George Nichopoulos, MD

with Rose Clayton Phillips

THOMAS NELSON
Since 1798

NASHVILLE   DALLAS   MEXICO CITY   RIO DE JANEIRO

Published in Nashville, Tennessee, by Thomas Nelson. Thomas Nelson is a registered trademark of Thomas Nelson, Inc.

Thomas Nelson, Inc., titles may be purchased in bulk for educational, business, fund-raising, or sales promotional use. For information, please e-mail SpecialMarkets@ ThomasNelson.com.

Library of Congress Cataloging-in-Publication Data

Nichopoulos, George, 1927–
    The King and Dr. Nick : what really happened to Elvis and me / George Nichopoulos with Rose Clayton Phillips.
        p. cm.
    Includes bibliographical references.
    ISBN 978-1-59555-171-9
    1. Presley, Elvis, 1935-1977. 2. Rock musicians—United States—Biography. 3. Presley, Elvis, 1935–1977—Death and burial. 4. Nichopoulos, George, 1927– 5. Presley, Elvis, 1935–1977—Friends and associates. I. Phillips, Rose Clayton. II. Title.
ML420.P96N53 2009
782.42166092—dc22
    [B]   2009041930

Printed in the United States of America

09 10 11 12 13 WC 6 5 4 3 2 1

For Daniel Brookoff, MD, PhD
and
Robert L. Green

CONTENTS

AUTHOR'S NOTE

George Nichopoulos, MD

Contrary to what I would like to confess, this is *not* an objective account of my life with Elvis Presley and what really happened between us during his lifetime and to us as a result of his death. My memories of our times together are emotionally based, anchored by the pain of living them. Even now my happiest times are clouded by the sadness of Elvis leaving us much too soon.

The account of my friendship with one of the most written-about personalities in history is my attempt to help readers understand a very private man, whose humble life conflicted so drastically with his famous public image.

It is as truthful as my memory can recall the facts, but it would be futile for me to claim that it is anything but tainted by the love I have for this fascinating and sensitive man, one of my dearest friends.

This story bears little resemblance to those of Elvis and me that I have read in other books. Everyone's story of Elvis comes, as mine does, from an interpretation of what we *saw* at the time, what he was willing to share with us, how others reacted, and how we were affected. Never did I imagine how ordinary actions and simple conversations would play out in the pages of history. Actions have consequences, and part of knowing ourselves is learning how others see us. People I have written about here will obviously feel the same way as they view my personal observations about them and my attempts to make sense of all we shared together. Writing a memoir is an exercise in separating fact from opinion, evaluations from judgment, and truth from wishful thinking.

I learned many lessons from my life with Elvis. I would like to believe that all of us close to him would have created different scenarios if we had known the end at the beginning. One of the cruelest aspects of death is that it deprives us of second chances.

Elvis's glamorous image changed with time, but not nearly as drastically as critics would have people believe. His decline, downfall, or unmaking, as other writers like to call it, has been grossly exaggerated—magnified by the tragedy of his untimely death. Elvis's life story, still today, focuses more on how he died than on how he lived. That is the biggest tragedy of all.

I doubt this book will set the record straight for those already invested in the "cover-up" theory or for those who relish the tabloid versions of Elvis's life. This book is for those who are open to a different perspective—an intimate look at my life with Elvis, our challenges, and the battles we won, as well as those we lost. It is for those who can profit from knowing how suddenly and drastically a person's life can be altered by incorrect perceptions that distort reality. In the end this is a story about a rush to judgment and the damage done when people choose to listen to others rather than think for themselves. Mainly it is about how I found my peace and learned to accept circumstances I could not change.

— Dr. Nick

October 29, 2009

INTRODUCTION

T hose of us who are patients, friends, and fans of Dr. George Nichopoulos (and there are many) have tried for years to persuade him to tell his story—what it was like to be the personal physician to Elvis Presley, one of the world's most famous entertainers. Because of his loyalty to his beloved friend, the doctor refused . . . until now.

I first met the distinguished physician in 1964. My doctor was out of town, so I went to the emergency room at St. Joseph Hospital in Memphis. I was twenty at the time and scared. I checked in with a painful infection that turned out to be minor and was easily handled with an antibiotic prescription. I recognized immediately that there was something very special about the soft-spoken, prematurely gray doctor with the strange name who was treating me. He had a gift. I was convinced by his gentle, intuitive approach that he was born to be a doctor. From that day forward, "Dr. Nick" became *my* doctor. Still to this day I call him if I have a medical question.

When my precious daughter Kimberley had an unusual medical challenge during her senior year in high school, I called Dr. Nick at home early in the morning—not the pediatrician who had treated her all her life. Dr. Nick walked through that ordeal with us and spent many hours doing the necessary research to help me find our way to a program in San Diego, California, that led to her full recovery and remission. His evident and genuine concern reassured us. That compassionate connection, which he forms so easily with people, is a vital part of who he is.

Over the years I have sent many of my friends, family members, and even strangers to Dr. Nick. The feedback has always been positive. His patients could fill another book with success stories about his medical knowledge and ability to correctly diagnose problems that were beyond the reach of specialists and which in many cases saved a patient's life.

My friendship with Dr Nick survived my moves outside the city of Memphis. He was my mentor. He inspired and encouraged me in the pursuit of my Bachelor of Professional Studies degree majoring in substance abuse. We have kept in touch over the past forty-five years.

I experienced one of my fondest memories of Dr. Nick while I was living in Miami, Florida. I was married and a new mother. Dr. Nick called with an invitation to attend a concert and meet Elvis. My husband and I drove to Jacksonville to attend my first-ever live performance. Afterward Dr. Nick took us to Elvis's suite to meet "the king." I was instantly struck with the magic of the man. When I commented to Elvis that his appeal seemed to be extremely broad—from young children to their grandmothers—he said, "I know, is that not amazing?" He excused himself for a minute and then returned with a diamond-encrusted belt he had received in Las Vegas. He was like a kid with a trophy and seemed genuinely surprised by his own fame. Elvis was charming and very humble. That was something else he and Dr. Nick shared.

Later I was invited to go on other tours. I was moved and deeply touched by the magnitude of the challenge that rested on Dr. Nick's shoulders. There were many people traveling with Elvis who apparently had agendas other than Elvis's good health. Dr. Nick's mission, however, was to prolong and enrich this fragile and gifted life. It seemed clear to me that Dr. Nick gave far more than he took from that friendship, as is his style. It was also obvious to me that Elvis knew Dr. Nick's being there was never about the money and certainly not about the fame.

One particular trip to Chicago reminded me of that. I watched, with the fresh eyes of an outsider, the drama that surrounded the entertainer, the boss, the CEO, who provided the income for so many people, and his observant doctor. The morning after the performance, we all gathered in Elvis's suite while he ate breakfast, since he didn't like to eat alone. It was very early and Elvis had just awakened. His hair was a mess. He had not shaved, and he was sitting in a blue robe watching the *Today Show* on television. There was a little small talk; Elvis would say something funny and everyone would laugh and then return to silence. Elvis made a disparaging remark when a famous entertainer began singing on the show. Feeling uncomfortable I left the suite and went downstairs to the hotel coffee shop, where I found an interesting book, ordered coffee, and started reading *You Were Born on a Rotten Day*.

Dr. Nick came downstairs and found me. I told Dr. Nick about the book, went back to my room, and started packing to leave for Dallas, the next stop on the tour. After we were all seated on the plane, Elvis walked on. He looked magnificent. I could hardly believe it was the same man. Like many people he cleaned up very well, but unlike the rest of us, he could not go anywhere without looking his best. Dr. Nick asked for my book and handed it to Elvis, who read it aloud during our flight, entertaining the entire group. Elvis loved to read, and he loved to laugh even more. It was very touching to see how Dr. Nick cared for other people's feelings and the extent he would go to brighten up their lives—even briefly.

I have often wondered what Elvis would think about all the attention given to his life after all these years. I feel sure he would be unable to imagine the problems faced by his close friend Dr. Nick. I believe he would be greatly saddened by what happened to this dear, caring man that took him away from his life's calling and all the patients he could have helped over the years.

The simple truth is that we are all wounded soldiers in God's army. This is, however, not another book about Elvis, the superstar with all the scars. It is a warm and loving story about the friendship between two men: one a talented and famous entertainer, the other a successful and gifted doctor. I witnessed firsthand how very important these two human beings were to each other, and it touched my heart. I am sure there were times that returning to his practice appealed to Dr. Nick and would have certainly pleased his many patients. Not being a person to give up on any patient, however, particularly the difficult ones, he weathered the storms and stood the test of time. I know that Elvis valued him for doing that.

In the autumn of his years, Dr. Nick tells his story in a way that is fresh, revealing, and inspirational. In so doing he reveals the shy, humble young man—the superstar whom you will fall in love with all over again. The bond between these two special people, as expressed so well in this book, will only enhance your memory of Elvis. The many friends, fans, and patients of Dr. Nick ask only that you read this book with a curious mind and an open heart.

Someone said, "We will be the same next year as we are today, except for the people we meet and the books we read." Read this book and be prepared to change your thoughts about the king and Dr. Nick.

— Patricia (Harp) Levine, BPS
October 10, 2009

REFLECTION OF A KING

Artist, Ronnie McDowell/Poster photographed by Frederick Toma.

"Some people want to believe Elvis a failure because admitting the magnitude of his success would make their own shortcomings unbearable. Others want to see Elvis as a king, some kind of savior, because granting him such stature places him outside the common realm, beyond criticism but also beyond emulation. Either way, those who hold these simplistic views are exempt from having to live up to the great challenge lives such as Elvis Presley's present to us: the challenge of seizing the chance to invent ourselves and, in the process, reinvent the world."

— DAVE MARSH
Elvis, 1982

ONE

KINDRED SPIRITS

Graceland, home of Elvis Presley, Memphis, Tennessee, the second most visited home in America next to the White House.

D r. Nichopoulos. Paging Dr. George Nichopoulos," announced the anonymous voice from the hospital intercom. At the same time, the beeper attached to my belt chirped.

What now? I thought, hesitating with my hand on the cold, steel exit bar, ready to push open the heavy side door. *May as well answer*, I thought, closing out the humid air on that smoldering hot day in Memphis—Tuesday, August 16, 1977.

"Dr. Nichopoulos. Paging Dr. Nichopoulos."

More chirping from my pager.

There had been a time when hearing my name called over the intercom was exciting for me—the same way I'd heard doctors paged on television: "Calling Dr. Kildare." That was sometime between my Boy Scouts days and medical school. Dr. Marcus Welby, MD, was my idol back then. Those were the days when doctors were the most respected members in a community—the link between life and death. I had liked Dr. Welby's approach, his gentle bedside manner, the way he was always available to his patients.

"Dr. Nichopoulos. Paging Dr. George Nichopoulos."

The personal pager on my belt beeped a third time.

What in the world is going on? I wondered, heading promptly to the nearest telephone and punching in the number.

"This is Dr. Nick," I said firmly into the receiver, knowing I would soon be heading in the direction of the call—Graceland, the home of my famous patient Elvis Presley.

"Dr. Nick!" The frantic voice was unmistakably that of Joe Esposito, Elvis's disciplined, Chicago-born-and-bred road manager, who seldom lost his cool. "You need to get here *quick*. Something's happened to Elvis."

"Calm down, Joe," I responded automatically.

Joe continued racing through his message: "I think he's had a heart attack."

"Is he responsive at all?" I asked, attempting to hide my concern.

Joe paused for a few seconds, then replied: "Yeah. When we tried to turn him on his back, I heard him breathe."

I sighed with relief. Before I could give instructions, Joe interrupted: "You need to get here quick," he repeated in a trembling voice. "I've called for an ambulance."

"On my way," I snapped, slamming the receiver back into its cradle.

Elvis had been doing very well health-wise, so this episode concerned me. I did not expect anything critical to be going on—especially nothing terminal. Since I had no other details, I tried to review what I knew.

I had swung by Graceland to see Elvis last night and left about ten o'clock when Ginger Alden, his current beauty-queen girlfriend, came in to accompany him to the dentist. As usual, the dentist was prepared to accommodate

Elvis's nocturnal schedule. When I talked with Elvis later, about two o'clock this morning, his tooth was still hurting. At that time he sounded very nervous; his conversation was rambling. He was muttering as if he was upset and didn't know how to explain it at the time, or as if someone was standing there listening.

He told me he wanted to play some racquetball. Since he had been under so much stress because of Ginger's refusal to go on tour with him, I thought playing racquetball might be good for him. I also wanted him to get a good night's sleep before leaving for the tour. Maybe that is all that had happened—Elvis had simply overexerted himself. At the same time, I knew Joe was definitely not an alarmist, yet his voice sounded anxious in a way I had never heard it before.

Certainly by the time I get to Graceland everything will be all right, I reasoned, trying to keep my eyes and my mind on the road for the six-mile drive. I was very familiar with the route I would travel—a fifteen-minute drive if I observed the forty-mile-per-hour speed limit—ten if I didn't.

My mind began meticulously running down a list of everything that had happened to Elvis in the past that could apply to the situation I might encounter—such as a seizure. I considered the different medications he was taking and any side effects or interactions he might be experiencing. Since Elvis had planned to play racquetball, I thought about the time I had to do CPR (cardiopulmonary resuscitation) on a player who collapsed on the racquetball court. That situation would have been doubtful for Elvis because he did not work out hard when he played doubles with Ginger. She was new at the sport.

Elvis was on his usual pre-tour liquid diet of mostly diet drinks and sugarless Jell-O and Popsicles. I had warned him that with only these in his system he could dehydrate. Maybe that is what happened. If Elvis had dehydrated, that could have altered his electrolytes and caused his potassium level to drop. In the worst-case scenario, that can create a cardiovascular event.

I sped past the busy commercial airport, with its early afternoon traffic. We planned to leave sometime after midnight from Memphis Aero, the city's private airport, on Elvis's jet, the *Lisa Marie*, for Portland, Maine—the first stop on his scheduled twelve-day, sold-out tour. Whenever we arrived at the airport to leave for a tour, excited fans and family were always there for a big send-off. The only thing lacking was a high school band playing Elvis's dramatic opening number, "2001: A Space Odyssey." That song was always on my mind when the *Lisa Marie* rolled down the runway and took to the air.

Despite my brief mental diversion, the echo of "Something's happened to Elvis" in Joe's nervous voice would not leave my thoughts for long.

AT LAST I was there—in record time. The wrought iron gates of Graceland were already open and I swirled in. Through the tall trees gracing the circular driveway, I could see the familiar orange-striped ambulance from the Memphis Fire Department. It was ominously waiting in front of the Southern colonial mansion Elvis referred to simply as "the house." My heart pounded as I prayed the situation would not be more serious than I had imagined.

As I pulled my car in behind the ambulance, I could tell Elvis was already inside it on the gurney. Rushing over, I hoisted myself up on the high back step to gain a position close to Elvis's head and the available emergency equipment. The loud chugging drone from the truck's diesel engine made it difficult to communicate with the paramedic. Charlie Hodge, a member of Elvis's band, and Joe climbed inside, and the heavy metal doors closed behind us.

Not knowing what had happened before I arrived at Graceland, I assumed my role in the resuscitation mode already in progress—treating Elvis as though he might have had a syncopal attack (loss of consciousness), seizure, accidental overdose, or cardiac arrest. Joe assured me again that he had heard air come from Elvis's lungs when he moved him. I had no way of knowing how long ago that had been.

I instructed our driver to take Elvis to Baptist Memorial Hospital. It was a split-second decision that I would not allow myself to second-guess. Methodist South Hospital was only a mile away, but Elvis had never been a patient there. I believed Baptist was where Elvis could get the best help the quickest. I could admit him expediently since his records were there; plus I was a staff doctor at Baptist, so I was familiar with the competent specialists who had previously treated Elvis at that location. Baptist also had a renowned Harvey team, a specialized crew who perform emergency cardiac resuscitation. I told our driver to radio ahead to Baptist so they could alert their Harvey team and make ready a room for Elvis Presley; he would be arriving by ambulance in respiratory distress. I then called for the head of cardiology to hurry to the ER.

Our driver eased the emergency vehicle out the front gates, where concerned fans had already started to gather—alerted by their unique grapevine communication system that mysteriously rolled into place whenever Elvis was in town. The emergency medical technician riding with us in the rear of the ambulance began running an IV. He allowed me to take the lead as we worked frantically the entire distance to the hospital, located just seven minutes to the northwest.

Elvis's pitiful—almost unrecognizable—face was swollen and blue, symptoms of cyanosis, a lack of oxygen in his blood.

Several things could be happening, I thought. *His condition could be due to toxins such as cyanide or carbon monoxide, or he could have had an allergic reaction causing his lips or epiglottis to swell. He could have choked or suffocated. One thing was certain: he needed a source of oxygen as quickly as possible.*

We tried in vain to intubate (put a tube down his throat to allow air in), but we could not position his neck properly to insert the tube. I was not able to see the vocal cords well enough to pass the tube through them into the trachea. As if the procedure itself were not delicate enough, I had the added pressure of knowing that the vocal cords at my fingertips were the instrument of one of the world's greatest singers. Unable to intubate him, we continued the bag breathing that the paramedics had started in order to force air into his lungs. He had severely bitten his tongue, which is common with a seizure or from the impact of a fall. Tiny red carpet fibers were in his mouth—remnants of his futile efforts to gain air; his face had most likely been submerged in the thick pile.

He had no heartbeat. Along the way the EMT and I alternated giving closed chest massage. We administered different medications in an attempt to stimulate his heart, but we were unable to get any sort of blood pressure or heartbeat on the heart monitor. Frantically we worked on different options that would increase Elvis's chances of being revived. Nothing we did brought a response. The longer we worked, the warmer and tighter it became inside the small emergency vehicle, where our hopes were decreasing along with Elvis's chances.

Finally we arrived at Baptist Memorial. The gloomy gray building housed one of the city's most respected hospitals, and I felt secure knowing I would be able to get the help we needed there. The EMTs jerked open the ambulance's metal doors and hauled out the stretcher. They burst through the battered doors of the emergency room entrance and wheeled the gurney quickly down the hallway into trauma room number 1, actually a small operating room already prepared to receive Elvis. I moved aside to let the skilled Harvey team take over.

The lead physician of the Harvey team stepped forward and shot life-giving stimulants into Elvis's body while all sorts of evaluations were going on simultaneously. No response. They placed paddles on Elvis's discolored chest and gave the order to discharge the electronic shocks—still nothing. I stared at the monitor in the distance. Six or eight beats in succession registered on the electrocardiogram machine.

Again a doctor injected stimulants directly into the heart and directly into the IV. Minutes went by—nothing. The electronic shock paddles charged again; another four weak beeps registered on the monitor. The time intervals were brief, with each beat occurring two to three seconds apart, then nothing but silence. The ringing in my ears grew louder and louder in those silent intervals as I strained to hear signs of hope. I slowly began to realize I would never again hear Elvis calling me by my name.

The attending personnel resumed talking—communicating about different things they could try that had worked before and might again. My eyes were foggy with tears. l could discern only blurred images ministering to the still body on the table that had once moved with such power and skill. My own body grew weaker and weaker, drained from anticipating the breath of life that never came.

Medically and scientifically I had suspected that Elvis was gone, but I just could not accept it. I wanted so much for it not to be true. I could not bear the thought of losing Elvis and of letting down everyone who had placed so much faith and trust in me.

The question for me had never been simply whether Elvis was dead or even *whether* we could revive him. The question was also, had so much time elapsed that if we revived him, he would be brain damaged? There is such a small window of opportunity to supply vital oxygen to the brain. Sadly, I reached the understanding that the air Joe said he heard Elvis exhale when he turned him over was just positional air movement.

The thought kept going through my mind that we were spinning our wheels in the emergency room, but I just could not give up. The doctors kept glancing my way, waiting for me to say the words that would put an end to their futile efforts to help Elvis reclaim his life. Finally, in a voice barely audible even to me, I said the dreaded words: "Stop CPR. He's gone."

The Harvey team slowly backed away from the table, removing their masks and revealing faces of absolute exhaustion. Slowly, with sad resignation, they began undoing all the IVs, breathing tubes, and EKG monitors—life support that had proved useless.

Gradually my shock began to dissipate, awakening me to the painful reality of the situation at hand. I could not imagine what lay ahead for his father, Vernon, still waiting back at Graceland. He needed confirmation; so did

Elvis's guys waiting in the next room. Somehow I had to regroup and find enough strength to face those who loved Elvis and were praying for him to pull through. My own feelings needed to be set aside; I still had a job to do.

After arriving at the hospital, Elvis's guys had been ushered into trauma room number 2. There was no sound from inside the small, cramped area until I opened the door, trespassing on the silence. The tears running down my cheeks put an end to their waiting.

"It's all over. He's gone," I said quietly.

Wails of disbelief filled the air.

There with Joe Esposito and Charlie Hodge in the sad space were Al Strada, a trustworthy aide who handled Elvis's wardrobe and other personal matters; Elvis's cousin Billy Smith, who was like a brother to him; David Stanley, a stepbrother, who worked as an aide and helped with security; and David's mother, Dee, who was married to, but currently separated from, Elvis's father. David and his brother Rick, known collectively as "the Stanley boys," had continued to work for Elvis throughout the disrupted marriage. Dick Grob, Elvis's chief of security, had arrived to take charge of the impatient press corps. Belligerent reporters were attempting to maneuver themselves into the scene for a career-boosting scoop on the status of Elvis's condition.

I wanted to stay with the guys so we could comfort one another, but there was an urgent need at Graceland, where hope was surely fading. There were other matters as well that I needed to discuss with Vernon that I knew would be hurtful.

It is very difficult for a doctor when he is a patient's friend. The patient and his family have more confidence in him; their faith in his ability is on an entirely different level. Everybody expected me to do something magical. They were anticipating that I would pull Elvis through because I had done that before during several serious events. The difference was this time I had not been present when the close call came. Sadly I discovered that despite all the precautions we had put into place, the people hired to look out for Elvis had not been there either.

DICK GROB AND Al Strada stayed at the hospital for security reasons, and Joe Esposito stayed behind to make the official announcement of Elvis's death at a press conference. I planned to call from Graceland to confirm that the Presley family had been informed, so the world could be told. Joe had been Elvis's point person ever since they were in Germany during their army days. He automatically knew what needed to be done before the story of Elvis's death leaked to the press. His first call was to Elvis's longtime manager, Tom Parker, whom the guys called "the Colonel." Joe had been Elvis's liaison with Parker and knew the urgency of canceling the impending concert dates.

Next Joe would call Elvis's ex-wife, Priscilla. Knowing how crude and insensitive some tabloid reporters could be, Joe wanted to make certain Priscilla heard of Elvis's death directly from him. He understood how concerned Priscilla would be for her nine-year-old daughter, Lisa Marie, who was spending summer vacation with her daddy at Graceland. The couple had remained good friends, thanks to the civility the mutual love for a child can bring to even the saddest of broken marriages.

The paramedics obtained permission to return to Graceland and for me to ride back with them in the ambulance in case we needed to transport Vernon to the hospital. Elvis's sixty-two-year-old father had a delicate heart, weakened even further just months before by a second heart attack. I have been told that there is no pain to equal a parent's loss of a child, no matter what the age. I prayed Vernon could survive his latest tragedy. He was already sadly familiar with death. He had watched helplessly the agonizing delivery of Elvis's stillborn twin brother in a tiny two-room house Vernon had built with his own hands. He had seen his wife Gladys pass away at age forty-six during a brief hospitalization. Now this: Elvis's sudden and unexplainable death.

THE SIZE OF the subdued crowd gathered outside the stone walls had grown considerably since we had left Graceland, but we could detect no activity inside as the ambulance pulled around to the back of the house. Without knocking I entered Graceland through the rear entranceway, the usual access for friends and employees. I had walked through that door many times during the past decade on a happy note. Never had I imagined I would be coming to carry out one of life's most painful missions.

Quietly I entered Grandma Minnie Mae Presley's room, where little Lisa Marie and other of Elvis's loved ones sat with his eighty-six-year-old grandma, waiting and praying. There were so many tearful faces: Vernon and his fiancée, Sandy Miller; Vernon's sister, Elvis's aunt Delta Biggs, who also lived at Graceland, where she managed the domestic staff; and two of the maids, along with other relations and employees who worked or lived on the property.

The instant I walked through the door, Vernon knew.

"Oh no! No!" he moaned.

The entire room began to weep—every single person in it. In all the years I had dealt with the loss of a loved one, this was unquestionably the most heart-wrenching scene I had ever witnessed. It reminded me of the old-time Greek funerals, where nearly everyone present joined in the crying and wailing.

After a brief period for the family, it was time. I walked slowly past the monitor on the kitchen counter, where I saw a swell of people milling outside the stone walls at Graceland. I removed the receiver from the telephone in the entry hall, dreading the wave of sorrow my call would put into motion, and punched in the number for the hospital.

"Joe," I said in a voice of resignation, "you can give the press its story."

Then our saddened group drifted into the den on the main floor that held the television set with the largest screen in Elvis's mansion. We braced ourselves for the formal news report from the press conference at the hospital. Numbed by the reality of the broadcast, we stared in silence at the TV screen—each of us choosing to process privately the complicated emotional void left after losing Elvis.

Even when trusted national news sources read the bulletin, many people thought it was a hoax. They had to hear the words again and again before the message would sink in: "Elvis Presley, the forty-two-year-old king of rock 'n' roll, died today in Memphis, Tennessee."

After he heard the official report, Vernon appeared subdued. I asked for permission to examine him and was relieved and pleased to learn he had no distress from chest pains. He was surprisingly coherent and focused and as ready to carry on as he possibly could be under such dire circumstances.

Finally I could no longer delay discussing the need for an autopsy. Dick Grob arrived from the hospital, and we explained the process and why it was necessary. We told Vernon that although his son was pronounced dead at the hospital, they considered Elvis dead on arrival. That meant there would be an investigation at Graceland to determine if Elvis's death was from suicide, foul play, or natural cause. If it was found to be by natural cause, then the medical examiner would release the body to the family, and Vernon could request that the hospital conduct an autopsy.

We all agreed we wanted the autopsy done to determine without a doubt how Elvis died; so Dick and I witnessed Vernon's shaky hand affix his signature to the necessary autopsy permission paper. That way, if death was determined to be from natural cause, the paperwork authorizing the autopsy would already be complete. In the meantime there were other matters that needed attention.

Dick Grob, Graceland's capable commander in chief, had trained with both the FBI and CIA. His background had fascinated Elvis, who was nuts about anything to do with law enforcement. Grob was also a former air force pilot. While he was at the hospital, protecting Elvis, Dick had aborted the departure of Elvis's musicians from Nashville on a plane bound for Portland and arranged to fly Elvis's advance team, already on the ground in Portland, to Memphis. Seeing him in action gave me a better understanding of why Elvis and Vernon had trusted Dick with many of their most serious and sensitive problems.

Charles Crosby and Ulysses Jones, the two paramedics who had escorted Elvis from Graceland to Baptist Memorial, had told police at the hospital that someone at Graceland said they thought Elvis had overdosed. This ignited rumors. Now that Elvis was dead, speculation about his cause of death was quickly growing.

Dan Warlick, chief medical investigator for the state of Tennessee, took charge when the official team arrived to examine the death scene. Warlick appeared not only young and energetic but also exceptionally directed and competent. His boss was Dr. Jerry Francisco, Shelby County's chief medical examiner and coroner. I later learned the rest of the slightly intimidating group included Police Lieutenant Sam McCachren, Homicide Detective Sergeant John Peel, and Assistant District Attorney Jerry Stauffer.

I was told that if Warlick's boss used the findings of Warlick's report to rule that the deceased died of *natural* causes, then the investigation would go no further and the body would be released to the family. If, however, Dr. Francisco determined Elvis's death occurred from *suspicious* causes, then the investigation would continue and the body would go to the county morgue, where the coroner would conduct an autopsy.

As Elvis's family physician, I had examined him within the last five days, so I was legally able to sign a death certificate at that time and stop the investigation that was taking place. I did not believe Elvis had died from any illness I had been treating, however, so I wanted the autopsy conducted to find out what had caused his death.

Warlick told me that when he arrived in Elvis's upstairs suite, where the body was discovered, the rooms had been straightened: the beds made and linens changed; the carpets cleaned and possibly scrubbed, particularly a stained spot where Elvis's face had rested. The team searched for drugs and drug paraphernalia; they found no drugs and only two large stainless steel syringes that utilize medication cartridges commonly used by dentists, not the type of syringes a person would use to inject drugs.

The detectives interrogated all the people who had been upstairs during and after the tragedy. They learned exactly where Elvis was lying when he was found, and Warlick carefully measured the distance from that spot to the place on the carpet that had been cleaned.

Warlick then talked to the maids, who proved to be a wealth of information. They had already told me that Aunt Delta had instructed them to clean Elvis's room after we left for the hospital. Their explanation was simple: "We always clean Mr. Elvis's room—first thing—when he leaves the house."

Warlick subsequently interviewed me. Seeing how tired I was after that interview, my son, Dean, insisted he give me a ride back to the hospital for the autopsy. I agreed without argument. I soon discovered Dean had an ulterior motive for his good deed.

Dean was an enthusiastic fourteen-year-old when I first took him to Graceland at Christmas to meet Elvis and his family. By the time he was nineteen, Dean was a competitive athlete; he taught Elvis and most of his entourage how to play racquetball. Afterward Elvis hired Dean as his aide and to help with security on tour. Dean had been working security at the mansion while I was at the hospital for the emergency. He could hardly wait to get me out of the house to tell me what had been said behind the scenes at Graceland after Elvis was taken away in the ambulance.

"AFTER THEY RETURNED from the dentist about 1:30 a.m., Elvis went upstairs with Ginger," Dean began. "That's when Elvis called you on the phone. Later he talked with Joe about tour details and met with Dick for about an hour and a half to go over security plans. After he finished his tour business, Elvis called Billy and asked him and Jo to play a game of racquetball with him and Ginger." (Elvis's cousin, Billy; his wife, Jo; and their children lived in a trailer behind the main house at Graceland.)

"When they returned to the house, the maid offered to make him something to eat, but Elvis passed since he was fasting," Dean continued. "She said Elvis looked 'hot and sweaty.' He told her he just wanted some ice water. Then Ginger, Elvis, and Billy went upstairs. Billy dried Elvis's hair, and when Billy left, Elvis called for Rick. It was about eight o'clock in the morning, and Rick was the aide on duty, but no one could find him. Then Elvis called your office, and you weren't there. He needed some sleep medicine, so he talked with Tish."

Tish Henley was a trustworthy nurse at the Medical Group where I had my practice, and she was in charge of dispensing medications to Elvis and Vernon. She and her husband, Tommy, the dependable groundskeeper and head of maintenance at Graceland, lived in one of the trailers on the property.

"After talking with Elvis, Tish called and told Tommy which medication to give to Delta for Elvis," Dean continued. "Then Delta took it upstairs to Elvis with a pitcher of ice water. After everything quieted down, Elvis started reading. He still couldn't go to sleep, but Ginger was sleepy. He went into his bathroom to read so the light wouldn't bother her. By then it was close to nine o'clock in the morning.

"Ginger said she woke up about two in the afternoon and phoned her mom. After they talked she hung up and went to check on Elvis. She knocked on his bathroom door, which was partially open. When he didn't answer, she pushed open the door. That's when she found Elvis lying facedown on the carpet. Ginger called downstairs for help.

"When the maids couldn't find David, who was supposed to have relieved Rick at noon, Al ran upstairs. Al called for Joe, and Joe called Vernon. When Joe couldn't reach you on the phone, he called an ambulance. Before it arrived, Vernon and Sandy were upstairs in the bathroom, where everyone was trying to get Elvis breathing. Sandy gave him mouth-to-mouth resuscitation until the EMTs arrived."

Dean was lost in his thoughts for a few moments. Then he pressed on: "Here's where things went wrong. Our work schedule had Rick on duty until noon, when David was to come to work. So where was Rick this morning when Elvis needed him around eight o'clock? Where was David when Elvis needed him this afternoon? Why weren't either of them at their posts?

"Something else is suspicious. The maids said they heard a loud thump from upstairs this afternoon sometime after one o'clock. Ginger said that might have been one of the times she woke up but went back to sleep. You know Elvis must have made a noise when he fell—shook the house, I'd think. Elvis wouldn't have glided to the floor *gently* like a feather. If David had been on duty, he would have heard that noise and checked on Elvis as he's hired to do.

"The maids said they thought Elvis was awake. They saw the buttons on the telephone light up a few times; then they heard the shower running in the upstairs bathroom that Elvis's girlfriends use when they are at Graceland.

They were also mystified that Ginger was fully dressed, with flawless makeup, when she sounded the alarm for Elvis. She had been sleeping for hours, right? I know firsthand it takes that woman at least an hour to get ready. What do you make of that?"

"I don't know," I answered, confused by all the new information. "All I know is when Elvis called me about his tooth hurting this morning, he asked if I could give him something for pain. (No narcotics were in his nighttime medication envelope.) I didn't have my bag at home, so I told him I'd have to write a prescription. He said he'd send Rick to get it. After we hung up, I called the house and confirmed that Elvis had been to the dentist. Then I wrote a prescription for a few Dilaudid tablets. Then I called the hospital's all-night pharmacy and told the pharmacist Rick was coming with a prescription for Elvis. That's the last time I saw Rick—at our house this morning around two thirty."

"I saw you talking with the investigator. How did that go?" Dean asked.

"That was Dan Warlick. He wanted to know why there were no medicine bottles in Elvis's bedroom or bathroom," I told Dean. "I explained it was because we gave Elvis his medications in envelopes to control his intake and to prevent him from accidentally overdosing on sleeping pills. I told Warlick that as far as I knew, the pills Elvis took this morning were medications I had prescribed that he had been taking on a regular basis, unless the dentist had given him something when he treated him hours earlier."

"When the investigators checked Elvis's bathroom, they were able to put together what they believed happened. He was either sitting down or getting up from the commode when some type of sudden event struck him. Considering Elvis's height and the distance from the commode to the damp stain found on the carpet, the investigator figured that Elvis stood up, took a step or two forward, and then collapsed to the floor. Elvis had red carpet fibers in his mouth, which would indicate that he was gasping for breath. He may have suffocated from the fibers; or it could have been an agonal response. That's sort of an automatic reaction the body has that keeps it functioning for a while after death.

"When people die they become *anoxic*, which means not enough oxygen gets to the brain. That can precipitate a grand mal seizure, which would account for Elvis's teeth biting almost completely through his tongue. A lot of things could have happened at the very end. The question is, what kicked it off?"

Dean was briefly silent; then he worked himself back into overdrive:

"There's a lot more to consider. The maids said Vernon asked them if they had seen either David or Rick go up or come down the back stairs off the kitchen before or during the time Elvis was upstairs with Ginger. Why would Vernon want to know that? Doesn't that strike you as strange?"

Before I could answer, we arrived at the hospital.

THE AUTOPSY OF Elvis Presley at Baptist Memorial Hospital was the beginning of a search for the truth that has never ended—an enigma that continues to ignite discussions even to this day. If it had not been for that single sheet of paper we felt we needed—authorizing an autopsy and signed by Vernon at Dick's request—maybe history would have recorded a different story of Elvis and Dr. Nick.

I entered the hospital, where Dick had delivered the signed form giving Baptist pathologists permission to proceed if the coroner's ruling allowed for a private autopsy. As I walked down the corridor I could see an assistant attorney general still stationed outside the room where Elvis's body lay. He was waiting to transfer the body to the city hospital for autopsy if that was what the coroner decided to do. The man was just receiving word that the medical examiner's office had completed its investigation and ruled Elvis's death was by natural cause. That meant there was no probable cause that would require the coroner to conduct an autopsy to determine the manner of death.

The hospital pathologists were now free to act on Vernon's authorization. This meant the Presley family would own the autopsy results; that is standard procedure in a private autopsy. The coroner's office does not usually perform an autopsy unless they are required to by the state in order to prosecute a crime.

There is a difference in the approach to an autopsy conducted by a hospital and a coroner's office. Hospital pathologists are *clinical* pathologists; pathologists in the medical examiner's office are *forensic* pathologists. Not only are their educational backgrounds and training different; their approach to analysis is different. A hospital autopsy is more of a learning tool than a legal tool. A coroner's autopsy is the legal decision on the cause and manner of death to determine if the death was the result of a criminal action.

BEFORE ELVIS'S AUTOPSY began, the Baptist pathologists and the medical examiner's office reached an agreement about how they could work together. They had a famous patient; they did not want to miss anything relevant and receive criticism over how the autopsy was conducted. I believe the overdose rumors that surfaced when Elvis arrived at the hospital could have made Baptist feel that having the medical examiner observe its private autopsy might be a wise move. I was told Dr. Eric Muirhead, the hospital's distinguished chief of pathology, would be supervising Elvis's "gross autopsy." That is the initial, overall visual examination of the body and its organs to gather observable information. The other phases, which are conducted later, are the microscopic and toxicology findings. The three phases combined are considered to be the "autopsy report."

Dr. Jerry Francisco would be present "in the capacity of a consultant." He would bring over his own staff: Dan Warlick, who had conducted the investigation at Graceland, and two pathologists. The job of the hospital pathologists would be the same as it always had been in cases where the two entities cooperated: they would collect the data and hand it over to Dr. Francisco: so he could make his ruling regarding cause of death. I was present at the autopsy for the same reason I always attended autopsies—I was the primary physician of the deceased and wanted to learn as much as I could about my patient.

For a moment I questioned whether Elvis was dead before the ambulance pulled away from Graceland or if he had died en route. All I had to go on when I boarded the ambulance was Joe telling me he had heard Elvis breathe. I reasoned that Elvis had to have been alive when we left Graceland. Why else would the paramedics have been transporting him? The paramedics would not have moved a dead body; they would have called for the police, as the law requires. My mind kept recycling the information, as I knew it.

As time neared for the process to get under way and Dr. Francisco walked into the autopsy room, I sensed Dr. Muirhead had an attitude problem with the medical examiner's arrival. I had heard about the strained relationship between Dr. Muirhead and Dr. Francisco. I could only hope their personality differences, if they did exist, would not affect the business at hand.

There were enough other factors already at work. Memphis had a history of political haggling between the Shelby County Court, which would later become known as the Shelby County Commission, and the agencies it was charged with funding. I had heard accusations from a patient of mine that a contingency in Memphis/Shelby County government was upset with Dr. Francisco and wanted him out of office. They felt he had sided with police on numerous occasions after a series of disagreements some regarded as incidents of police brutality. The allegations were usually along racial lines, as many problems in Memphis tended to be.

Solemnly the members of the two pathology teams began drifting into the autopsy room toward the place where Elvis lay waiting to provide us with answers in the only way he could. I looked for a place where I could subtly brace myself. It was excruciating to see Elvis so exposed on the autopsy table. He had been a man of such pride and privacy. I felt the urge to cover him with a blanket, as I would have wanted someone to do for me. I wished there were a more humane way to reveal the secrets death holds.

Dan Warlick began the gross autopsy by examining Elvis closely, head to toe, apparently looking for bruising, needle tracks, or injection sites. None were found. Warlick was meticulous; I had never seen so much attention to detail in an autopsy. I knew I would need to take notes on what was taking place, to review when my mind could focus more clearly on the meaning of what I was observing.

The autopsy team continued their laborious examination, looking diligently for causes of sudden death, such as a ruptured aneurysm or a pulmonary embolus (a blood clot in the lungs); none were found. There was no evidence of hemorrhaging, no killer heart attack, no evidence of infection of the heart valves. Most diseases causing sudden death were eliminated.

Dr. Francisco had agreed to a press conference at eight o'clock that evening so that reporters could meet their hectic late-night news deadlines. We realized the world was anxiously waiting for answers regarding Elvis's cause of death. About half the members of the autopsy team, as well as me, left to meet the press. The others stayed behind to complete their specific duties.

MEMBERS OF THE press corps huddled tightly in the specified room, hoping for the ruling on Elvis's death. Dr. Francisco acted as spokesperson, and Dr. Muirhead appeared as the hospital's pathology chief. There were two pathologists from Dr. Muirhead's staff and two pathology assistants from the medical examiner's office. Of course I was present: Dr. George Nichopoulos, personal physician of the late Elvis Presley.

We walked into the assigned room—most of us wearing our trademark white lab coats—and took our seats in the conference room chairs behind the large table where an array of tape recorders and microphones were placed in front of us.

MEMPHIS PRESS-SCIMITAR, WEDNESDAY, AUGUST 17, 1977

— Staff Photo by Glenn Peterson

'CAUSE OF PRESLEY DEATH WAS A HEART ATTACK' Dr. Jerry Francisco, left, Shelby County Medical Examiner, discusses the findings of an autopsy performed just hours after the death of the Memphis singer. With Francisco at a press conference last night were from left, Dr. George Nichopoulos, Presley's personal physician; Dr. Eric Muirhead, director of pathology at Baptist Hospital; and Dr. George Bale, asst. director of pathology.

On cue and in a direct and confident manner, Dr. Francisco announced: "The ruling of the autopsy is that the cause of death is cardiac arrhythmia due to undetermined heartbeat. There are several cardiovascular diseases that are known to be present . . . [Dr. Francisco explained those.] It may take several days [to determine the cause]; it may take weeks. It may never be discovered."

He acknowledged that Baptist Memorial pathologists would continue lab examinations to complete their findings. Dr. Francisco added in a steady voice: "He was using medication [actually several medications] to control his blood pressure and for a colon problem, but there is no evidence of any chronic abuse of drugs whatsoever."

The remaining doctors at the table sat silently throughout Dr. Francisco's announcement and while he answered reporters' questions. None of the doctors made any effort to add or dispute the information Dr. Francisco shared with the press.

That seemed odd to me. I was told later that since the press conference was scheduled for before the autopsy would be completed, Dr. Francisco and Dr. Muirhead had agreed that Dr. Francisco would announce that the autopsy results were inconclusive. Instead Dr. Francisco startled the pathologists by making two definitive statements: Elvis died of cardiac arrhythmia due to unknown causes, which may never be determined; and there was no evidence of drug abuse.

The pathologists would later claim they did not participate at the conference because they were embarrassed by Dr. Francisco's diagnosis. I thought their faces revealed a deeper emotion, somewhere between contempt and anger. If Dr. Francisco had agreed to give the ruling he discussed with Dr. Muirhead, then he had broken his word. The hospital pathologists may have felt he had dismissed the results of their efforts before they were given an opportunity to present them.

It is true that Dr. Francisco was the person responsible for ruling on Elvis's cause of death. In the end it was his call; the medical examiner's word was the only one that officially mattered. Or was it? The press conference underscored, as nothing else could, that a battle had ensued regarding the autopsy results. Sides were drawn: Muirhead vs. Francisco. I had no idea where I fit into the equation as Elvis's personal physician.

Next, the microphone was passed to me, and I answered reporters' questions. They inquired about rumors of Elvis using hard drugs.

I answered, "Elvis had been taking an appetite suppressant earlier to curb a weight problem, but the medication was not an amphetamine."

At that time, among newer doctors, prescribing amphetamines was an acceptable practice for weight control. Older doctors frowned on the treatment because the potential for abuse was beginning to be recognized.

"If he were using cocaine, I would have known about it," I told the reporters. "Just five days ago I gave Elvis an extensive physical. At that time he was getting over an eye infection and a sore throat, but overall he was a healthy man."

When the press conference ended, I understood the questions had not. My initial reaction was that the reporters seemed dazed, maybe even disappointed that they did not have a more sensational story to report—for the time being anyway.

After the press conference, I returned to the autopsy room, where certain specialists on the team had remained in order to continue the tedious job of carefully collecting and preparing samples for microscopic and toxicologic studies. Warlick had stayed with the body during the press conference, and he later shared with me that he felt there was "a reverence about it and a quiet sadness" throughout the entire autopsy process. His assessment was comforting to me. Elvis deserved nothing less.

From a colleague I learned two sets of physical samples were being prepared for two separate studies of the microscopic and toxicology materials: one for the medical examiner and another for Baptist. Dr. Francisco's samples would be delivered just blocks away to the lab he generally used, the University of Tennessee Center for the Health Sciences. Baptist pathology would send its samples to Duckworth Laboratory at Methodist Hospital for analysis, as they always did. It was strange to me that Baptist, the largest private hospital in the country at that time, had no toxicology laboratory. I would wonder later, amid the heated controversy over the autopsy results, if the hospital pathologists were trying to prove their competency because they did not have their own tox lab, or if they were trying to prove their need for one. Whatever the motivating factor was in Baptist Memorial's quest to confirm its diagnosis of Elvis's death, it fueled a controversy that has never died.

ON THE RIDE back to Graceland from the hospital after the autopsy, Dean informed me of the unprecedented outpouring of grief at the mansion that had necessitated calling in additional officers for crowd and traffic control on Elvis Presley Boulevard. The only way to enter Graceland now was through the private rear gate.

Confusion inside the mansion had diminished, but its painful effects were still evident. Each familiar face reflected the anguish of being unable to reverse a loss no one had expected and no one wanted to accept. I had planned to talk with Vernon about what I knew at the time regarding Elvis's condition, but when I saw him watching the televised tributes to his son by some of the most famous people in the country, there was no way I could intrude on his opportunity to reflect on the importance of Elvis's life in its broad historical context.

At the end of the longest day I could remember, I headed home to the sensitive, sad welcome I knew awaited me. Elvis had endeared himself to my wife, Edna, and our two daughters, Chrissy (whom we lovingly called Kissy) and Elaine. My daughters had known Elvis for almost as long as they could remember. Edna had had a mothering influence on him. Elvis was family to all of us.

Dean stayed at Graceland a while longer. Many unresolved issues remained, and Dean was still working for "the boss." He wanted to do his part to see that "everything runs smoothly for when Elvis comes home."

"HAVE YOU HEARD any additional details about the services?" I asked Dean on the phone as I prepared to leave the next morning for my routine hospital rounds and office duties.

"The viewing will still take place at the house between three and five o'clock this afternoon," Dean said. "Vernon has decided to hold the funeral at Graceland because of security and to make it easier on Grandma."

"Allowing fans inside Graceland at a time like this could be a disaster," I cautioned, remembering how difficult crowd control was at concerts when fans were emotional. "I think holding a private service at the house tomorrow is definitely the best move with all the celebrities coming to town. Otherwise the funeral could turn into a media circus."

"Yeah, the *National Enquirer* already has a helicopter circling Graceland, and Dick and Joe are trying hard to accommodate the working press."

Then Dean added, "Elvis is coming home at noon."

He advised me to get to Graceland as early as possible to spend some time with Elvis. I also wanted to check on Vernon and his mother. Sometimes there are serious repercussions after the initial shock of a loved one's death wears off. Priscilla had arrived to take care of little Lisa in the way only a mother can.

AFTER I ARRIVED at Graceland, I witnessed the scene Dean had been unable to fully describe. The crowd, now estimated at close to seventy thousand, surrounded the front gates and spilled into the street, making Elvis Presley Boulevard impassable. Inside the stone walls, the Red Cross and fire department paramedics had set up a medical aid section to help those overcome by physical and emotional exhaustion. Some fans had been standing without food or drink since the night before to maintain their spots in line. The heat was brutal, with temperatures soaring well above a humid one-hundred-degree mark. Stricken fans lay on stretchers and blankets, waiting to be treated so they could return to their positions in line for a chance to pay their respects to their idol.

Literally hundreds of floral wreaths and bouquets covered the front lawn.

Courtesy of Dick Grob

Paramedics aid fans on the grounds of Graceland, August 17, 1977.

Air National Guardsmen stood at strategic points along the fence line and outside the front doors of the mansion. Their presence reminded me that this was the funeral not only of a world-famous entertainer but also of a soldier who had served his country with dignity and honor, making sacrifices that many men and women in that era with a lot less to lose had refused to make.

Although at concerts I had seen thousands of fans who appeared to adore Elvis, the depth of love their presence represented never fully registered with me. I do not believe Elvis had any idea that beneath their adulation was such an honest and deep affection. I could relate to their emotion because I knew Elvis and loved him like a brother, but it was difficult to understand such intense grieving by those who had known Elvis only as an image and a sound.

Solemnly I entered Graceland to pay my respects, as the fans would do later. Elvis rested just inside the door in a copper casket on the marble foyer under the gleaming crystal chandelier. I talked to him for a while and imagined he was listening. In one way or another I kept saying, "I hope you can see all this—how much people love you."

I knew how his fans felt; I was one of them.

ALMOST FROM THE beginning Elvis and I had been kindred spirits. We were amazed at the parallels in our personal lives. We both grew up in small towns labeled by a stigma that instilled in us the need to prove our worth to others.

Elvis was solemn the day he shared with me the shame he had felt when his dad was sent to prison for altering a check to buy food for his family. It was obvious how much Elvis loved Vernon when he described the day "Daddy was taken away from Momma and me." Unable to afford to live in a house of their own, they bounced around, boarding with cousins. His hometown of Tupelo, Mississippi, was a small rural spot where menial day labor jobs, involving hard work and long hours, were the best most people could do. During that period ministers, doctors, and policemen were the most respected men in town.

Elvis found comfort in church, where, as a little boy, he and his lonely

Courtesy of Terry Quinley

Elvis with Policeman Leon Quinley while visiting at Lansky Bros. on Beale Street in 1954.

mother were accepted—free to worship without judgment. He felt secure in this special place where he discovered his talent, a gift he could share to make people happy, even if just temporarily. Elvis submerged himself in his singing and found refuge; the world disappeared, and his spirit was redeemed. Supported by the belief that all things were possible, he became an avid adventurer, chasing dreams.

When it came time to serve his country, Elvis did what he was asked to do to the best of his ability. He had learned that pride is found in a job well done. His humility, seasoned by growing up in poverty, gave him respect for others and allowed him to remain one of them, no matter how much his accomplishments set him apart. He was a gentle, kind, and caring spirit. His daring, fun-loving exploration of all life had to offer made every encounter with him enriching in one way or another.

I, on the other hand, was just proud to have known him. Elvis knew I understood his plight because of our similar upbringing. I was born a Yankee in Ridgeway, Pennsylvania, and transplanted to Anniston, Alabama, a small postcard-perfect Southern city. My parents were Greek immigrants, and we were the "only ones in town." I, like Elvis, had to walk miles to school each day for an education that did not come easily. Instead of a traditional house, my home was in a building above the family restaurant, where my father, Gus, worked long, tiring hours to provide us with the necessities of life. My mother and I were exceptionally close. She could barely speak English and could read and write even less of the language; I had to interpret our world to her in my faulty Greek.

Since there was no church of our faith in town, the Episcopalians welcomed us in as one of their own. They allowed me to become an altar boy and sing in the choir, which diffused the isolation I felt from being "different" from all the other kids. In addition, Scouting gave me a sense of accomplishment and provided adventure and ways to escape into a different world, where I could be self-sufficient. As I succeeded in Scouting and athletics, the guys accepted me as one of them. From that time on, hanging out with the guys always gave me a strong sense of belonging.

Elvis and I enjoyed talking about our days in the army. We both had been stationed in Germany and liked the German people, whose lifestyle was so much like that of home. It was there he met his wife-to-be and the mother of his child, and it was there I found my beloved career. It was while working in the army medical corps that I decided to become a doctor. We shared an

Nichopoulos Collection

Dr. Nick and his U.S. Army buddies from the 98th General Hospital, Munich, Germany, 1947.

Rose Clayton Phillips/Photo by U. S. Army Sgt. Ira Jones

Elvis with U.S. Army buddies in Friedberg, Germany, spring of 1959.

interest in medicine and spent numerous hours discussing the spiritual, emotional, and physical aspects of healing. Our years together had indeed been a blessing to my life.

SLOWLY, AND IN no planned order, family members, friends, and staff came individually to the viewing to spend private time with Elvis. One of the heartbroken was George Klein, Elvis's longtime buddy, dressed like an ad in *GQ* magazine. A popular local deejay known as "GK," he was a welcomed presence to the hectic scene Graceland had become. His knowledge of Elvis's acquaintances and his diplomacy made him the ideal person to handle the numerous requests from movie stars and dignitaries for coveted space in Elvis's funeral procession.

When the public viewing began, the fans filing by the casket were orderly, respectful, and sad beyond belief. By that time people were so accustomed to seeing fans faint, it was hardly a distraction any longer. The "fallen," as we called them, received prompt medical attention and faded back into their place in the crowd. After the viewing ended, Elvis's guys moved his casket from the foyer to the spacious passageway separating the living room from his cherished music room.

The next day that same once-joyful area took on a solemn ethereal glow. Folding chairs replaced familiar furniture, and floral wreaths filled every imaginable space—their perfumed sweetness a gentle reminder of love's desire to comfort the grieving. Elvis's gleaming casket took a revered place between the brilliantly colored stained glass panels at the end of the room, with his piano close by.

Naturally Elvis's service opened with prayer and music. Some of his favorite singers sang old-time gospel songs in a perfect harmony that resonated to the sadness in our souls. I could not concentrate on the eulogies. I was preoccupied with memories of how much Elvis had loved gospel quartet music and how fearlessly he took its message into places it had never gone before. For the first time I realized the irony of the king of rock 'n' roll singing spiritual songs in the showrooms of Las Vegas and Lake Tahoe while jovial patrons sipped cocktails.

Elvis had spread the Word in his own unique way—making traditional hymns part of his concert music mix in arenas all over the country long before contemporary Christian music became a popular genre. Elvis never seemed to

August 18, 1977

SERVICE
— PRAYER —
BILL BAIZE — SONG — WHEN ITS MY TIME
JAKE HESS — SONG — KNOWN ONLY TO HIM
— TALK — JACKIE KAHANE
STAMPS — SONG — HOW GREAT THOU ART
— TALK — REV REX HUMBARD
KATHY — SONG — MY HEAVENLY FATHER
— PREACHER — REV. C. W. BRADLEY
STAMPS — SONG — SWEET SPIRIT

EXTRA SONG — HIS HAND IN MINE

Notes for Elvis Presley's funeral service at Graceland, August 18, 1977.

worry about whether his fans would accept the gospel songs; his only concern was how well he could sing them.

Throughout the service my eyes kept returning to the tender sight of Elvis's grandma and dad, tired and frail, holding up as well as could be expected for a family who would soon be burying a part of themselves.

Vernon had selected me to serve as a pallbearer, and I was profoundly honored. After the dignified ceremony ended, our nine-man group took Elvis in his casket into our hands.

What a privilege, I thought, *to be among Elvis's friends carrying him to his final resting place.*

Edna and I rode with Vernon in the first limo directly behind Elvis, who was leading the way as he always had. Members of the police force held their hats over their hearts, while members of the Air National Guard saluted the

Courtesy of Dick Grob

Funeral procession of the king of rock 'n' roll on Elvis Presley Boulevard, Memphis, Tennessee, August 18, 1977.

man who had touched the hearts and enriched the lives of so many people around the world.

Fans and citizens, who appreciated the dreams Elvis fulfilled and the spirit with which he broke all the rules, gathered quietly along Elvis Presley Boulevard for the short ride to Forest Hill Cemetery. A respectful and protective police motorcycle escort flanked the gleaming white hearse, followed by a string of pristine white Cadillac limousines holding those of us known to be closest to Elvis's heart. Each person must have realized, as I did, how fortunate we were to have shared the brilliant life of this remarkable man.

After entering the hollowed, stone mausoleum, we pallbearers placed Elvis's casket on the empty stand waiting to receive him. His ailing father moved slowly forward to speak to Elvis one last time. Somehow he had summoned enough strength to carry out this final act of love for his only son. Lisa Marie stood shyly by the casket of one of the most famous men of our time and whispered good-bye to her daddy. It was over. Only Al and Dean remained behind until Elvis's casket took its place behind the long, black curtain that would temporarily cover the place entombing the king of rock 'n' roll.

Elvis Presley's interment in the mausoleum at Forest Hill Cemetery on Elvis Presley Boulevard, August 18, 1977.

SADLY AND SILENTLY we returned to Graceland, where seeing Elvis walk through the door would never again be a possibility. For many of us it would be the end of our times together. Friendships would be broken without Elvis, the link who connected us. His death dealt us a double blow.

The emotion of the day had depleted everyone's energy, and our close-knit

On their way to meet the press. (left to right: Tommy Henley, husband of
Elvis's nurse and also Graceland employee; Joe Esposito, Elvis's road manager;
Dick Grob, chief of security)

group began to disburse. I was impressed that Grandma, the strong-willed
matriarch of the Presley family, had survived the ordeal of the past three
days so well. Her greatest need now seemed to be for someone to listen to
her talk about the sweetness of her grandson—how he never left the house
on a trip without kissing her and saying good-bye—things that matter
most to a grandma. Knowing how the pain of loss robs the soul, my lovely
Edna saw Grandma's need and filled it with patient understanding and
natural grace.

From across the room, Dean, who had finally returned to Graceland, was
signaling for me to meet him outside.

"What's up?" I asked, after saying good-bye to various friends on my way
to the patio.

"Dad," Dean said, with a sigh of relief, "Dick just told me Vernon is not
making any personnel changes for the time being, so I report to work tomorrow as usual."

Press corps from around the world gathered inside the Graceland gates.

"And listen to this," Dean continued, while looking around to make certain we were alone. "Dick said Vernon asked him 'to find out if someone *killed* my boy.'"

I stared back in disbelief, but Dean was not finished.

"I also heard some reporters down at the front gates saying they would not rest until they discovered what part drugs played in Elvis's death."

Elvis's life story had taken a turn for the worse; mine would not be far behind.

TWO

RAISING THE BAR

Courtesy of Dick Grob ©

When I walked into my office at the Medical Group the day after Elvis's funeral, my eyes went immediately to a neatly autographed photo he had given to me that was hanging on my wall: "To my good friend and physician, Dr. Nick, Elvis Presley." The truth of his death was still almost impossible to comprehend. It left an enormous gap inside me. Many of the days and nights I had not been with Elvis, I had mentally devoted to him. In a real sense I now felt cheated—deprived of the gift of Elvis's spirit that had motivated and challenged me in so many ways since we first met.

The day I was first introduced to Elvis was a brisk Sunday afternoon, February 26, 1967, my day to be on call at the Medical Group. I was leisurely sifting through a stack of mail when a call came in from the doctors' exchange. It was Charlie Hodge, whom I'd met at a New Year's Eve party. The Memphis physician who had been treating Charlie's good friend and employer was unavailable. Could I make a house call?

"I'm at the office," I said, "just bring him here."

That seemed simple to me, since the Medical Group was centrally located in midtown Memphis.

Charlie was silent for a moment; then he said, "Dr. Nick, it would be much better if you could come here. He's in a lot of pain, and the automobile ride would probably aggravate his problem."

So I headed to my destination: the Circle G Ranch in Walls, Mississippi, ten miles south of Graceland. After I parked my car, Charlie escorted me across the dusty gravel road to a trailer. Behind the squeaky door was a dark room where Elvis stood smiling with his hand outstretched. He introduced me to Priscilla Beaulieu, his beautiful, dark-haired sweetheart at the time. After a round of cordial introductions, Elvis politely excused us and led me into another room for better light and greater privacy.

Elvis blushed a warm pink, turned around, wiggled his jeans down over his hips, dropped his underdrawers, and bent over slightly to reveal a severely reddened buttock, inflamed from a week of horseback riding. There was also bright blistering on his inner thighs that seemed very painful to him. I treated the sensitive areas gently with a cool, topical ointment and gave him a prescription for an antibiotic to avoid infection. He took the incident in stride but was obviously embarrassed. After the treatment, he confided that he needed to leave the next day for what he called a "fairly physical type movie." Then he said, "I don't think I'm going to feel like going."

Before I left, Elvis had a request. He told me his grandma had a history of heart disease and had been sick for several days. Since I would be passing Graceland on my trip back to Memphis, he wondered if I could stop and examine her. Naturally I agreed; I could not wait to see the interior of Graceland.

After I met Elvis's grandma, Minnie Mae Presley, who appeared to be in her midseventies, I was glad I had come. She had a bronchial infection in addition to asthma and was having difficulty breathing. We chatted for a while; I warned her of the signs of pneumonia and left several prescriptions.

Then Elvis called and told the maid to ask if I could return to the ranch. *I'll just call him and ask what he needs*, I thought; but Elvis was not near a phone when I called, so I drove back to the Circle G.

Elvis explained that the cast and crew were in Hollywood, ready to shoot his new movie, and he had decided his saddle sores were still too painful for him to travel. He knew it would be expensive if he didn't show up on time. He thought "the Colonel" needed to be informed he would "be delayed" so that he could utilize the two days for some other aspect of the movie.

Elvis decided it would be better if *I* told Parker of the dilemma; he called him and quickly handed the phone to me with a mischievous grin. Parker asked that I "encourage Elvis to get to Hollywood as soon as his health permits."

As I was driving out the gate, one of his guys waved me down and said, "Elvis wants to know if you can come back."

Well, I thought, *at least I saved gas.*

"If you've got a few minutes, I'd like to show you my land," Elvis said.

I guessed he was feeling better after my treatment. We climbed into a heavy-duty, dusty white pickup, and Elvis drove us over a good part of his 163 acres of beautiful, rolling fields. We had a nice visit. I found Elvis to be a naturally warm person and an interesting conversationalist. I got the impression he simply wanted to talk to someone different from the guys in his inner circle and to share his pride in the setup they had put together.

Charlie later told me that Elvis had bought all the trucks and house trailers I had seen for his guys—as well as their horses and Western outfits—the whole deal. The ranch was like a new toy that Elvis enjoyed playing with. He had created this insular world in an attempt to enjoy a normal life. In all the years that followed, I would never again see Elvis look as relaxed as he did that day.

When I finally got into my car to leave, Elvis said he had another reason for asking me to return: "I forgot to thank you."

It was a kind, sincere remark, the first of hundreds to come.

"If you really want to thank me," I said, "you can let me go home and not call me back."

Elvis thought that was funny and enjoyed a good chuckle. I told him I was not joking, but he didn't believe me. That was the beginning of the decade-long friendship between the king and Dr. Nick.

THE NEXT DAY I went to Graceland to examine Elvis again and to give him copies of the letters I had mailed to Parker for the insurance company. I obtained a very brief medical history to insert into his patient file. At that time Elvis confided that insomnia had been a major problem for him throughout his life, and he sometimes took sedatives to help him sleep. He also shared that he occasionally took amphetamines to stay awake when he drove across country (since he didn't like to fly) and to make the early morning call times on the movie set.

"What I most need to know is if you have any drug allergies," I said.

"Yes, sir," he replied. "Codeine makes me itch."

I thought that was peculiar; most people allergic to codeine complain of nausea more than anything else. Elvis said he took codeine for injuries on the movie set and for occasional headaches.

Since he planned to live mainly on the West Coast, where he would be making three movies a year, Elvis told me he would appreciate it if he could call me regarding any health problems when he was in Memphis.

I told him, "Of course," but after he left, I didn't expect to be treating him again.

Courtesy of Joe Esposito

Relaxing on the set of the movie *Clambake* in Hollywood during March 1967. (left to right: Joe Esposito, Shelley Fabares, Elvis Presley)

THREE MONTHS AFTER we met, Elvis and Priscilla married in a private ceremony in Las Vegas, Nevada. With his packed schedule for making movies and recording soundtracks, Elvis wanted to stay on the West Coast closer to work. He had homes in both Los Angeles and Palm Springs, California.

By Christmas the newlyweds arrived at Graceland to await the birth of their only child. The event had all the makings of a Hollywood movie. Elvis called the office on February 1, 1968, to tell me Priscilla was ready to deliver. I was not expecting her to go into labor as quickly as she did.

The Medical Group was less than two miles from Baptist Memorial Hospital; but by the time I got there, Elvis and Priscilla had already arrived. He was pacing in a small waiting room with members of his entourage who had tagged along and were milling around in the hallway, waiting for Elvis to break out the cigars he had brought along to celebrate the personal yet historic occasion.

The only professional photographer I can remember was from the Associated Press and had a big Speed Graphic camera. After the baby arrived, Priscilla kept telling the nurse to "hold back the press" so she could get dolled up. She was still groggy, and a nurse was helping her fix her hair and makeup. Finally, Priscilla looked ravishing. The big moment had arrived.

Elvis walked into Priscilla's room to meet his newborn baby girl. She was so delicate; Priscilla was proud—and relieved; Elvis was beside himself with excitement. All he could do was grin and keep looking back and forth from Priscilla to Lisa Marie with a sense of wonder. We took pictures, and I stayed with the happy parents for a while before returning to my office. That's when I noticed Elvis was so excited he had forgotten to pass out the cigars.

MY NEXT MEDICAL *emergency*, as they always were with Elvis, came during his marathon recording session at American Studio early in 1969. This album was to be the followup to his hugely successful 1968 NBC-TV special, now commonly referred to as the "Comeback Special." He was really pumped about recording in his hometown with a young, hotshot Memphis band that had a string of chart-topping hits. But three days into the recording session, Elvis came down with a terrible case of laryngitis that turned into tonsillitis with a fever. That is when I noticed his illogic regarding medicine. I had gone by Graceland and left some medication at his bedside, with clear instructions regarding how he should take it. When I returned the next day, the medicine was all gone.

"What's happened to your medicine?" I asked, fully expecting him to say he had spilled it.

"I took it," he answered, proud of himself. "That's what you told me to do."

"That was a week's worth of medicine," I said in disbelief. "You *couldn't* have taken all that in one day."

I was stunned, wondering how he could possibly be awake and communicating normally. That was naturally a red flag to me that Elvis had a high tolerance for certain medications.

"I need to get well quick," Elvis reasoned. "I've got an album to finish."

"Medicine doesn't work that way," I tried to explain; but it was useless. Elvis was one of those people who believed that the quicker he took all his medicine, the faster he would get well.

ELVIS HAD WON over an immensely enthusiastic grassroots audience by traveling throughout the United States from the beginning of his career in 1954 until he joined the army in March 1958. After being honorably discharged, he performed only two live dates; those were in 1961. After that fans were forced to experience Elvis through a string of movies and soundtrack recordings. On July 31, 1969, things changed. Elvis returned to singing before a live audience for an invitation-only show held at the International Hotel in Las Vegas. His Vegas debut was a widely anticipated event.

Extremely worried about how he would be accepted by his fans and showbiz critics after such a long absence, Elvis assembled a group of celebrity guests and excited hometown friends he had flown in for the event. He wanted lots of familiar faces in the audience when he stepped onstage for the first time in nearly a decade.

There was a magical quality about that night—the anticipation in the crowd. My radiant wife, Edna, said it felt like the entire room was hyperventilating; that was a pretty apt description. No one knew what to expect from Elvis the movie star in his first role as himself. Then he emerged—"fit, trim, and gorgeous," as one reporter would say. Elvis was literally riveting; his nerves were in high gear. His charisma, his incredible voice, his sexy moves—the audience went absolutely nuts.

Afterward the group partied like crazy in Elvis's hotel suite celebrating his success and the resolution of any misgivings he'd had about returning to live show business.

"We might never see anything like this again," I told Edna, as many of the rich and famous joined Elvis's hometown friends.

Elvis walked around the room and personally thanked each person he had invited for attending. He held out his trembling hands and wiggled his legs illustrating what was going on inside of him before he looked out and

Courtesy of Joe Esposito

Elvis returns to live performing in Vegas at the International.

saw friendly faces in the audience. Elvis made everyone feel special—like we had each contributed something important to the success of the night.

The next day Elvis signed a five-year contract to play a monthlong engagement at the International Hotel twice annually. Parker had arranged for RCA, Elvis's record label, to record several of the dinner shows for a live album during that first engagement. Elvis was ecstatic.

After a few tapings, however, Elvis shared with me how stressful it was trying to record a live album while performing a show. "That's a lot for me to think about at one time. I'm busy singing and performing—then they tell me to remember to look like I'm having fun."

It was obvious Elvis welcomed the challenge and wanted to share every bit of the experience with his friends; those, I would learn, were lifelong traits. By the end of his first monthlong stint of fifty-eight shows, Elvis had set all performance records for the famous Las Vegas strip. He could not have been more enthused about the new direction of his career.

When Elvis returned to Vegas in 1970 for his first annual January engagement—another fifty-eight shows in twenty-eight nights—he invited us again. Edna was as excited as Elvis and decked out just as pretty—new clothes, new hairdo. Although the turn-away crowds were as large as those lucky enough to be seated, we were treated to a table down front with the movie stars. The message was clear: Elvis's guests got celebrity treatment.

On that trip there were a couple of significant things happening: Elvis had a cold, and his voice was not in the shape he wanted it to be. The air in Las Vegas is really dry, and Elvis was not accustomed to the effects Vegas's weather could have on his throat and sinuses. People get what they call "desert throat" that can be especially troubling. Elvis suddenly realized how convenient it was to have a doctor on hand. He did not have to send one of his guys out an hour before a show to find "someone good" to take care of him, which was not always practical or possible. Elvis would get truly upset if there was something wrong before a show—especially with his voice. Getting concerned about his throat would accelerate whatever else he was experiencing and make it worse.

Elvis's anxiety level before every show was like that of an athlete before a game; but as soon as he walked onstage and heard the first note and warm receptive applause, the nervous energy melted into focused concentration. He went through a metamorphosis. I would be talking to this keyed-up individual one minute; then he would burst onto the stage and I could not believe he was the same man. I would watch him perform his choreography, and think, *That* cannot *be Elvis up there.*

The more his fans became involved in his performance, the more energized Elvis would get; his fans charged his battery. By the time a show ended, he would be literally rattling from the vibration of his body's explosive energy. It would take quite a while for that excitement to dissipate.

WITH ALL THE publicity surrounding the "Vegas Elvis," Parker saw an even greater opportunity to promote "his boy" on a bigger stage. He booked Elvis as part of the Texas Livestock Show in the Houston Astrodome. In a ceremony before the show on February 27, 1970, Elvis's entourage—me included—manned a dozen convertibles and circled the football field. Elvis kept looking up and smiling confidently in every direction at hundreds of rows of waving people. He told me later all he could think about was, *how do I sing to this crowd?* The arena was smelly and the acoustics awful, so by showtime Elvis was a nervous wreck.

From the beginning of his career, Elvis had preferred playing intimate settings, where he could look into the faces of an audience and make an emotional connection. There were no chairs on the ground in front of the stage in the Astrodome; there were no closed-circuit television screens to take him closer to the people; there was just Elvis standing in a vast, open space he referred to as "the floor of an ocean."

When showtime arrived, Elvis sang from the bottom of his soul to the top of the rafters, drawing from his incredible inner strength. Despite his own personal reservations about being able to sell enough tickets to fill the enormous space and translate his songs in any meaningful, emotional way, Elvis broke all previous concert records—six sold-out shows in three days.

WHEN ELVIS RETURNED to Vegas in August, I began going out there three or four days in advance as he was preparing for his show. Then after the show got under way, I would go back to Memphis to treat other patients and then return to Vegas for the closing. By that time Elvis had met a physician who worked on call for the hotel who would take care of him when I was not present. I had obligations in Memphis that prohibited my going more often.

It was during that set of engagements in Vegas that Elvis told me about a kidnapping threat he said proved to be "real and serious." He was specifically worried about the safety of little Lisa Marie and added security around his Los Angeles home. Elvis was a news buff, so he was acutely tuned in to the media's coverage of violence. At that time there was a lot of publicity surrounding the first anniversary of the murder massacre of actress Sharon Tate and her friends by the Charles Manson cult in Beverly Hills.

In a prior year had been the assassinations of Dr. Martin Luther King Jr., on a hotel balcony in Memphis, and of Robert F. Kennedy, in a hotel ballroom in Los Angeles. Both locations were within miles of places Elvis frequented, so he felt the events were "too close to home." Elvis believed assassins bragged about their killings; and if they were out to get the biggest names they could, then Elvis Presley was surely on their list. Maybe Elvis was slightly paranoid about his safety, but given the historical context of the situation, I could understand his fear.

Adding to the stress over kidnapping and possible murder attempts, there were people rushing the stage in an effort to get to Elvis. As part of a solution, Elvis had customized tour jackets made for his bodyguards, his aides, and a few friends, who regularly traveled with him as I did. It was not an ego booster or marketing ploy. Elvis wanted to know precisely where his security was stationed during a concert in relationship to where the hotel or arena security was posted, so he would know where his best help was if trouble broke out. Security was a constant problem wherever Elvis was; it did not start and stop with concert performances.

Although the tour jackets created a presence for Elvis's security, they also created a problem no one anticipated. Once people could identify who belonged to the Elvis Presley show, Elvis began receiving increased complaints about strong-arm tactics of some of his bodyguards, who had not been professionally trained to handle crowd control. He also had a couple of bodyguards with short fuses as far as their tempers went.

Elvis's security concerns instigated his decision to obtain deputy sheriff badges for all the places he had residences, to enable us to carry concealed weapons. Elvis wanted the guys who worked for him, plus me, to take the required classes and exams with him so everyone could qualify for a gun permit. It was a real "guy" thing for the group. We spent many hours honing our skills at police firing ranges. Elvis met Dick Grob while Dick was a police officer in charge of the Palm Springs firing range. Dick was considered the best shot in the area, and that pleased Elvis immensely.

Acquiring firearm permits took Elvis's interest in guns as a hobby to a whole new level. It precipitated his becoming an avid collector of unusual and valuable firearms. He also purchased guns for everybody in his group, which the press had dubbed the "Memphis Mafia," to protect him and them from any threats, actual or perceived.

Elvis was truly into police work. He liked the action; it was a change of pace for him. He would listen to police scanners, hop on his motorcycle, make it to the scene of a crime before the cops arrived, direct traffic, and perform any unofficial police business he could get away with. He would even pull over speeding drivers and give them verbal warnings about breaking the law. Since Elvis was an honorary captain in the Memphis Police Department and a gun-carrying special deputy for Shelby County, the law enforcement officers seemed to look on Elvis's escapades as a notch above what would be considered a concerned citizen's arrest, although he never actually made any of those.

On occasion, if Elvis made it to the scene of an accident before the police, after they arrived they would have to ask him to leave because he would be

attracting a crowd. Most policemen seemed to get a kick out of how dedicated the king of rock 'n' roll was to "acting" like a police officer. Some in the
Memphis Mafia may have thought it was silly, but Elvis truly dug it.

PARKER ARRANGED FOR the Elvis Presley show to go on the road on
September 9, 1970, for his first tour since the fifties. Elvis realized more than
ever what an easy target he would be on center stage under the spotlights,
traveling from city to city. Elvis would also be filming the MGM documentary *Elvis: That's the Way It Is* that would bring even more publicity to him
and the particulars about his life on the road.

There was a lot going on in Elvis's career—much of it in uncharted territory. He was entirely responsible for putting his stage show together. He was
also developing his personal business organization to take care of his needs
on the road, separate from what Parker, his record label, RCA tours, and his
booking agent handled. He oversaw his costume design, his band, and his
choreography. It was an enormous undertaking.

There was a tremendous amount of mental pressure bearing down on
Elvis that, when combined with the physical stressors on his body, was taking him to an increased level of anxiety. Elvis's life had quickly gone from a
balancing act to a juggling act; making movies and recording now seemed
simple in comparison to the complexities of life on the road.

More and more Elvis wanted to know if I
could "get away from Memphis for a while." He
would say he had a couple of things he needed to
discuss with me that he really could not talk
about over the phone. He would rationalize my
coming to see him in California or wherever he
was as getting me "out of Memphis." Elvis could
not understand the preparations I had to make
in order to leave my other patients. After I arrived
he did not seem to want anything I considered
very important other than my companionship.

Universal Pictures Press Photo

Only occasionally in those days was Elvis what
I might call *sick*. I finally realized that what Elvis
wanted was a sounding board for his ideas. He
needed someone he could trust to simply *listen*
to him to relieve the pressure.

Elvis plays a doctor in the
movie *Change of Habit*.

WHEN ELVIS BEGAN his January engagement in '71, he complained about not feeling well. He suffered from the flu for several days and "couldn't get going" like he wanted to on stage. This time I stayed in Las Vegas without my family for a couple of weeks, but it was really hard on me. The time away caused a lot of problems at home and in my practice.

Six other doctors had to divide the time necessary to take care of my patients. With the different schedule dictated by travel and shows, it was hard for us to connect to discuss what needed to be done for my hospitalized patients. It was a burden on the other doctors to cover for me, and often they would want me to work weekends and nights to cover for them when I returned. Reluctantly, Elvis understood. I had been in the Medical Group for only four years when I met Elvis, and my practice was continuing to grow.

My field was internal medicine and I loved my work, especially diagnostics. I had studied so many years preparing for certification that I was not happy unless I was putting to use what I had learned to help others. Still I encountered some medical challenges that—as an internist—I did not feel fully equipped to handle by myself. When these arose, I always sought opinions and expertise from the top medical specialists in their respective fields. As Elvis began to rely on me more for treatment, it became even more important that I follow that procedure. When necessary I would sometimes take a doctor I was consulting with me to see Elvis for a personal, "hands-on" diagnosis.

One such time was March 16, 1971. That was the day I received a telephone call from Nashville telling me that Elvis had a terrible pain in one eye and had to leave his recording session and head to a doctor's office. As usual, Elvis did not want to go into the hospital, which is what the doctor recommended. Luckily, I knew the Nashville ophthalmologist, Dr. Spencer Thornton, who had seen Elvis. He had been one of my professors in medical school, and I called him right away.

Dr. Thornton assured me that Elvis was in serious condition, and he did not advise his returning to Memphis. With Elvis's extraordinary pain and the fact that the pain was inside his eyeball, where the nerve fibers and blood vessels are located, the problem was extremely dangerous and could even threaten Elvis's eyesight. Dr. Thornton felt I needed to get involved right away.

Nashville's Baptist Hospital had a hotel attached to it for out-of-town families who were visiting patients at the hospital. Dr. Thornton arranged for Elvis to go there, and I was to bring Dr. David Meyer, the top ophthalmologist in Tennessee, to give a second professional opinion.

We chartered a plane, whose pilot, Fred Smith, later became a good friend of mine. (Fred started Federal Express, the original overnight package delivery service.) As we proceeded on our two-hundred-mile trip, I updated Dr. Meyer on Elvis's medical history. Elvis had been dealing with migraine headaches due in part to his hypersensitivity to light, often triggered by the spotlights he had to contend with while performing onstage. Additionally Elvis suffered from Reiter's syndrome. This is a disease that is initially generated by infection in genetically predisposed individuals and is characterized by reoccurrence of arthritis, conjunctivitis, and urethritis. It had caused glaucoma, a buildup of pressure in the eye, at an earlier age than was normally experienced. The disease plagued Elvis throughout his life.

After we arrived at the hotel, our introductions were cordial but brief. Dr. Meyer immediately examined Elvis's right eye; Elvis quickly complied with everything he was asked to do. Dr. Meyer did not waste any time in giving Elvis the news.

"Elvis, you're in terrible shape," he said. "You *are* in severe pain; I'd say a maximum grade ten. I do know why."

At first there seemed to be a sign of relief at the doctor's statement. That did not last long.

"When I press on your eye," Dr. Meyer continued, "it feels like a marble—stone hard; normally it would feel like a grape. But that's not all. Your cornea, the front surface of your eye, is steamy-looking, totally opaque, because the pressure in your eye is so great. Pressure should normally be ten, perhaps fifteen, sometimes *maybe* even twenty. Do you know what the pressure in your right eye is right now?"

A weak "No, sir" slipped from Elvis's lips.

"Well, yours is over *eighty*," Dr. Meyer said, with strong emphasis on the high number.

By then there were six of us in the room listening to every word, and we could all see Elvis's spirits sink.

"Mr. Presley," Dr. Meyer continued, "your pupil has no movement. This is a very bad sign—a very serious condition."

He helped Elvis back into bed and continued with his frightful diagnosis in a compassionate voice. "We can do one of two things: we can make a hole in your iris, which is surgery; or I can give you an injection of steroids immediately and dilate your eye so we can break this open. If I don't do something right now, repairing your eye will be of no value. You won't have any vision in it."

It was obvious to all of us that Dr. Meyer was not treating Elvis like a celebrity; he was treating him just as he would treat any other patient in a dire emergency. We all understood the bottom line: if Dr. Meyer did not act immediately, Elvis could become blind in his right eye.

Elvis looked up directly into Dr. Meyer's eyes and asked, "Well, David, have you done one of these before?"

It was just like Elvis to crack a joke to relieve the pressure.

Dr. Meyer smiled, appreciating Elvis's question. "Yes, Mr. Presley, I've done this before. I think I can do this. I have to put this shot directly into your eyeball. But it's the lesser of two evils."

Then Dr. Meyer paused before he continued: "I need to know, can you sit still?"

Elvis nodded affirmatively. It was evident he was suffering excruciating pain and not looking forward to the prospect of even more.

At Dr. Meyer's instruction, an assistant furnished by Dr. Thornton brought an extremely bright light into the room and positioned it as requested. I felt bad for Elvis, knowing how sensitive he was even to normal lighting conditions. Dr. Meyer instructed Elvis to *please* not move, explaining that a needle the length of the one he was going to insert into his eye would be very, very close to all the critical structures a person uses to see. He explained that there is not nearly as much room as one might think inside an eye. Dr. Meyer was extremely convincing.

Understanding how grave such a delicate operational procedure could be, I told anyone who wanted to stay in the room to brace himself in a position so as not to distract Elvis or the doctor in any way. Barbara Leigh, a beautiful young actress and the girlfriend of the MGM president who had filmed the documentary *Elvis: That's the Way It Is*, had flown out for Elvis's recording session. She was present for moral support and quickly moved to Elvis's side and took hold of his hand.

Dr. Meyer deadened the white of Elvis's eye, inserted a speculum to hold the eyelids open, and with steady hands injected the long needle full of steroids directly into Elvis's eyeball. The tension in the room held us spellbound as we watched Dr. Meyer's talented hands work. Elvis gave no signs of wincing. Sooner than I expected, Dr. Meyer leaned back and resumed breathing at a normal rate. Almost immediately the pressure in Elvis's eye began to drop. Dr. Meyer was impressed with Elvis's flawless performance.

"What discipline!" Dr. Meyer boasted. "Elvis did not move; he was tremendous. He was incredible!"

By then Elvis was no longer "Mr. Presley" to Dr. Meyer, who went on and on praising the actor for what may have been the role of his lifetime.

Later, while we were discussing the situation, Dr. Meyer agreed that Elvis's self-control could have come from his karate training, which I had told him about on the way to the hospital. "It was an incredible display of courage and concentration," he told me.

Within a few hours Elvis's condition was greatly improved. Convinced there would be no immediate complications, Dr. Meyer and I returned to Memphis.

Elvis had to wear an eye patch for a few weeks, and from that point on he wore dark glasses even on cloudy days to diminish the risk of damage to his sensitive eyes. To show his gratitude to the good doc for saving his sight, Elvis sent Dr. Meyer an impressive contemporary metal desk equipped with a television, a tape recorder, and other gadgets for the new office he had just opened. Dr. Meyer became Elvis's friend, a welcomed guest at his live shows, and one of his medical consultants for the rest of his life. The "eyeball episode" remained one of Elvis's favorite stories and grew more intense each time he told it.

As FATE WOULD have it, the demand for tour dates increased substantially, so Parker expanded the road tours, sandwiching in dates between Elvis's Las Vegas engagements. In most cases the largest arena in small towns on the itinerary could not accommodate the demand for tickets; many of the dates would require Elvis to perform two shows a night just as he did in Vegas. Elvis decided to lease a jet and hire a full-time pilot in an attempt to simplify some of the traveling nonsense.

On July 20, 1971, Elvis opened his first engagement in the High Sierra Room at the Sahara Tahoe Hotel in Stateline, Nevada. In what was by then business as usual, Elvis broke all records for two shows. A month later his performances would pack the showrooms and again break records. These were perhaps the best-received shows in Elvis's career as far as his audiences' response. He was playful and enthusiastic and musically in top form.

Fans were unaware that these back-to-back performances were taking every ounce of Elvis's energy. The climate change affected his sinuses and throat, as did the troublesome smoke-filled rooms in Lake Tahoe and Vegas. The nearly blinding, bright spotlights were another source of continuing aggravation—a trigger for his migraines and a detriment to his sensitive eyes.

What kept Elvis going was the reaction of his audiences. The better their response, the more intense his performances became—the more he gave of himself. Soon exhaustion was a key factor in his complaints. I think people did not realize that Elvis's shows were extremely athletic performances. No one expects a pro football player or even a pro basketball player to regularly perform more than one or two games a *week*, unless he is in a tournament or it is play-off time.

Elvis always had a tournament-type schedule, and the pressures that go with that. He was regularly performing one or two shows a night on every date; yet Elvis didn't get much sympathy when he did not feel well. He was a man who appeared to have it all, and he was expected to be above such ordinary human frailties as allergies, colds, or exhaustion.

Many times Elvis's illnesses were intestinal and did not respond quickly to over-the-counter medications. This was a serious problem for Elvis, who had to perform before hundreds or thousands of people who expected him to be onstage on time. At first I had passed off the problems as symptoms due in large part to his nerves, loss of sleep, and inconsistent diet, but Elvis's lack of stamina appeared to be more than a lack of energy and severe incontinence. Something else was going on.

By mid-'71 the fun associated with beginning to tour again had turned to hard work—slowly at first, but picking up speed as dates were checked off the calendar. The number of shows, the amount of travel, the pressure of being in peak form, the drain on his voice in multiple shows night after night would have been absolutely unrealistic for any other entertainer; but for Elvis it was expected. These were factors critics never seemed to consider when expecting Elvis to be perfect each time out. Traveling was grueling for the time and the energy it took; and once Elvis arrived at his destination, the real stress began.

During his August engagement in Las Vegas, an overwhelming demand for tickets caused the addition of an unprecedented third show in a single night. The next night Elvis complained of the flu, but performed. The rest of the engagement went downhill. Unfortunately his scheduled year-end tour included more dates than usual. Before it was over, he began having eye trouble again from glaucoma. The bright lights continued to aggravate his migraine headaches, and even when wearing dark glasses, he preferred the comfort of rooms with dim lights.

ELVIS SHOWED NO enthusiasm for returning to Vegas at the end of January 1972. Priscilla had moved out of Graceland with Lisa Marie and into her own apartment in Los Angeles. I attributed Elvis's mood to depression—the traumatic letdown when a commitment fails, no matter who is to blame.

Elvis began complaining more about his bodyguards' inability to handle various security issues. I figured it was just anxiety over his upcoming two-day stop in New York City for his opening in Madison Square Garden. Advance tickets to all four shows sold out in one day—an incredible feat for that time period—raising the bar for his showstopping performances.

Since he had never before played the Big Apple, media attention was intense. Parker scheduled a press conference, and Elvis made even bigger news with his quick quips and outrageous offstage attire. Elvis did not like to give interviews; I knew he particularly did not want to do the press conference in New York City. He did not like meeting dignitaries, mayors, or whomever before his shows. He did some of it, but he really hated it. He thought social obligations distracted him; he wanted to think about his show—what he was going to do.

As usual, I stayed with him in the dressing room at the Garden until he got onstage. He paced the room like a caged animal waiting to be unleashed to devour his prey. The level of Elvis's concentration was incredible. When I looked into his eyes, they appeared fixated on some invisible object no one but he could see. I imagined his karate training had taken him into an unknown zone.

RCA Records recorded a live album to sonically cement the Madison Square Garden milestone into history. Elvis performed brilliantly. Even today when Elvis's greatest performances are highlighted, the series in the Garden remains a triumph.

Unfortunately, the success of the event was marred by a personal problem that Elvis discussed with a longtime friend.

"When he called me, he was really upset," our friend told me, remembering Elvis's situation. "He had no idea that Rick and David Stanley [his aides and stepbrothers who worked with him at Graceland and on the road] had been using drugs, and he had just found out. Elvis was venting his disappointment and wondering what he could do. He felt the people around him should have been more protective of them."

Elvis had a rule about his people not using drugs or drinking alcohol while they were working for him. Because the Stanley boys were related to him as well as being his employees, it created a difficult situation for him. Also, he cared about them, so it was particularly hurtful. From what Elvis said, I think he felt responsible for the Stanley boys because he had encouraged them to begin working for him when they were just teenagers.

Courtesy of Joe Esposito

Elvis and Joe Esposito leave Tulsa, Oklahoma, for the next stop on a busy itinerary.

The touring went from exciting to routine much sooner than anyone expected. This was especially noticeable after the success in NYC. It seemed for Elvis and even for his band that the larger the gig, the greater the thrill, and the harder it was to get up for the next "where are we now?" town.

Elvis held himself to a lofty standard, giving the best he had for every show. He always wanted to feel good for his audience—for everybody. He wanted to be the leader, the Indian chief, and set an example for his musicians, his crew, and the guys on his personal staff. While he was on tour, Elvis expected perfection out of everybody—no screw-ups. This kept pressure on him, as well, to make certain nothing went wrong. It was a huge commitment and a heavy responsibility. Elvis wanted people—and companionship—he could count on.

COMING HOME TO Memphis even briefly in July of 1972 provided Elvis with a little "hang time," and everyone enjoyed being together in a relaxing environment. It was obvious Elvis had missed his Memphis friends, and he picked up doing the usual things, like attending movies at the Memphian Theatre. It was here Elvis met Linda Thompson, a willowy beauty and at that time the Miss Tennessee Universe crown holder. She would become a significant relationship in Elvis's life for the next four years.

Many stories exist about Elvis the legendary lover, primarily when he was making movies—how he was very sexually oriented in his relationships with his women. I cannot account for that. During the times I was with him, I never saw him attempt to prove he was a sex symbol. Elvis, for the most part, was extremely attentive to his dates and wanted the woman at his side to be the main attraction. He always wanted her decked out with the necessary jewelry and attire—to stand out so everyone would know she was his girl.

Photo by Jeanne LeMay Dumas ©

Elvis and Linda Thompson at the beginning of their great romance.

He wanted people to see that he had the most beautiful girl in the room. Linda's beauty said everything that needed to be said about him as a man and his sexual prowess. She definitely read Elvis's needs and played her role affectionately to the hilt. Linda doted on Elvis and always kept the mood light and happy. Everyone in his entourage liked her, and I could tell that pleased Elvis even more.

LIKE NO STAR before him, Elvis's music making had established him as the ultimate pop-culture icon. Still, no one could have foreseen that his next entertainment coup would make Elvis a household name around the world—even for people who could speak no other word in English. Tom Parker had found a way to make Elvis's dream of touring the world come true—in a sense. Fans in forty countries would be able to see Elvis "live," essentially without his leaving his home turf.

The plan was for Elvis to arrive in Honolulu, Hawaii, on January 14, 1973, and at 12:30 in the morning perform a concert that would be beamed live via satellite to most of the countries of the Far East, including Japan and Australia. The show would be beamed from Hong Kong to the Chinese mainland and by delay broadcast to thirty countries in Europe. Since satellite transmission as well as videotaping was in its infancy, lack of technology had prevented most people around the world from seeing Elvis perform in concert. That would now change.

Most people did not know that Elvis had done a complete run-through the night before in front of a live audience, as sort of a dress rehearsal for the people who could not get tickets for the sold-out special the next night. It also was a spectacular show. Elvis chose the twenty-three songs he sang and arranged his own choreography, putting everything he had into the presentation of the ultimate Elvis on a worldwide stage.

For the satellite show, he was draped in a white cape with red, blue, and gold stones studded to form the American (bald) eagle. Elvis was the image of the USA that 98 percent of Japanese television viewers took to bed with them that night. More than one billion people, the largest audience ever reported to have been assembled, actually watched Elvis do his thing. That onetime live global event was the most expensive television spectacular in history, with the highest ratings ever recorded. After an utterly awesome performance, Elvis spent hours patiently singing additional songs to be inserted in the U.S. version of *Elvis: Aloha from Hawaii* that would be rebroadcast later.

Every review I have ever read praises Elvis's near-perfect performance at the event, which was later best described as "an incredible feat of monumental proportions." It was exactly that.

After long days and sleepless nights performing and recording for the event, Elvis was totally depleted. Before he returned to Vegas to pick up where he had left off, I asked him what he thought about the phenomenal year he was having and the historic feat he had just accomplished. He did not answer; he just stared into space. Elvis would never again be the same.

LESS THAN TWO weeks after the Hawaii satellite event, Elvis returned to play Vegas. Before he could get off to a good start, he called me about a throat ailment. He was so hoarse that his Las Vegas doctors had advised him not to perform. He was understandably depressed.

A short time later I heard that Elvis had come unglued, gone "totally wild," after a security altercation that proved to be only excited fans. Linda called for the Hilton Hotel doctor to sedate him. His rant went on for days, with the doctor checking on him periodically. When I was informed of the incident by phone, I could not decide whether I was glad I had missed the ordeal or sorry I had not been there for Elvis. One thing was certain: this did not sound like the Elvis I knew.

After he completed that troubled engagement, Elvis would not leave Vegas. One of my patients who worked for Elvis called and confided in me that he did not know what to do. The rest of his guys wanted to go home to their families. That was when I began to notice an increase in the complaints plaguing Elvis when he called me. From this point on he began canceling shows in Vegas. Busy treating my patients in Memphis, I was somewhat out of the loop. I was only told he was under the care of more than one doctor there.

Elvis had been performing two shows a night in Vegas and often two shows a night on the road before traveling to the next city. I thought his grueling schedule was what had Elvis so stressed and exhausted. When we talked by phone, I could detect his agitation, which I interpreted as frustration.

In May everything caved in. The Sahara Tahoe overbooked its theater and had near riots when ticket holders were unable to be seated. Elvis was extremely frustrated over his continuing problems with security. Reports from the road said Elvis was not looking good and his voice was weak. Elvis had looked fantastic the last time I had seen him in Hawaii at the satellite special; I just could not understand what was happening. Then he canceled the rest of his Sahara dates and returned to Los Angeles to rest. When he did not return to Memphis, I was disappointed, knowing that he would be back on the road in a couple of weeks.

After Elvis's next tour began, my receptionist alerted me to an "extremely important" phone call from Vernon. I remember how pitiful his voice sounded when he asked, "Could you come out and see if you can do something for Elvis?"

That was in June 1973. I had not seen Elvis in six months, and I thought I had better go check on him. I had no clue I would be walking into one of the most frightening situations of my career.

I HAD JUST arrived in St. Louis, Missouri, and was unpacking my bags in the room next to Elvis's. Other members of the entourage were downstairs, ready to leave in the limo, but Elvis was a no-show. No one had seen or heard from him. Joe hurried upstairs and began pounding on Elvis's door. When he did not answer, Joe gained access with his extra key and found Elvis still in bed. Joe hollered for me—frantic. I grabbed my black bag and dashed into Elvis's suite.

He was still in his pajamas, with a sheet pulled halfway across him. He was barely breathing, fading in and out of consciousness. He had lost control of his bowels and kidneys and soiled himself; these are usually signs of a seizure. My first thought was his blood pressure had bottomed out again. Once before he had had trouble with Sparine, a medication for depression that another doctor gave him. I had no idea what type of medications Elvis was currently taking, but I did know what I was seeing were not signs of a drug overdose.

One of the things I remember the clearest is how badly my hands were trembling as I worked to draw the liquid stimulant into the syringe. Elvis's skin was damp and cold when I touched him to administer the shot aimed at regulating his breathing. Joe and I tugged at his clothing until we managed to get him completely undressed. Then we practically dragged him into the bathroom, where we struggled to get him into the bathtub we had filled with cold water. Slowly Elvis began to respond. I worked with him until his vital signs gradually improved, and then Joe and I helped dress his limp body for the stage.

By that time Parker had made it into Elvis's room and was huffing and puffing, lifting his cane into the air, shouting something about having Elvis onstage "if it's the last thing you do."

I kept speaking softly to Elvis to reassure him that the worst part of his scary ordeal was over. Within the hour his bewildered audience watched as a semiconscious Elvis struggled to repossess his body. He seemed to be half-asleep until midway through his performance.

I was grateful Vernon had been worried enough about his son to call for help. Elvis was as close to death that night as a person can get without expiring. Like most things regarding Elvis's health, the incident was misconstrued as a drug overdose.

I was convinced at that time that Elvis's condition was a reaction to a medication he had been taking. I had no reason to believe otherwise. Elvis had been under the care of more than one doctor for several months, and none of them had communicated with me regarding the medications they were prescribing. Since none of his entourage had confided in me about his bizarre behavior on the road and their suspicions of drug abuse, I did not even consider a drug overdose.

AS A DIAGNOSTICIAN I looked at Elvis's bloated appearance, his full face and swollen hands, attempting to understand what could have caused such drastic physical changes in such a vitally handsome man in a period of just six months. I asked him for time to work on resolving some of his health issues, but he had to hurry back to Los Angeles. For the first time I detected a deep hurt inside Elvis that he would not allow to surface for discussion. He was agitated and preoccupied—a distant shadow of the megastar from the Hawaii satellite special just months before.

Carese Rice Collection

Ten weeks later, on October 9, 1973, Elvis's divorce became final. *What's next?* I wondered.

Elvis leaving the Hilton Hotel in Atlanta, Georgia, July 3, 1973.

The original Baptist Memorial Hospital was located on Madison Avenue in the Memphis Medical Center when Dr. George C. Nichopoulos joined its staff in 1963. The Union Avenue wing where Elvis would be hospitalized several times between 1973 and 1977 is at the top of the picture.

Within three days I had my answer. I received an urgent call from Graceland, where Elvis had arrived from California on a chartered plane. He needed medical attention but refused to go to the hospital. His breathing was labored, and those with Elvis suspected pneumonia. Could I come? Thinking back to the incident in St. Louis, I did not hesitate. I hastened to Graceland for a personal assessment of Elvis's condition.

If I had not known the person before me so well, I would never have recognized him as Elvis. His skin on his face and hands was puffy. His lips and eyes were swollen grotesquely. His breathing movements were labored; his stomach distended because he was swallowing a lot of air to get more oxygen. After administering a shot to stabilize his breathing, we began giving oxygen. I attempted to identify the cause of his edema (swelling), suspecting either an allergic reaction or congestive heart failure.

I knew Elvis had a family history of heart disease and wanted to have a specialist check his heart as soon as possible. I wanted to honor Elvis's request to remain at Graceland, but I doubted that would be possible. I called my nurse, Tish Henley, who agreed to come to Graceland and keep watch over Elvis until I could return. Unfortunately Elvis's situation did not improve, and remaining at Graceland was no longer an option. An ambulance transported him in a semicomatose condition to Baptist Memorial Hospital.

Our first task was to get him stabilized. As soon as possible after that, I called in a well-known cardiologist for a second opinion. The other doctors and I had ruled out congestive heart failure as being responsible for the fluid buildup, but we wanted Elvis evaluated because of possible hereditary heart disease. At this point all the specialists whom I had called in for consultation agreed Elvis was experiencing an acute drug reaction. Given Elvis's cushingoid characteristics (his abnormal bloating, swelling, and muscular weakness), we surmised the reaction was most likely to some type of steroids. His stomach was swollen because his megacolon was full of feces and air that could not be drained.

One of the doctors alerted me to black-and-blue marks at different intervals on Elvis's body; I had no explanation for their origin. Only Elvis would be able to explain the marks when he became communicative.

We knew at this point that he had hepatitis. We discovered the hepatitis from tests we ran to determine the cause of his fatty liver, which we had already identified. Lab tests later revealed that Elvis's edema was from Cushing's syndrome, as we had suspected when he arrived at the hospital.

Cushing's syndrome is a disease created from an excess of corticosteroids taken either by mouth or shots or produced by adrenal glands, sometimes as the result of a tumor. The most common cause would be massive injections of steroids either self-inflicted or administered by physicians. We doctors decided Elvis's disease was most likely caused by his body's long-term intake of steroids, although I had no prior knowledge that Elvis had been taking steroids. These were not steroids that bodybuilders use, but steroids that people take for asthma and for colitis.

I called Dr. David Meyer to deal with what he later described as "eyesight threatening glaucoma." The condition had continued to plague Elvis despite his efforts to treat it daily.

Dr. Lawrence Wruble, a renowned gastroenterologist, was brought in to evaluate what appeared to be a gastric ulcer and to determine any possible damage to the liver from the hepatitis we had detected. I had consulted Dr. Wruble by telephone while I was on tour with Elvis earlier and discussed Elvis's bloated appearance. I had told him of Elvis's bouts with overweight, adding that his condition was clearly not fat. Now Dr. Wruble could see for himself. Elvis's face and body had never before ballooned to this extent over such a short period of time.

MANY DRUGS AT that time were new to the field and often still quite experimental. They could cause severe side effects if doctors were not extremely cautious. The extent to which many of the drugs were addictive was not known, particularly the amphetamines that were commonly used before antidepressants were available. The amphetamines gave people energy, suppressed their appetites, got them active, and made them feel better; so doctors felt they might be good for depression for a quick fix.

Elvis had told me he began taking amphetamines in the late fifties to adhere to his early-morning-to-late-night filming schedule. Looking back at the length of time Elvis said he had been taking these medications and the time he said he had been off of them, I knew I needed help evaluating this part of his condition. I called in Drs. David Knott and Robert Fink, two leading psychiatrists who were also involved in detox.

After Elvis became alert enough, we had a long-overdue conversation. Elvis denied abusing drugs and was reluctant to discuss his black-and-blue marks. He said to the best of his knowledge they were marks from acupuncture needles. When we explained that was impossible because acupuncture needles do not leave bruises, Elvis admitted that the acupuncturist had also used syringes to administer shots.

With Drs. Knott and Fink beside me, I told Elvis he needed to level with us. He had almost lost his life, and his road to recovery depended on his being truthful. Elvis finally admitted that Dr. Leon Cole, a Beverly Hills physician, had been treating him for constant neck and back pain that had been inhibiting his ability to perform. In a conference call with Drs. Knott and Fink beside me, Dr. Cole told us he had administered a six-week course of Demerol shots, along with large amounts of cortisone, to ease Elvis's back and neck pain.

Moreover, Dr. Cole informed us that Elvis's injections contained Novocain, to reduce pain at the injection sights. Dr. Cole said he was unaware that Elvis might have been taking other drugs.

Elvis looked at me sheepishly and said he was not the only one of the guys who had taken Dr. Cole's shots. I reminded him that he was the only one in trouble from it, and that was what mattered to me. I could tell Elvis was hurt. He felt we were judging him unfairly. But we had to level with him:

"Elvis, you are badly addicted to Demerol. Your body has been poisoned by the combination of drugs in the shots. Taken in combination, the drugs were stronger than if taken separately; you became addicted in a short time."

It was difficult to tell from Elvis's response what those words meant to him. He propped himself up higher in the bed and swallowed hard. The trio of doctors intimidated him, especially with these words:

"This is not going to be easy for you. You are so addicted that the only thing we can do is start you on methadone. It's a synthetic substitute narcotic that we use for heroin addicts, but it is the safest thing to use while your body weans itself off of Demerol."

Dr. Knott would be in charge of the detox. He would put Elvis on phenobarbital, a crystalline barbiturate used as a sedative, to prevent withdrawal symptoms; then he would place him on a methadone regimen.

"It will take a six-week course of intensive therapy," Dr. Knott told Elvis, "but I think we can get you free of drugs, including your recreational use."

For decades euphoric drugs, such as alcohol and heroin—and more recently marijuana, LSD, and cocaine—had destroyed the talent and lives of many music greats. Everyone in his group knew how Elvis felt about avoiding those vices and other street drugs, so it was understandable that his face would register a look of morbid shock. I knew Elvis wanted to get well; but I also knew from earlier comments that he thought seeing psychiatrists was a sign of weakness, and he was determined, no matter what, to present a strong persona to everyone around him.

While Linda stayed with Elvis in his hospital room, Joe Esposito and I decided to go to Graceland and see if we could uncover "some stuff" we were told Elvis might have brought from LA. We headed to his master bedroom suite and began a thorough search. Unfortunately, we found a stash of medications. Small vials of liquid disturbed me most, especially since they were not labeled and I had no idea what was in them. Our discovery also yielded three supersized pharmacy bottles containing a thousand Spansule capsules each, which I had not prescribed for Elvis.

Disturbed by the situation, Joe reluctantly admitted to me that Elvis had been receiving medications from various doctors in Las Vegas and LA and that the results had been extremely alarming on a number of occasions. I was stunned; up to this point no one had mentioned a word to me about any medical emergencies Elvis had experienced—much less overdoses. Worse yet, I had no idea of the regularity of these occurrences.

Later Al Strada approached me. Al, who had ambitions toward premed at UCLA, was Elvis's personal aide and worked more closely with him than most of the other guys. Al told me he had become so concerned about Elvis and the medications available to him that he had taken it upon himself to sneak pills out of Elvis's medicine bottles and flush them to deplete Elvis's supply.

We devised a method for making placebos of the capsules by taking capsules apart and substituting artificial sweetener for the medicine that was supposed to be inside the capsules. We recruited other members of Elvis's entourage to help us.

I began searching for pharmaceutical companies that made placebos, to see if, as a doctor, I could order them to use in the treatment of a patient I had reason to suspect was drug dependent. A *placebo* is actually a fake pill. It looks exactly like a real pill, but it doesn't act like one unless a patient is so suggestive that just the idea that he is taking medication creates the same effect as the real medicine would have on him. Placebos are primarily used in research as a substitute for medicine in a study to measure the effect the medicine has on the patient, relative to the reason for which it was given. Since Elvis was so suggestive that even a vitamin B12 shot could really get him going, I felt that the placebo would be useful for my goal.

I was saddened and hurt that Elvis's use of prescription drugs had been kept from me. I realized that the guys' loyalty was to Elvis first. I learned later, however, that some of them were even keeping Elvis's drug intake a secret from one another.

I was grateful that Elvis was in Memphis, where I could oversee his recovery, but I knew I could not continue to treat him effectively if he was going to obtain and use medications from other sources. I had a choice to make. Either I could confront Elvis and tell him to find another doctor; or I could continue to treat him, knowing I would probably never have complete knowledge of or control over what, if any, additional medications he might take. I only knew for certain I never again wanted to see Elvis in the life-compromising conditions I had seen him in twice in the last four months. I needed time to decide what to do.

ELVIS RETURNED TO Graceland on November 1, 1973, free from the addictive medications that had caused his hospitalization. From that time on I was able to work with him more closely on his specific health-related issues that had led to his seeking pain medication and overmedicating himself. First I focused on treating his insomnia, which I felt was a contributing factor to other problems he had been experiencing. I suggested he enter a sleep clinic I had located in Arkansas, one of the few in the country. He was not ready to do that.

So we tried an experiment. I told Elvis to stay awake as long as he could until he fell asleep without sleeping medications, no matter how long it took. I asked Sam Phillips, another patient of mine who owned a recording studio and several radio stations, if he would have a "sleep tape" made for Elvis that might aid his ability to fall asleep.

I told Elvis proudly, "For the first time in eons, Elvis Presley has no place he *has* to go and nothing he *has* to do. You can read, watch TV, and do whatever you want."

Unfortunately the experiment did not work. Elvis did not sleep for three days and nights, so his doting cooks took advantage of his waking hours by serving all the favorite dishes he had missed during the many months he had been away. He might not be able to sleep, but he could eat; and he did. Obviously I had to change my plan, so I decided to concentrate on Elvis's diet instead.

At that time Elvis's weight problem was more fluctuation caused from bloating than it was from gaining actual pounds, but still I believed his diet might be contributing to some of his health issues, particularly those involving his chronic intestinal problems. It was necessary with the strenuous work Elvis did onstage to find an appropriate diet that would work for him. He had a bad habit of reading about a new fad diet in a magazine and just having to try it. He had this thing about wanting to "lose weight the fast and easy way." One time just before he went on tour, somebody came up with a no-calorie Jell-O diet. Elvis ate Jell-O ten times a day until he got full. To his dismay he lost zero pounds.

I tried to encourage his cooks to substitute fruit for sweet desserts and a low-carbohydrate diet for their Southern cooking with butter and sugar, even in vegetables. I asked them to reduce the starches and skillet-fried foods. They just stared back at me as if I were crazy. I got it. Elvis was their boss, and they would cook what *he* told them to cook. I realized then it was going to be easier to control Elvis's diet on the road than at Graceland. It became obvious that, like most people, if he could not sleep, he would eat; so we were forced to reintroduce some type of sleeping aid into his medication regimen. This time, however, I needed to devise a new plan for administering his meds.

It was time for another serious conversation with Elvis. I told him I could not trust him to continue handling his own medicines. I was not accusing him of *deliberately* taking too much, but I had talked with some of his people who said sometimes he had taken something when he was half-asleep to be sure he could go back to sleep. He might not need it at that point, because it takes a while for some sleeping pills to work. I told him I believed that unintentionally overmedicating could have created a lot of his problems earlier on the tour.

I said, "Let me handle your medications. You call me if you need me."

The plan worked well for a while, but then he got to the point where he would say, "Hey, I'm an adult. Why can't I handle my own medicines? Why do you have to babysit me?"

"We've tried dispensing meds the other way, and you saw what happened," I told him. "This is the only way I can be responsible for your medications."

AFTER RESTING FROM his hospitalization for ten days, Elvis left for Palm Springs. Then he headed to Los Angeles to visit with Lisa Marie. When he returned home, he dove into a stressful two weeks of recording at Stax studio. He had trouble getting the band members he wanted for his sessions because of the holidays and problems with his song selections. Overall the event was a total disappointment to him. When the ordeal ended, Elvis was unusually lethargic. I was growing more concerned.

I thought Lisa Marie's visit at Christmas would lift his spirits unless there was a medical basis for the signs of depression I was continuing to notice. I talked with Elvis about seeing either Dr. Knott or Dr. Fink for a follow-up consultation. He declined, saying he thought he could work through the situation on his own.

Maybe Elvis's body just needs more time to heal from the train wreck it has been through, I thought.

Because of his illness, his adrenal glands had not been functioning normally before his hospitalization. Afterward they were able to continue to produce sufficient adrenal hormones under normal circumstances, but not in stressful circumstances, whether physical or emotional. By the end of the year, it was obvious that Elvis's depression was creating physical symptoms and that he needed support through either counseling or medication. Since he was not asking me for pain medication at that point, I thought his detox had accomplished our goal. Usually his pain and major stressors were associated with touring, and for the time being he had a reprieve from that.

I was beginning to see in Elvis's eyes what I had seen in other patients in the past. Some illnesses are life-altering incidents that scar people physically and emotionally for the rest of their lives. I think he finally had come to understand that actions have consequences, which sometimes cannot be reversed—even if you are Elvis.

THREE

EXTREME MEASURES

Nichopoulos Collection

After Elvis's traumatic hospitalization in 1973, I became officially on call as Elvis's personal physician. Our first victory was convincing Tom Parker to cut Elvis's twice-yearly, monthlong Las Vegas engagements down to two weeks each, beginning in January 1974. We thought that was a huge move in the right direction and were grateful we succeeded. Elvis's first trip to the stage after his recovery was one of his best performances ever, and he received favorable reviews from the critics throughout the stay.

After the Vegas engagement my son, Dean, went with me to check on Elvis at Graceland one afternoon. Elvis had always been interested in hearing about my kids' adventures, and he knew that Dean was ranked in the national top twenty in racquetball in his age group. Elvis also knew I played racquetball, because I would often stop by Graceland when he was in town, on my way to or from a workout.

We started talking about ways Elvis could stay active, and Dean agreed to teach him to play racquetball. Elvis was still actively involved in karate, but karate takes a great deal of concentration at the level he was on. It was not exactly relaxing for him. Besides, Elvis loved for everyone to be involved in whatever he did, and not everyone in his group was capable of mastering karate. Dean said he could teach Elvis's guys and their wives or girlfriends to play the sport at a level of competence they would all enjoy. That sold him on the idea.

Carese Rice Collection

Montgomery, Alabama, March 6, 1974.

Racquetball is athletically quite demanding, both physically and mentally, if you work at it. We thought the sport would be a great solution for Elvis's need to escape boredom, avoid temptation, and get exercise—a fun approach to weight loss. A solid, hard-fought game could melt away pounds and neutralize stress—just what Elvis needed. We planned to get started after he returned from his approaching tour.

Despite the fact that people who traveled with Elvis told me his shows were much better when I was with him than when I stayed home, Parker treated me as if I were a hanger-on. He could not see the need for a physician to be on tour with Elvis and would go out of his way to avoid speaking to me. That changed after Parker hurt his hip and I fixed it with a cortisone shot. Then he realized that a doctor on tour could be a good thing.

By that time Elvis and Parker were engaging in verbal confrontations regarding their business concerns. Their heated conversations visibly upset them both. They began finding ways to successfully avoid each other but could not escape the complications that resulted from their failure to communicate.

ELVIS PLAYED MEMPHIS in the spring of 1974 for the first time since 1961. The response was incredible. After four shows booked for March 16 and 17 quickly sold out, Parker added a fifth one for March 20. I had noticed as we toured cross-country that Elvis's musicians generally feared playing their hometowns more than anywhere else. I guessed the local crowd was tougher; the band felt they had more to prove, and they cared more about the people they were proving it to. I was paying close attention to Elvis's reactions. He did appear to be more nervous than usual before the shows; but, as always, when the first note sounded, he was back to being the king of rock 'n' roll.

By that time I had seen hundreds of shows, and for the most part they did not change a lot. The order of the songs Elvis sang was pretty routine, but not his performance. If there were songs the audience wanted to hear that were not on the list, he would work them into his act. Elvis had a great ability to tune in to his audience and know what they wanted. His natural sense of pacing was amazing, and he proved it by thrilling the spillover crowd at that fifth show with a performance lasting more than an hour and a half. Luckily, RCA was there to record the event, which they later released under the title *Elvis: As Recorded Live On Stage In Memphis*.

Nichopoulos Collection

Happily clowning on stage during an afternoon show at Mid-South Coliseum in Memphis, April 17, 1974.

WHEN ELVIS LEFT a couple of months later for his semiannual Tahoe engagement, I felt confident enough with the progress he had made since his release from the hospital just to travel out for the opening and return to Memphis. My capable nurse, Tish Henley, whom Elvis knew well by then, planned to go with us and stay for the remainder of the tour. I had learned after an incident—when Elvis woke up and took sleeping pills he did not need—that I could not give him bottles of medicine to take on his own. I certainly could not give him vials, even if the shots contained only vitamins. And I was using placebos for his pain as much as possible. I needed Tish there to make the judgment call regarding what Elvis needed. I called her "the sergeant" because of the way she barked out orders to Elvis and his associates.

While in Tahoe, a pivotal event drew the line for Elvis regarding his bodyguards. Dick Grob, who was in charge of security, witnessed an event in which Elvis's bodyguards had a rough time getting an unruly fan, who had consumed too much alcohol, off of Elvis's reserved floor. The incident was exaggerated in the tabloids, which claimed Elvis had stood by and watched the altercation. Dick knew the episode would trigger a lawsuit, although he could swear Elvis was not even present when the incident took place.

Carese Rice Collection

Vegas, August 1974.

Elvis's increased anxiety level did not help his health issues. His weight kept fluctuating, despite his efforts to stay active, and he became so frustrated by his inability to stabilize his weight that he would make disparaging remarks about it. Some people have implied that Elvis's drug usage increased with his beltline. I do not agree. If anything could account for Elvis's belief that he needed drugs, it was his stressors, especially the number of shows he had to perform with little time for rest.

Elvis's Vegas opening in late August 1974 was a huge disappointment to him. He surprised the audience with some new songs and received only a mild response, which obviously upset him. The next night he felt compelled to return to his regular repertoire but decided to work more karate moves into his routine. The fans loved it, and critics praised his show. They mentioned that he "looked fairly trim" and seemed to be "having a ball."

Elvis was just like a kid when things were going great for him, and at that point they were. I was particularly relieved that critics, fans, and his management were responding well to the shorter performance schedule of two weeks, rather than a month at a stretch.

It was during this engagement that Elvis met Sheila Ryan, an attractive, shy, and genuinely sweet actress, who joined him at the end of the run. The new couple stayed in Vegas to visit other entertainers' shows and relax with some downtime, just as he had done when he first landed in Vegas. I thought it was a good sign that his health had bounced back.

Before returning home to Memphis in September '74, Elvis purchased a Stutz Blackhawk automobile, his all-time favorite car. He gave another Stutz to a Las Vegas doctor and good friend, Dr. Elias Ghanem. When he returned home, Elvis began celebrating his success with his hometown friends. He purchased a doublewide trailer for cousin Billy Smith so his family could live at Graceland. Charlie Hodge, who already lived at Graceland, received a boat. Elvis drove all over Whitehaven with Mary Jenkins, his cook, to find the perfect home for her and then bought it. He was not finished, however. One night he bought eleven Lincoln Mark IVs and five Cadillacs and gave them to various friends for Christmas.

Carese Rice Collection

Dayton, Ohio, October 6, 1974.

After a successful tour, Elvis was determined to share the bounty with people he cared about. Usually his big giveaways were either because he felt good about a really successful tour or because he had offended someone and felt guilty. The problem was that once Elvis gave something to one person, he had to keep on giving because others in the group would look as if they had been slighted; Elvis could not stand to hurt anyone.

ON THE FIRST stop of his fourth tour of '74, Elvis was onstage only thirty minutes before he had to leave with a high temperature. A couple of days later he was on course again, giving a terrific show at Notre Dame. Two nights later he stunk. Entertainment reporters were going crazy trying to figure out what could be wrong with the king that his physical appearance and performances were so inconsistent. I had stayed in Memphis; but before the week was over, I got another one of those sad telephone calls from Vernon. He was upset over how Elvis looked and pleaded with me to meet the tour in Stateline, Nevada, where Elvis would be performing for the next ten days.

He was a mess when I arrived. One of his doctors had joined him on tour and treated him with a medication that caused his blood pressure to fluctuate. Elvis was having difficulty keeping his balance and was experiencing problems regarding muscle control. To make matters worse, on the first day of the Tahoe engagement, he was served with a $6.3 million lawsuit relating to his bodyguards' alleged beating of a fan in the spring. He was visibly upset for days and stayed in his room with Sheila.

After he closed at the Sahara Hotel, Elvis told me he was going back to Los Angeles to see about a house he had for sale. I later learned from Sheila that they went immediately to Las Vegas because Elvis wanted to see Dr. Ghanem about his new sleep diet. Dr. Ghanem had concocted a liquid nutrient supplement that would supposedly reset a person's metabolism to allow him to lose weight while sleeping. It sounded custom-made for Elvis. He loved that idea and decided to try it. Elvis and Sheila stayed in a suite Dr. Ghanem had built onto his private home for his celebrity clients. Elvis stayed knocked out, asleep, on the liquid nutrient for what I was told was three weeks.

When I learned of the sleep diet, I was not surprised. Elvis was always looking for shortcuts. I talked with Elvis many times about trying to get some normalcy in his life rather than a quick fix. He would follow a routine until the newness wore off; then he would go right back to the same old thing he had always done—just as most dieters do.

Elvis spent Thanksgiving with Linda Thompson in Santa Monica, California. I knew about that, but I did not know at the time that afterward he returned to Dr. Ghanem's house for another round of the sleep diet. I learned the mixture was based in papaya juice, heavy in sugar, and pumped into his system by IV. Elvis was already a borderline type 2 diabetic, plus he took in more calories drinking papaya juice than he would have on a normal diet. The worst part, however, was the diet clobbered his colon. A person needs physical activity for the colon to function properly.

As Elvis slept, his colon failed to empty, increasing the potential for further complications from years of intestinal and bowel problems. By the time he finished the "sleep diet," he had gained ten pounds. He was really mad. When he returned to Memphis, Elvis said nothing to me about the papaya juice diet, but he looked much heavier than when I had last seen him. I tried to convince him that he needed to come into my office and let us run tests on his liver and evaluate the causes of his edema, but he was acting silly about it—just blowing off the suggestion.

Through concerned aides I learned of suspicious-looking packages arriving through the mail and of one of Elvis's guys attempting to secretly retrieve parcels from the airport. Elvis, they cautioned, had taken a renewed interest in his copy of the *Physicians' Desk Reference*. He sometimes got into trouble by thinking he could learn everything he needed to know from a book—like if he used the *PDR*, he would know as much about drugs as a doctor knew.

Elvis did not read the *PDR* and memorize it as people claim he did. If a person were to examine a *PDR*, he would know how impossible memorizing parts of it would be. Whenever I started him on a new medication, Elvis wanted to know why he was taking it and what side effects he could expect. He would read a few books on certain health matters and think he knew what was happening in his body and how to treat it himself.

By the end of 1974, Elvis had all the symptoms of severe depression but still would not agree to resume the therapy he had begun in the hospital a little more than a year before. We talked many times about his needing help for his insomnia, which I felt was a central issue in his depression. When the body is unable to sleep, it cannot heal. The worst part of sleep deprivation is that it puts a person in a hypervigilant state, which contributes to anxiety and irritability.

Most people will crash after a time and catch up on their sleep—rejuvenate themselves. Elvis could never do that; he could rarely sleep more than three to four hours at a time. He continued to sleepwalk. He might get to the deep sleep level his body needed, but it was interrupted after a brief period. Still, Elvis would not consider the possibility of going for treatment. I was getting fed up.

ON JANUARY 29, 1975, I got a call from a frantic Linda Thompson at Graceland saying Elvis was struggling to breathe. Without going to Graceland to check on him, I called for an ambulance to transport him to the hospital, where I'd meet him. This was my chance to get some answers.

After Elvis was stabilized, we started a battery of tests to give us some explanation for his distended stomach that was obviously pushing against his lungs and causing breathing difficulties. Unfortunately tests revealed high levels of barbiturates in Elvis's bloodstream, as well as the narcotic Demerol. I was heartsick. During the next two weeks, we worked to discover the cause of his edema and the extent of damage, if any, to his colon and liver.

I had no way of knowing when he had resumed taking Demerol or how long he had been on it. I also had no idea where he had obtained it, so I ordered a detox while Elvis was sequestered. I figured it could not hurt. I was wrong. The media later used it against us, by arguing that his detox was evidence that Elvis was a drug addict.

One thing we had learned during his hospitalization in 1973 was that in order to be content enough to stay put, Elvis needed his hospital room to be like home. His guys got busy creating a comfortable abode, covering the windows with aluminum foil and having a direct telephone line installed.

It was during this hospitalization that one of Elvis's guys informed me that a doctor had mailed Elvis some drugs "to get well." We could not identify the substances because they were not labeled. I knew that just because Elvis had received the package did not mean he had requested it. I also wondered if the pills were some naturopathic substances, like the ones Elvis bought from Sweden. I asked Vernon if we could have the pills analyzed, but he was not willing to pay to have that done.

After that a local doctor came to visit Elvis and gave him some medications without informing me. When I found out, I called the doctor and asked him what was going on. He said the pills were placebos and for me not to worry. The bottle was sealed from a factory; those pills *were* real. I wondered then if some doctors just gave Elvis medication without his asking for it, so they could stay involved with him and on his good side. I was disappointed in Elvis for not telling me he was seeking additional medical treatment in town, and I was angry with the other doctors for their lack of professionalism. I was also put out with myself. I wondered why I was so hung up on reforming Elvis. Why couldn't I just patch him up and let him go?

During that hospitalization Vernon suffered a heart attack and entered intensive care. This shifted Elvis's nervous system into high gear. He took advantage of the opportunity to ask for extra sedatives from the young nurses. I knew Elvis was upset about Vernon, but I also knew his game was on.

When Vernon's condition warranted his moving out of ICU, he had a room that adjoined Elvis's two-room suite. Now two Presleys, father and son, received smuggled food from the Graceland cooks. Baptist Hospital was getting more like home every day.

After a ten-day stay, Elvis was ready to leave the hospital. There were two reasons at that time why we could not classify Elvis a drug addict as people most commonly use the term. Elvis could bounce back in such a short time during a detox, and his body underwent no detectable trauma as a result of a possible withdrawal from addictive narcotics. He was psychologically dependent, but an addict? No.

Up to this point Elvis had been calling me on the phone if he woke up during the night and needed more medication than what I had left with him during my visit earlier in the evening. I would often drive from my house to Graceland in the middle of the night and give him additional medication if I felt the need justified it after I arrived and evaluated the situation. Now it was obvious to me that I needed to develop a different procedure for handling his medications. I needed somehow to maintain control of the medications I was prescribing for him.

Nurse Tish Henley had moved into a trailer behind Graceland when her husband, Tommy, began working for Elvis as his groundskeeper and head maintenance man. We decided I would evaluate Elvis when I was at Graceland (which was at least four or five times a week) and leave his medications with Tish. She would place the pills I instructed her to administer to Elvis in small, brown envelopes so the aides could give them to him at the appropriate times.

The medications were given in three doses during a twelve-hour period in small, brown envelopes. These were regular medications that sometimes required more than one dose a day—high blood pressure and diabetes medication, antihistamines, and medicine for his kidneys, colon, and arthritis, etc. The medications varied according to different circumstances, whether he was on tour, recording, or at home between such events. The second envelope contained a sleeping pill. If he needed an additional sleeping pill, it was given in a third envelope. I never included injectables in the envelopes as it was reported later on television. For one thing the envelopes were too small to hold a loaded syringe; for another, I would never allow anyone to give Elvis a shot but Tish or me.

The envelopes were sealed for privacy and protection so that no one could add or take away any of the medications. Although that was not the way Elvis preferred it, he had learned during the past year I was not going to give him bottles of pills to take at his own discretion.

After he was discharged from Baptist on February 15, Elvis was in good health. With his opening in Vegas a month away, everyone joined together to keep him active. Dean had investigated the racquetball situation and was ready to go. We started playing on the courts on the Memphis State University campus (now the University of Memphis), at the athletic club in east Memphis, or at the downtown YMCA, playing at nights when club members were not using the courts.

Because of Elvis's unconventional hours it was difficult at times to locate an available court. But when we did, he dived into his lessons. Most of his leisure activities at Graceland were between the hours of midnight and six in the morning. I never really knew how much Elvis's nocturnal lifestyle was dictated by his desire to avoid fans when he was out and about and how much of it was due to his insomnia that kept him from sleeping. I just know he was comfortable being a creature of the night, so our racquetball sessions were usually between 10:00 in the evening and 4:00 in the morning. I barely had time to shower before heading for the hospital around 6:30 a.m.

I also know Elvis loved to win in whatever he did, so he wanted me to be his partner. I'd had more hours at racquetball than the rest of the entourage, and that gave us an edge. If I couldn't play, he'd pick Dean. Since Dean had taught the others how to play, he knew their capabilities and weaknesses. By choosing one of us as his doubles partner, Elvis shrewdly eliminated his toughest competitors.

DESPITE THE UPS and downs in his health, Elvis returned to Las Vegas in March 1975 and did twenty-nine shows. Toward the end of April, he hit the road and toured the South and Northeast, doing almost sixty more concerts.

Sometimes Linda Thompson would be with him, sometimes Sheila Ryan. I never knew whose face would meet me at the door. To complicate matters, he would occasionally add other young models and starlets to the rotating list. When I asked him how he kept up with who was with him, he flashed one of his big grins, letting that serve as his answer. Obviously he had worked out some type of code.

Elvis, Dr. Nick and Charlie Hodge deplane a chartered jet.

ELVIS LOVED PERFORMING, but he could only do just so much of it. The killer was the length of the tours—going through a tour for usually twenty to thirty nights straight. I tried to convince Parker it would be better for Elvis if the tours could be divided up; maybe go out for ten or twelve days, return to Graceland, and then hit the road again. Parker just would not take my suggestion seriously. I knew from my own experience of traveling with the entourage how exhausting the pace was, mainly because of the way it disrupted the sleep cycle. I knew it had to be even worse for Elvis because of his already compromised sleep patterns. In 1975 he became overwhelmed with it all.

His third tour of the year got off to a rocky start. Sheila was not available to accompany him; she had become seriously involved with actor James Caan and apparently was looking for a way to break off her relationship with Elvis. Elvis was not taking the hint. To spare his feelings, Sheila and Joe Esposito concocted the story that she had an ear infection and couldn't fly on the tour. Elvis got busy and found a low-flying aircraft that would allow her to make the trip. As Sheila began to pull away, Elvis became more determined than ever to make their relationship work.

Elvis genuinely cared for Sheila; he had bought her a horse to ride at Graceland and had invited her to move in with him. It must have been difficult for Sheila with her gentle nature to finally say good-bye; it was probably even more difficult for Elvis to realize it was time for him to open the door of his cage and let Sheila go free.

Another reason Elvis was so desperate to keep Sheila was that he could not spend the night without a woman by his side. He often talked about having to "train a girl" or needing to "break in a new one," as he put it. He wanted his girl to anticipate his needs as the guys did who worked for him.

Carese Rice Collection

Afternoon show in Long Island, New York, July 19, 1975.

Elvis went into the dumps; rejection held a particular sting for him. No matter what Joe or I or anyone else did, it was not enough to pacify him.

The trouble started during a show in Cleveland, Ohio. It continued the next night in Nassau, New York. Finally, when it occurred a third night in Norfolk, Virginia, the victim of his insensitivity confronted him. Elvis had been making disparaging personal remarks to the audience when introducing Kathy Westmoreland—a young, pretty backup singer, whom he dated from time to time. Kathy told Elvis sternly he'd better stop. He did.

But he started up again. This time he aimed his inappropriate words at the Sweet Inspirations, one of his backup vocal groups. Two of the Sweets walked offstage, and Kathy followed. All I knew to do was let the situation run its course. Immediately after the show Elvis got on the plane, and with little notice we headed to Greensboro, North Carolina, and another bizarre incident occurred.

After arriving in Greensboro around midnight, Elvis claimed he needed to see a dentist. We located one. The dentist took care of whatever the emergency was, then Elvis took a box of over-the-counter medications he certainly did not need and put it in a brown paper sack, which he carried proudly toward the door. My head was still churning with the ill mood of the tour and the direction it was taking. Nevertheless, I made a terrible mistake. I reached out and took the coveted brown bag from Elvis's hands and told him I would keep it for him. The fact that I did it in front of other people embarrassed him. Elvis did not like what I had done; I did not like the manner in which I had done it in front of onlookers. He could tell I knew my move was not the best one I had ever made.

After we returned to the motel, Elvis stomped around in his room like he had joined General Patton's army. He slammed doors so hard they vibrated until the windows rattled. Then he disappeared into his bedroom.

During his Greensboro concert later that evening, Elvis apologized to the Sweets for his conduct the night before in Norfolk. The audience, of course, had no clue what he was talking about. Later that night, Elvis returned alone to the dentist for more work on his tooth. He was determined to accomplish his mission without my interference.

The following day we had another confrontation. Elvis always had a bus for those of us flying on his plane, so we all could go together from the hotel to the airport. When we were leaving Greensboro, someone had a great idea that turned into a dumb move, knowing Elvis as we all did.

Someone said, "Look, Elvis won't be at the airport by eleven o'clock— probably not until late afternoon. We're all hungry; let's stop and eat."

Accustomed to having to wait on Elvis, we agreed—eight or ten of us— and stopped at a Dairy Queen. There we were, enjoying our meal, chatting and eating, when suddenly a motorcycle policeman and Elvis's limo zoomed down the street. We all jumped up together in a panic, ran out the door, hopped on the bus, and took off after him.

When we arrived at the airport, Elvis was livid that our bags weren't loaded. Since he was ready and we weren't, Elvis flew away leaving us standing with our luggage in the middle of the runway. We toted our bags to the tiny, private airport terminal and pondered what to do. We waited and worried for two or three hours—just as Elvis planned for us to do. Finally we saw his trademark plane cutting through the sky—returning for us. Elvis had relented; everyone cheered the sight of our impending rescue.

I hadn't appreciated Elvis's kiss-off when the plane had left us stranded. I interpreted his act as a childish maneuver and was making arrangements to buy my own ticket and return to Memphis. I was glad at that point that I did not work for Elvis. His show of force was more aggravation than I needed. Then I realized Elvis had made his point: he was showing his band that he was boss. Whether or not he was on time had nothing to do with their responsibilities. I later learned that his band members were fined if they were not loaded on their designated bus at the specified time. Elvis ran a tight ship—not a cruise liner.

After their feelings of relief wore off, Elvis's band began threatening to quit. By the time we finally deplaned in Asheville, no one wanted to go onstage that night. Word somehow got back to Elvis, and he knew he was in big trouble—facing a band boycott. His reaction to the crisis was swift and effectual. He sent a courier to retrieve Lowell Hays, the personal jeweler to the king of rock 'n' roll. Lowell traveled in the entourage for just such emergencies, so he wasn't difficult to locate.

Elvis started buying "I'm sorry" gifts for everyone he had offended and those who might have suffered fallout from the incident. It was the largest purchase of jewelry imaginable. There were so many "suffering egos" when word got around about Elvis's noble act that the jeweler ran out of merchandise and had to call his brother to fly in on their company plane with another load of jewelry. Elvis bought it all.

His father, recuperating from his heart attack, joined us at the motel in Asheville a short time later. I was standing next to Vernon, talking to him about his recovery progress, when Elvis strolled out of his bedroom to greet his father. Elvis had a small pistol concealed in his hand, and as he put his arm around his father, his pistol accidentally fired—or at least we all thought it was an accident. Elvis always had a gun or two on him, and it wasn't unusual for him to shoot out a television set if he felt like it. Elvis was mad at me for embarrassing him earlier; but he wasn't mad enough to shoot me. The gun was aimed at the wall across from where I was standing, so we were all shocked when the bullet ricocheted off a metal chair and hit my chest, stinging as it grazed the skin.

With his father just having had a heart attack, the incident could have been very serious. I believe the noise from the shot scared Elvis as much as it did everyone else in the room, but he tried to make a big joke of it. After the excitement died down, I went into his room, where he wanted to know if I had "doctored the doctor." We discussed the events of the preceding hours and the seriousness of what he had done.

Backstage in Asheville, Elvis wanted me to give him a shot to calm him down. He was still agitated and wanted a narcotic, but I told him I didn't think he needed it. At times like this, when I felt it was going to be useless to argue, I'd give him a placebo and let it go at that. Many times when a person gets depressed, narcotics will provide an "up" feeling, as well as relieve pain. I didn't believe he was in pain. I thought he just wanted to change his bad mood. When Elvis was stressed-out to the max, he would always go back to something that made him feel good. This approach is particularly common among people who abuse alcohol, which Elvis did not use.

Carese Rice Collection

Elvis introduces Kathy Westmoreland to their audience in Cincinnati, Ohio.

One thing that always seemed to make him feel really good was creating the element of surprise. Many times he would do this by playing jokes on people; other times he'd do it by giving people extraordinary gifts. It was a euphoric escape for Elvis; he'd feed off other people's excitement. Some of Elvis's guys said his spells of generosity were often the result of his being high on amphetamines. I think that was a judgment call on their part that most people I know would disagree with. Actually I think the act of giving was more an attempt to boost his spirits than the results of a pill's effect.

Even after what could be called "the world's largest legal jewelry heist" in Asheville, Elvis bought thirteen Cadillacs for some of the other people whom he had offended on the tour—including Kathy Westmoreland.

Later, Elvis would turn to Kathy for companionship in some of his loneliest hours. I was grateful she'd had the wisdom to see through his hurtful actions and forgive him; I knew he was too.

WHEN THE TOUR ended, Elvis asked me if I could resume my nightly visits to Graceland. After each of his hospitalizations, I had made it a habit to stop by on my way home from the office. We would chat and talk about what kinds of activities he was going to do that night—racquetball or movies, etc. That was not a problem at first. Elvis did not get up until around six o'clock in the evening, which was after my office hours and hospital rounds. Once I got to Graceland, however, it was another story. I was stuck. Elvis always wanted me to stay for three or four hours; then I would really be in for it when I finally got home.

I justified my actions by explaining to Edna how important it was to keep Elvis occupied so he would not fly off to Vegas or someplace and get into trouble. Edna told me our kids and she needed me just as much as Elvis did. So I began trying to build a team to work toward helping him stay occupied in healthy ways. That's why I was so encouraged by his involvement in racquetball; the sport was a solution for a lot of my concerns.

Elvis was rather awkward in his athleticism. Even in touch football he was uncoordinated. He had mastered karate and its subtle and precise moves, but racquetball presented a different challenge. It was fun playing with him, though. If he got tired, Elvis would just call "time," even if the ball was in midair; then he would sit down and double up laughing. He would knock the heck out of the ball, hit another player, and just fall over laughing. That would start everybody else laughing—even the person who got hit and had a huge, burning welt as a result. The whole entourage enjoyed those times. I think Elvis's real goal in "horsing around" was so that we would not notice he really was not great at racquetball.

ELVIS LOVED WATCHING college and pro football on television, and he particularly enjoyed attending Memphis Southmen games at Liberty Bowl Memorial Stadium, where we would watch the action from the press box. If word leaked out that Elvis might be at the game, attendance would pick up; he really liked that part. It was comical, though, because people would spend more time looking over their shoulders to get a glimpse of Elvis than they would watching the game.

One night Linda Thompson, Barbara and George Klein, and some of the bodyguards went to the game with us. Barbara still worked for me at the Medical Group, but she had by this time married George, who had become a local celebrity deejay. Elvis's eye wandered over to a pretty, young hostess, JoCathy Brownlee, who was working in the press box. She was Barbara's friend and a physical education teacher. JoCathy also knew Linda from their days at MSU, so they all chatted for a while. After a night of flirting, which Elvis loved to do, he asked me to track down JoCathy so he could call her for a date.

Great, I thought, *Elvis and a P.E. teacher—what a perfect match! It would sure make my job easier.*

They had their first date. Elvis gave her the customary new car and diamond ring and then invited her to go with him to Las Vegas. JoCathy could not accept his invitation to travel with him because she was joining her mother on a junket to Vegas that George Klein had arranged. So Elvis had Linda meet him in Vegas.

A couple of days later, Elvis and his entourage, me included, headed to Vegas. I cannot recall the details of why we were flying on a smaller aircraft than usual, but we were. There was sort of a wind shear as we approached Dallas, and the pilot overcompensated. The plane unpredictably and instantaneously dropped a substantial number of feet—literally taking everyone's breath away. Elvis panicked.

Although the oxygen masks dropped, Elvis couldn't seem to calm himself enough to inhale the oxygen into his lungs. He fell to the floor next to an air vent, so that he could feel the air on his face. Elvis insisted the pilot land the plane. After we checked into a motel, I gave Elvis a shot to calm him. He rested for a while, and then we resumed the trip. Elvis had attempted on other occasions to explain his panic attacks to me, but I had not realized the incredible level of fear they induced until I witnessed it firsthand.

After arriving in Las Vegas, Elvis was physically depleted from the traumatic episode on the plane. I had other concerns about his stamina. He had been playing racquetball rigorously and had dropped twenty pounds, but he had not improved in the manner I had anticipated after his release from the hospital.

During his opening show Elvis had to sit down onstage, which was unusual. I knew he wanted to show off for JoCathy and her mother, whom he had looked forward to meeting. Mrs. Brownlee lived in Mississippi, where Elvis's deceased mother had been reared. Elvis was giving the Brownlees the royal treatment. He had flowers waiting for them in their hotel room and insisted they be his guests while in Vegas. Elvis had even arranged for JoCathy and her mother to sit ringside and share a table with Linda.

Two girlfriends sitting together, I thought. *No wonder this guy has panic attacks.*

Elvis rested after the opening show and redeemed himself at his midnight performance. But after three miserable nights, it was clear I needed to hospitalize him again. His colon problems were causing complications; he either was delayed getting onstage or could not stay onstage once he got there. As one might imagine, nothing could have been more embarrassing than having people whispering about his bowel difficulties.

The fact that his luggage concealed cases of laxative solutions for his almost daily medical prep made it impossible to hide his sensitive problem from those who traveled closely with him. Unfortunately, some of them even joked about it. Now he was bloated to the point that the excess air pushed his diaphragm against his lungs, making it difficult for him to breathe. When he exerted himself, it affected his usually strong vocal projection. It was obvious to everyone that he was extremely uncomfortable and struggling to get through the show.

After the first night's performance, I tried to convince Parker that Elvis was not going to make it through the engagement. Parker told me he felt certain I would "be able to keep Elvis going."

Finally I told Parker, "Elvis is sick; he needs to go home."

We left Las Vegas about six in the morning on August 21, 1975. Elvis entered Baptist Hospital after we deplaned in Memphis.

Elvis's opening in Vegas had been disastrous. This time it was not that he was overweight; his stomach continued to be distended in spite of his loss of weight. What had alarmed Elvis, Parker, and me even more was that he could barely sing. Reviewers had been commenting for a while that Elvis seemed to gain or lose twenty pounds from one performance to the next. No matter what their other comments had been, most critics were highly complimentary of his voice. Now Elvis's singing was in jeopardy because he was unable to project from his diaphragm due in part to his abdominal distension.

At the hospital I worked quickly to determine the causes of his extreme tiredness, which I still suspected was partly because of adrenal fatigue. At that moment what had caused the condition was not as important as jump-starting his system. Since he did not have pneumonia and was still complaining about shortness of breath, I thought he might possibly have early stages of COPD, chronic obstructive pulmonary disease. Now in addition to high blood pressure, he also had high cholesterol. He still had intestinal and bowel mobility problems, which we were attributing at that time to medications he was taking. I needed desperately to determine what was going on with his liver, so my regular team of consultants returned to duty.

In the midseventies we doctors were hampered by the technical limitations of the equipment available to us. We were able to identify Elvis's enlarged liver and found that he had fat infiltration; we searched for information in his system regarding the fatty changes that were going on. Since Elvis used a lot of Tylenol for inflammation associated with the arthritis in his neck and spine, we questioned whether Tylenol had caused the changes; we knew that was possible, but not likely. We recommended he check into the Johns Hopkins Hospital for evaluation and elaborated on our need for him to help us learn more about his escalating medical problems. He refused to go.

I called my pastor, Father Nicholas Vieron, and asked if he would be kind enough to stop by the hospital and visit with Elvis. I had been a parishioner at Annunciation, the only Greek Orthodox Church in Memphis, since 1955, when I was an intern. I often called on Father V when I had a hospitalized patient scheduled for surgery and was unable to reach a minister of the patient's own faith to bring comfort and spiritual support. Father V had visited with Elvis on previous hospitalizations, and they had formed a relationship based on their mutual love for the search for truth.

"My association with Elvis was limited to my visits when he was a hospital patient and my conversations with him about faith, religion, and things beyond," Father V told me, reminiscing. "Elvis, a gracious young man, especially to his elders, had a desire to learn more about the early church. I shared with him such books as *The Incarnation* by St. Athanasios, the *Philokalia*, and sermons by

St. John Chrysostom—most of them fifth- and sixth-century Christian writers. Elvis was also interested in some of the sacred ancient church services, such as the one about exorcism. I only had a copy of that service in Greek. I recall making an English translation available to him. Elvis wanted me to make a copy for him because he felt he was surrounded by evil and jealous spirits.

Lord, have mercy.

O Lord our God, the King of the ages, Almighty and Pantoerator: You create and transform all things by Your will alone. You changed the seven fold furnace and the flame in Babylon into refreshing dew and preserved your Three Youths safe. You are the physician and healer of our souls, and the security of all those who hope in You. We entreat and beseech: banish, expel and cast away from your servant (*Name*) every diabolic action, every satanical attack and assault, every evil influence and harm and the spell of the evil eye caused by malevolent and evil people. And if this has occurred because of beauty, or handsomeness, or prosperity, or jealousy, or envy, or the evil eye, Master, lover of humanity, stretch forth Your mighty hand and Your powerful and sublime arm and in Your watchful care look upon this Your servant and visit him (*her*), and guard him (*her*) with an angel of peace, a mighty guardian of body and soul, who will rebuke and expel from him (*her*) every evil design, every sorcery and the spell of the evil eye of corrupting and envious people, so that Your servant, defended by You, may sing with thanksgiving: "the Lord is my helper and I shall not be frightened."

Elvis was respectful not just to my pastor but also to my father, Gus, whom he called "Mr. Nichopoulos." Dad was a Shriner, and Elvis somehow knew a lot about their beliefs. He became interested in a very rare and very expensive book, *An Encyclopedia Outline of Masonic Hermetic Qabbalistic and Rosicrucian Philosophy*, Golden Anniversary Edition #2114. He wanted to read it, but it was out of print. Elvis decided he would just have the book reprinted. It's a huge book—larger than those coffee table–size family Bibles you see. While he was at it, Elvis got two copies: one for him and one for my dad. Then he had both of them *autographed* by the author, Manley P. Hall.

Elvis would read parts of the book and underline passages and write notes to Dad about his thoughts on certain things. I could tell that while Elvis was reading, he was searching for something—which religion best fit or had his beliefs in it. After he gave Dad his book, Elvis would call and discuss those special passages with him because Elvis respected Dad's beliefs.

AFTER ELVIS WAS released from Baptist Memorial, the seriousness of his condition called for extreme measures. Tish, whom Elvis respected for her competence and her wonderful disposition, had been distributing Elvis's medications since the time he was released from the hospital in January. Now Elvis's medical condition required he have two additional nurses splitting shifts inside Graceland. They were stationed in Lisa Marie's bedroom, down the hallway from his master bedroom suite. My goal was to have nurses with Elvis around the clock, to make his quarters as close to a hospital environment as possible, so he would follow more seriously our detailed instructions for his recovery.

There were times I think Elvis really enjoyed being a recluse; there were other times he had no choice. Sometimes he could not leave Graceland because the fans at the front gates would follow him; other times they gave him respectable space to move about freely. Elvis savored some advantages to his cloistered time. He loved to read, meditate, and watch TV. Elvis was more self-educated than anyone else I knew. He always took two or three trunks of books with him on tour, and he had bookcases full of volumes in his room at Graceland.

One of his favorite books, which we discussed many times, was *The Prophet*, written by Kahlil Gibran, a Lebanese poet, philosopher, and artist who moved to America in the early 1900s. The book contained so much about God and love and living, and it really inspired Elvis. He would sit up in bed and read aloud from it for hours. He made notes in the margins and highlighted phrases that went along with what he believed. I gained a lot of insight into Elvis from what he read; it helped me characterize who he really was and what he wanted from life.

Elvis relished his hours of solitude—not having somebody hovering over him all the time as his guys did when he was on the road. The downside to Elvis's dropping out of sight was that the drug rumors would resurface.

As Elvis continued to grow stronger, we spent even more time playing racquetball. The more we played, the more trouble we had locating a court. The sport was gaining in popularity, and a lot of prominent Memphians, particularly doctors, were becoming enthusiasts. Elvis finally decided he would build his own racquetball court behind his house so that we would not have to "fake the fans" at the front gates or "chase all over town" looking for a place to play.

There were some days when Elvis did not have much interest in playing aggressively, but he continued to "suit up" and liked the idea that he was doing something wholesome for himself. To keep him motivated, Dean and

I had designer racquetball outfits made with his name on them—even special racquetball gloves. We also ordered customized racquets. He would get just as excited over the racquets as he would a new guitar. His favorite racquet was "Red Guitar," named for the logo we had placed on it. Finding a present for Elvis was always a challenge, but it was a great reward to see the look on his face when he received a gift that he would not have thought to buy for himself.

After Elvis decided to build his own court, he dove into designing plans and overseeing the construction of his racquetball facility. He included a weight room and a music room so he could relax—however he chose—literally in his own backyard.

IT WAS DURING that time that "El's Angels," as we called Elvis's motorcycle motorcade, began paying visits to the Nichopouloses' modest home in east Memphis. His visits were unannounced and sometimes happened at night, while the rest of the world was sleeping. The first time he paid us the honor, he arrived at dinner like a landing helicopter.

Edna covered her ears and hollered at our daughter Elaine to "get outside and see what your friends want before they make us all deaf!"

"I don't have any friends who ride motorcycles," Elaine said.

"Oh, no! It must be Elvis!"

Edna looked horrified.

There at the back door stood Elvis, politely waiting for someone to answer his knock.

"What do we do?" Edna asked. It was the first time I had seen my wife without a backup plan.

"Open the door," I laughed. "He can see we're home, and Dean's with him."

The problem was there had been a mini disaster at our Kinsmen address. Edna's dryer had broken. Harking back to her pre–electric dryer phase, Edna had ingeniously hung our clothes up to dry—panties, bras, socks, and towels—conspicuously displayed in every door, nook, and cranny, or strung up on makeshift clotheslines throughout the house.

Edna was mortified. She just stood there as if she were nailed to the floor. I opened the door with a cordial welcome, acting as though nothing were out of order. I thought an explanation would be more information than he needed. Being the nice Southern gentleman that he was, Elvis kept staring at my face, doing his best to ignore the swinging underwear he had to push aside to get through the door and into the next room, which was not much better. Somehow the purpose of Elvis's visit has escaped my memory. It was something he felt important enough at the time to cross town to discuss, but I think he was so shocked by our home décor that it slipped his mind as well.

We had a relatively short, awkward visit. Edna kept offering Elvis something to drink that he consistently refused in order to avoid more confusion. After I walked him to the door, Elvis asked if I would step outside with him for a minute.

"Look, Dr. Nick," Elvis said sympathetically, "I can't have my doctor living like this."

It was obvious he meant no disrespect. It was also obvious that a house for the Nichopouloses' had gone on Elvis's list of things to get done. That's how it all began. Elvis started prodding us to look for a new house. With three teenagers running amok, plans for a larger house had been on our minds for a while. Elvis wanted to hear them all. We realized for the first time that all of the houses Elvis had purchased for himself, for several of his bodyguards, and for Linda and her family had been turnkey homes. This would be the first time he would see one go up from hammer to nail.

Elvis was totally into it. He wanted a bedroom built for him so he would have a "Graceland Getaway" on the outskirts of Memphis, rather than having to go to the Howard Johnson motel down the street from Graceland when he wanted privacy. He had definite ideas about how he wanted the living

The House That Dr. Nick Built
A truly modern house from the 1970s.

This boldly modern house must have caused quite a stir when it was completed in 1977, because Memphis never really embraced modern architecture, especially in houses. High-style modern architecture of the late 1960s and '70s reflected America's heightened awareness of the environment. Modernist houses tried to be totally integrated into their site. They had strong horizontal massing, tent-like roofs with deep overhangs, and "open" plans with the main rooms flowing over changing floor levels that defined spaces and functions. Exposed beams, fieldstone walls, skylights, and dark wood trim emphasized the environmental look. Broad expanses of glass gave a strong visual connection to the outside, where terraces and built-in planters merged with gardens and water features. These elements originated in the 19th-century Arts and Crafts movement and developed through its descendants, the Midwestern Prairie School architects, most notably Frank Lloyd Wright, and the California Craftsman tradition of the brothers Charles and Henry Greene, best known for the Gamble House in Pasadena. This Memphis house evokes images of Wright's 1930s studio at Taliesin West in Scottsdale, Arizona, and Charles Moore's 1960s design for the Sea Ranch residential resort in California.

Contemporary California architecture had a direct influence on this house built for Dr. and Mrs. George Nichopoulos. Dr. Nichopoulos was Elvis Presley's personal physician. He said that he and his wife liked contemporary houses; they especially liked the way the living room and den were open to each other in Elvis' house in Beverly Hills, and they wanted that same openness in their house. Prominently sited on the crest of a low hill, the house is clad in stone and redwood siding. A trio of shed-roofed dormers punctuates the façade; one dormer defines the entrance and creates a dramatic space in the entrance hall.

The foyer, living room, den, and din-

ing room radiate from a central, two-story, glass-walled, skylit atrium. The living room is two steps below the foyer, the den two steps below the living room, and the dining room is several steps above the den. The dining room has a coffered ceiling and a shimmering cascade of prisms for a chandelier.

An open-riser stair with a robust wooden balustrade ascends from the foyer to the second floor, where the balustrade continues along both sides of a bridge leading to suites of guest rooms. From the bridge, you get a view of the entrance pergola, seen through the foyer chandelier which has a dozen smoked-glass globes arrayed at varying heights.

The living room and den have sloping ceilings accentuated by dark beams. Both rooms overlook the pool terrace and the backyard. A massive fieldstone wall with fireplaces and raised hearths separates the two rooms. A television is built into the stone wall on the den side. The bar in the den has a fieldstone base and a full-width, mirrored backsplash, modeled very closely on the bar in Elvis' Beverly Hills house. An exercise room and racquetball court are behind the den.

The kitchen and breakfast room are between the racquetball court and the dining room. Their sky-blue cabinetry is a vibrant accent in these large spaces with white walls and high, sloping ceilings. The family bedrooms and a small chapel are in a wing opposite the racquetball court, across the pool terrace.

Whether seen as retro-chic or still avant-garde even after a quarter century, this thoroughly modern mansion would be a groovy pad for a large, active family or for entertaining on a grand scale. ∎

5564 Cottingham Place
6,900 square feet
6 bedroom, 6 1/2 baths; $589,500
Agent: John Giovannetti
Realtor: Traditional Properties,
788-1752, 753-4007

Nichopoulos Collection Personal Copy of *The Memphis Flyer*, March 1, 2001 room and den to open onto a swimming pool. Edna was cool with Elvis's ideas up to a point, but she had firm plans of her own.

When we got to the place where we could not make heads or tails out of the blueprints, Elvis decided to have a scale model built. That's when he really got excited. He decided there would be enough materials left over from his Graceland construction to build a racquetball court in our basement.

"You need a place to go when the dryer breaks," he laughed, reflecting on the incident that had jump-started the house.

In the middle of all that excitement came the delivery of his customized airplane, the *Lisa Marie*. Elvis gathered up everybody for her maiden voyage to Las Vegas. After that he looked for every excuse he could find to fly somewhere for something.

IT DID NOT take a new airplane to get Elvis excited. It could be something most people find routine—like hamburgers. It all started innocently enough, but it turned into an obsession that would keep Elvis hooked for years.

One night my family and I were all sufficiently stuffed after dinner at the Kinsmen address, when I looked at two nice-sized Greek burgers remaining on Edna's Corelle platter.

"I bet Elvis would love your burgers," I told Edna.

"Well, take these to him," she said, moving to the kitchen counter to place the prized patties into a doggie bag for the king.

Driving to Graceland I was thinking, *Man, these sure smell good! Maybe I should just keep them.*

By the time I walked into the house, I was drenched in the aroma seeping through the hot aluminum foil. It did not take Elvis long to dig into his home-cooked Greek meal. He didn't say a word. His head nodded and eyes danced with every chew. Finally he licked his lips.

"Man, those were good!" he exclaimed. "I gotta have some more of those."

And so it began: our big, fat Greek burgers became an Elvis compulsion. Our daughter Kissy would gather up the neighborhood kids and pack them into the car for a ride to the mansion to deliver burgers. The burgers were also cooked via telephone instructions from Edna to the Graceland cooks, who never got the seasoning quite right; mixed by Dean at Elvis's Palm Springs address, in meat loaf style to avoid the bun; and even fried by Dean and me in the kitchen of a Hilton hotel, to the hotel chef's horror. Whenever the king got the urge, we found a way to make it happen.

The topic of conversation was Greek burgers whenever Elvis talked with Edna on the telephone. "Now, what's in them?" he would ask over and over. "Why can't anyone make them taste like you do?"

Elvis decided it was just one of life's great mysteries.

One night we had supped on a batch of Greek burgers at Graceland before leaving to take in a movie. Elvis was in a particularly good mood, although he seemed to be procrastinating more than usual. My family finally piled into our big, white Cadillac while Elvis slid behind the wheel to drive. He and I were in the front seat, talking about Armageddon, one of his and my daughter Elaine's favorite subjects. When we stopped at a traffic light, Elvis reached slyly behind him into the backseat where Edna was sitting and placed a small box into her hand, whispering, "Shhhh."

Edna told me she could hardly wait to get inside the theater. She practically ran into the privacy of the ladies' powder room. After lifting the lid of the tiny box Elvis had given her, Edna literally held her breath. There in the soft velvet flashed an awesome ring—a beautiful cluster of marquise-cut diamonds.

"It's gorgeous," Edna whispered into Elvis's ear as she thanked him with a huge hug after returning to the lobby.

"I hope I got the recipe right," Elvis smiled as a son would do wanting to please his mother.

We learned later that Elvis had commissioned his jeweler to design a ring with multicolored diamonds representing the ingredients in Edna's Greek burgers: bronze for the meat, pale yellow for the onions, slightly tinted green for the peppers, clear for the bread. Only Elvis could have thought of replacing cooking ingredients with diamonds—a lasting gift for a nurturing gesture.

ONE NIGHT I got a call from Dean in Vegas. He had a story he wanted to tell me:

So we're up in Elvis's suite, and we're talking food. What would be good? What you hungry for?—that kind of thing. Dick told us about this quaint little hole-in-the-wall Italian restaurant with *great* food not far from the hotel. Elvis was listening, and he got all excited. So I said, "What do you want us to bring you, Boss?"

Well, Elvis thought for a few seconds, then jumped up. He was going with us. He pulled on his sweat suit, hooked on his dark glasses, and he was set to go.

We started walking down the hall toward the elevator. Elvis turned to look over his shoulder every few feet. He got in. We rode down. He hung back for a minute till Dick got completely out the elevator and motioned that it was okay for him to walk across the lobby to the exit.

Elvis looked from one side to another and said in a tone we could barely hear above the casino slot machines, "Think anybody will recognize me?"

"Naw, Elvis," I told him. "You got your DEA jumpsuit and sunglasses on, walking out of the Hilton at night. No one would ever guess who you are."

I walked faster in front of Elvis to prepare our getaway. "I need a Hilton car," I told the valet as I'm thinking, *No problem.*

"We don't have one," the valet said nonchalantly.

I was not prepared for that. "Man, I got Elvis coming out. Right *now*! I need a little help here."

The valet got all flustered. He looked around and then said, "See the guy over there in the cowboy hat—old Tex? When he gets his date out of the car, you grab that one."

I couldn't believe it! Old Tex's car was this huge Lincoln—top-of-the-line—and this valet was telling me to *grab* his car. He doesn't even know who I am. I just said, "Elvis," and he's gonna hand me a Lincoln.

"Look, you gotta have it back in *two* hours," the valet whispered real fast. "He's going to the show. You gotta have the car back when he gets out."

I looked up, and here came Dick and Elvis, hiding in his disguise, walking right toward me. I motioned for Dick to get behind the wheel. Naturally he was the one to drive the "hot car" with Elvis inside; Dick's a former Palm Springs police officer, you know. I slid into the back seat real fast, like I didn't know those guys up front.

We got to the little restaurant, and Elvis loved it. We ordered, ate, and were out of there in ninety minutes flat. Dick wheeled the Lincoln back up to the Hilton entrance, and I dropped the keys into the valet's hand. He was kind of nervous by that time.

"Thanks, man," I told him. I think I'm showing my gratitude by getting the car back on time. Right?

Dick and I kind of shielded Elvis walking back into the Hilton, un-recognized.

We made a sneaky trip back up to the suite so Elvis wouldn't be disappointed that there was no mob scene.

We settled in, and I waited till Elvis got over the excitement of his night on the town. Then I told Dick and him about the "hot car" that carried us to the neat little hole-in-the-wall restaurant.

Elvis just stared at me like he's not believing it. I thought, *Oh no, I'm dead.* He said, "What? You mean that valet did that for us—gave us a car to use?"

Whoa. I was thinking that valet impressed Elvis a lot more than the meal had. "Yep," I told him. "He sure did." I was proud.

"Well, I think we need to show him we appreciate it," Elvis said and walked out of the room.

Next thing I knew, I was handing over the keys of a brand-new Trans Am to the valet. He's shocked, like, *Is this a joke?* Guess he'd never got a tip even close to that. Made me feel real good.

AS FAR AS his daily life was concerned, Elvis was a creature of habit. He felt comfortable doing things in a certain order; that was about the only stability he had in his life. Elvis's work schedule varied, as did his medical needs, so I decided to develop a plan to ease the complexity of his having to take various medications at different times of the day and night at home or on the road. We developed one protocol for life at Graceland and another protocol to prepare him for his shows. These protocols would vary slightly depending on where he was performing and what was going on with him health-wise.

On show day usually someone would wake him up about three or four in the afternoon, and he would start with black coffee. Then he would take some sort of appetite suppressant, sometimes innocuous-type things or sometimes amphetamine substitutes. After that he'd take a decongestant and his blood pressure medicine. Then he would eat and relax for a few hours before getting ready for the show.

I thought if I could get Elvis's medications on some sort of routine like he was on in the hospital, we would have better control of any possible side effects from the medications interfering with his performances. His nights and days were twisted around, but he still needed to take meds and vitamins regularly spaced between whatever else he needed to do to prepare for a performance. That ran a gamut from antacids to eyedrops.

I had a certain philosophy regarding administering medication. I'd prescribe the lowest dose possible so I could more easily adjust the doses and

This "protocol," written by Dr. Nick for Tish Henley to use when traveling on tour with Elvis, is a copy from the original, which disappeared when the doctor's car was burglarized in 1977. It reappeared years later when it was submitted as court evidence. The "Dil mixture" referred to on the document actually meant "diluted"—not "Dilaudid," as prosecutors claimed.

push the drug as far as it needed to go rather than pushing it to toxicity, the point at which a person could become sick from the medication. It made sense to me to use two or three drugs of a weaker value so they would not reach toxicity. Later, drug companies started doing that—putting two or three drugs in small doses in one capsule. They were not doing it much in Elvis's day. I also felt the medications could have a better effect when prescribed in increments from the time he awoke until he went onstage some five or six hours later.

After he suited up on tour, I would give him a vitamin B12 shot. Elvis thought B12 helped him. That was a popular therapy in the seventies, so he had read a lot about the benefits of these shots. They supply an energy boost but also increase the appetite, so he had to be reminded of that. If he had some congestion, depending on its location and how problematic it was, I would decide whether to give him an antihistamine or a placebo. I would have to give him something for congestion because he was afraid he would "clog up" without it. That was one of his phobias.

There were a lot of things going on with Elvis's eyes. He kept getting conjunctivitis from the dye used in coloring his hair. Elvis had always loved black hair, and because he was prematurely gray, he had it dyed regularly. He also had his eyebrows and eyelashes dyed black, and the dye would irritate his eyes when he sweated. In fact, originally the purpose for Elvis wearing the scarves around his neck was to be able to wipe his forehead to keep perspiration from falling into his eyes. After the ladies saw a scarf touch his face, they just had to have one, and his tradition of tossing scarves to the fans began.

In the latter years he developed photophobia from the bright lights. I often put a local anesthesia in his eyes. Since the anesthesia didn't last long, I thought it was just some psychological thing; but I did it. It did prevent Elvis from having to rub his eyes during a performance when excessive sweating would get into his eyes and cause them to become irritated. I was willing to accommodate him with whatever would not hurt him. I had learned the hard way that I had to choose my battles.

He had developed the routine of taking a voice shot while he was in Las Vegas where it is so dry. Dr. Sidney Boyers, a throat specialist, developed the secret concoction, a combination of three or four different herbs; some say it was snake oil, a steroid, and a secret ingredient (rumored to be liquid cocaine). There was no medical justification for it that I could find, but Elvis swore it helped. There were times when his throat felt exceptionally dry, and he wanted us to take the liquid mixture in the vials we used for the shots and apply it in drops directly onto his vocal cords.

It did not matter how his throat felt before he went onstage; he thought a treatment would prevent something bad from happening. Of all his phobias, his main fear was having his voice crack or not being able to project as well as he should.

Decongestants and B12 given as shots were routine for him as well. Elvis felt in order for something to be more effective, it had to be given in a shot; so we had a difficult time getting away from giving Elvis his medications in shots, particularly on the road, where his medications needed to be fast acting. From what I have heard, every time Elvis took a shot, people around us thought it was some type of upper (an amphetamine), downer (a sedative), or painkiller (a narcotic). That simply was not true. After we got backstage, about four or five minutes before he would go on, I administered eyedrops.

After-the-show assessment of Elvis's condition was more difficult. For that reason, throughout the show I would watch his movements closely from the audience to determine whether his actions could cause a neck or back injury, since pulled muscles rarely got the rest time they needed to heal. There were a few songs, like "Poke Salad Annie," that I could tell by the way he moved when he sang them whether he had sustained an injury.

I did not want Elvis coming offstage and tricking me into thinking he needed something for pain when he really didn't. When I evaluated his pain to be moderate to high, I would use a diluted shot of Dilaudid. I needed a medication that was quick acting for the pain because many times he would have to return to the stage in a few hours. I coded two different strengths of Dilaudid that I had mixed with B12 or saline so I could give him the smallest dose possible. A high level of pain can cause a rise in blood pressure, which could be especially dangerous the way Elvis exerted himself. I had to judge from situation to situation what was best.

No sooner had we put the protocol in place than I was told by some of his aides that Elvis was going to other physicians to get medications that I would not give him. If I was going to be his primary physician and he was my responsibility, then I needed to be the doctor to take care of him. It is professional courtesy when one doctor treats another doctor's patients for that doctor to call the primary physician and tell him or her what he is doing.

When I learned who the doctors were and called them, they were embarrassed about what they had done. Elvis was entitled to choose whatever physicians he wanted, but if I was going to treat him, I needed to know what, if anything, other physicians were administering. I needed to have the information available in order to determine if something I had given him was causing a reaction or a particular side effect, or if it was from some other substance he was taking. Often people do not realize how dangerous some vitamins and nutrients can be when combined with certain medications.

I tried to solicit full cooperation from those who were closest to Elvis on a daily basis to identify what drugs or supplements he might be getting from other doctors. The episodes people described during which he was obviously most adversely affected by drugs always seemed to happen in Palm Springs, Las Vegas, or LA. If I had seen Elvis during those reported situations, I could have better assessed what was going on at the time. I had to form an opinion based on what was described by only a couple of people who brought me into the loop with information about what they had seen.

Those who had expressed their concern for him were already on board with the program devised for the control of medications I had not prescribed. A few of Elvis's guys were harder to convince. I tried to explain in detail, as logically as I could, to everyone involved that if we did not control the situation, it would affect not only Elvis but also their jobs. If Elvis didn't work, they didn't work. They finally got that.

I had to use a stronger approach with the few people working for Elvis who abused alcohol, marijuana, and street drugs on their own time. Elvis would have fired them on the spot if he had seen evidence of their using drugs while they worked. They thought they were using on the sly. Users always think no one else knows. It was a tightrope. I wanted to get my point across in a way that would prevent these people from running to Elvis and ratting me out. There were a couple of guys who were continually tattling. They wanted Elvis to think they were looking out for him—that he could trust them more than anyone else—but it had the opposite effect. Elvis did not like dissension, and people who caused it did not last long in his employment.

There was somewhat of a turnaround about that time. If the pilots flew out of town, they would call me. If someone had to go to the airport for Elvis, he would call me. Sometimes someone would pick up a package and bring it to my office. Elvis's use of recreational drugs was always a sporadic thing as far as I could tell—a diversion when he was under extreme stress. Some stories have surfaced about Elvis experimenting with street drugs, but I never saw any evidence of that.

Elvis and his guys viewed me as the "run to" doctor for when they got *really* sick. In some ways I was like a parent, who often is the last to know what is really happening with his kids when they are out of sight.

INSTEAD OF HIS annual New Year's Eve party, Elvis closed the year performing in concert in Pontiac, Michigan, setting a world's record for a single show. An audience of 62,500 people attended, and Elvis made a reported record gross of eight hundred thousand dollars for a single performance by a solo artist. That night Elvis had a right to be more nervous than ever. He had brought along a plane full of hometown folks for the event, including his longtime friend Bill Browder, who had worked as his RCA Records promotion man.

Now a popular country music recording artist known as T. G. Sheppard, Browder had two number one hits of his own that Elvis really liked: "Devil In The Bottle" and "Tryin' To Beat The Morning Home." Elvis had talked T. G. into canceling a lucrative New Year's Eve gig and going with him for support. Nothing he said, however, could calm Elvis as showtime neared. Elvis kept imagining all kinds of terrible things that could happen onstage. He finally fixated on losing his voice. He began insisting that I fly in a throat specialist to treat his vocal cords.

"Wait, Elvis," I said, desperately seeking a solution. "I know one of the nation's top throat specialists, and he lives right here in Pontiac. I'll get on the phone and track him down."

"Hurry!" Elvis said, continuing to pace.

I located the number and hoped it would connect me to my friend.

"Dr. Fred, this is George Nichopoulos. How would you like to see Elvis's sold-out concert in a couple of hours?"

His affirmative answer set the plan in motion. I told Elvis I was leaving for the lobby to meet the doctor.

"Here's the deal," I told my friend after he arrived and I could fill him in on Elvis's phobia of the hour. "You're the only one who can ensure that the show goes on tonight. You've got to be good at what you are about to do."

Dr. Fred borrowed my laryngoscope and a few other instruments and placed them in his own black bag. Then we were off to see the king of rock 'n' roll. Elvis was polite as usual and attentive to the "specialist" I had solicited to care for his delicate and priceless vocal cords.

"Okay, Elvis," said Dr. Fred as he prepared to examine him, "open wide. Relax. Hold real still. Relax. Take a deep breath. This will just take a minute. There. We're all done. You are now relaxed and ready to go woo the crowd."

He's hypnotized him, I thought.

Then I realized he was probably just using his basic skills for his new role. After all, what more could I expect from a *gynecologist*?

Elvis gave a superb performance that night, but the big story reported by the press was that he had split his pants. That was not uncommon. Elvis often "split out" because of the extended leg stretches and karate kicks in his routine. For some reason the media preferred the "fat and forty" hook for their news stories. They had been using it that year since his fortieth birthday on January 8 as if it were some big scoop. That's how Elvis ended 1975. He again achieved what no one before him ever had, only to be mocked for his imperfections.

FOUR

"HERE . . . SOMEWHERE."

Elvis's vacation rental house in Vail, Colorado.

One of my best vacations ever" was how Elvis referred to our experience in Vail, Colorado, on his second trip there in 1976. He rented four condos and a huge house with big fireplaces and lots of windows showing the slopes from everywhere in the house. Elvis insisted I bring "my girls," which meant Edna and my daughters, even though Elaine had to be back in school in two days for exams. We went home after the weekend and then returned the next week for the remainder of the ski trip.

Courtesy of Jim Baker

Linda Thompson and friend brave the cold while on vacation with Elvis in Vail, Colorado.

Linda Thompson was with Elvis, and we stayed in the house he had rented for them. Kissy and Elaine were extremely fond of Linda. She had a wonderful spirit of generosity and gave freely of herself in a warm and caring way. She taught my girls how to make snow cream and played Monopoly with them for hours. As for Elvis, he began a series of what Kissy and Elaine called "Elvis's Life Lectures."

"Elvis had gone to Vail for his forty-first birthday earlier in the month," Elaine, who was only sixteen at the time, remembered. "He told us, 'Maybe it's true life begins at [age] forty. I feel like I'm just beginning to live; like my whole life is ahead of me.' I thought maybe he meant a 'normal' life, since I didn't think he'd ever had one."

"He'd tell us to stay away from drugs and how they could mess up a person's life," Kissy added. "Elvis bought snowsuits, ski boots, and gloves for everybody who was on the trip. He even paid for everybody to take skiing lessons so we all would have a great time."

"Elvis took Kissy and me with him to the Denver police station, and we met these two nice policemen I still remember who showed us around the station," Elaine told me. "Kissy and I laughed about the visit, thinking it was probably a field trip for 'Elvis's Life Lessons' course that he kept preaching to us. Then he bought Linda a new car and had it delivered to the house. It was a beautiful two-tone blue Cadillac, and she was so excited."

ONE DAY THE glare of the sun on the snow in the house of windows was too much for Edna. She developed a severe migraine headache.

"My head was throbbing, and everybody wanted to do something to help," Edna remembered.

She just wanted to be left alone, but Elvis was unrelenting.

"I can make it feel better," he offered. "Let's just go into my bedroom and let me work on you."

"Daddy, you freaked," Elaine reminded me. "You should have seen the look on your face. Elvis saw it, and that just egged him on worse."

"Well," Edna continued, "Elvis took my hand and led me into his bedroom, leaving my family behind. He shut the door—hard. He shook his hands like a magician readying himself to perform some hocus-pocus. I thought, *What is this man going to do to me?*

"Elvis started massaging my forehead; then he moved to my neck and shoulders, then down my back—all the time repeating Bible verses. He was so sincere; it was all I could do to keep from laughing. 'How we doing?' Elvis wanted to know. His question seemed to signal a knock at the door."

"What's going on in there?" I asked.

Of course, I had a right to know; at least I thought I did. That was the legendary Valentino of our time in his bedroom with my wife.

"Fine. It's all gone," Edna lied to Elvis. She didn't have the heart to tell him he wasn't helping at all, and she knew I was getting antsy.

"Thank you, so much. You've got really good hands," Edna told Elvis.

I guess she figured he'd heard that line many times.

Elvis pranced around proudly like a little boy bringing home a good report card. He bragged to everyone about how he had healed Edna's migraine headache.

While Elaine and I packed for Memphis, Elvis asked Dean if he wanted his girlfriend to come back with us when we returned in a few days after Elaine finished her exams. Elvis had already asked me to bring some of his guys' wives back on the return flight. Dean opted instead to bring Missy, his six-month-old St. Bernard. Elvis got all excited over the puppy coming to play in the snow, so we set out for Memphis to retrieve the new group of playmates.

ELVIS WAS A maniac when it came to speed. He loved anything that ran fast—cars, motorcycles, roller coasters, horses, snowmobiles. At two or three o'clock each morning, Elvis would man his snowmobile for a ride up the ski slopes. We parents tried to convince Elvis that snowmobiles were not made for the slopes and someone could get killed. But because of his fearless nature, he thought that was nonsense. Two things happened to change that.

One: the man in charge of prepping grew tired of having his glass-smooth snow slopes streaked at daybreak, so he called the police. They caught Elvis in the wee hours of the morning with his goggled night riders—my three kids included. They had trespassed beyond the Red Line, the caution line used to prohibit skiers from going too far up the mountain. Naturally Elvis went to the very top, taking his night riders with him. As they were preparing to make their second descent, a loud helicopter arrived with blinding bright lights. Elvis just knew he was busted—no more riding snowmobiles on the slopes.

"That's what we all thought," Elaine explained. "But when the police approached us, Elvis flashed his own badge back at them. Snowmobiling was still on."

"It could have been really bad," Elaine added. "I kept thinking, *Don't shoot! It's Elvis.*"

At an early age she had learned there was magic in that name.

The second incident occurred when Elvis made up a new game.

He was talking to the younger set: "What about those saucer things?"

Those "saucer things" were not as heavy as a snowmobile; and they were much worse for their riders. They were disks like garbage can tops, just big enough for a double-X behind, with no place to hold on and no way to steer. Both my daughters, who were part daredevil like Dean and Elvis, went for it. So the goggled night riders gathered again at the top of this huge slope, all set to go—all in a row—with Elvis in front, the perpetual kid and leader of the pack. After about a dozen such trips, Dean was ready to stop and go on to the next big thing. Elvis was not ready to give it up.

"Just one more time," he commanded.

Elvis gave the signal and off they went, going no telling how fast in their little disks down the slopes. Dean gained speed, faster and faster. He was whizzing along, until he went smack—hitting a fence post head-on.

"I'm dead!" he hollered.

"Then shut up," Elvis told him, laughing.

But after examining Dean's leg beneath his padded snowsuit, Elvis announced, "Looks like you got big trouble."

He called for an ambulance, and when it arrived, he climbed in without even removing his ski mask. Dean was hollering in pain but laughing at Elvis—still in his ski mask, playing doctor for the EMTs.

"All the way to the hospital, Elvis kept touching my leg, lifting it, turning it. He was really concerned, but he was about to kill me," Dean recounted. "Finally we arrived at the hospital. I pulled out my Blue Cross Blue Shield insurance card with Elvis Presley Enterprises printed on it and handed it to the busy receptionist. She must have thought she was being cute, 'cause she smirked back, 'Yeah. So where's Elvis?'"

Still wearing his ski mask, Elvis looked all around, left and right, up and down; then he answered mischievously, "He's here . . . somewhere."

"And *who* are *you*?" the receptionist shot back.

"The Lone Ranger," Elvis replied matter-of-factly.

But she had already returned to her paperwork, paying no attention to the silly masked man.

X-rays showed Dean's knee was badly sprained and bruised with contusions. He was relieved. The last thing Dean wanted was to cause trouble for Elvis after he had brought his entire family, including his puppy, to Vail on a winter excursion.

Since Dean was in so much pain and from out of town, the doctor gave him pain pills right on the spot. When they left the hospital, Elvis generously offered to keep Dean's medication for him.

"You gotta be kidding!" Dean told his boss.

Elvis raised his eyebrows and chuckled in his trademark style when Dean refused to let him cop his painkillers.

When we left for home, we thought Dean would be returning on the next flight to Memphis with Elvis and his entourage. That was not the case. It turned out that Linda needed to be in Los Angeles for some movie auditions, and Elvis decided the group should go with her for moral support. Dean was horrified. He still had Missy with him. They all flopped in Linda's apartment, where Dean later survived one of his most embarrassing experiences: walking Missy, his husky St. Bernard pup, on a leash down Santa Monica Boulevard. Elvis thought it was hysterical.

"I asked if you wanted to bring your *girlfriend*," Elvis hollered from the apartment balcony.

That was as close as he ever came to saying, "I told you so."

ELVIS'S FIRST TOUR of 1976 started in March after he had been "off work" basically for three months. To mark the occasion Elvis called and asked me if Kissy and Elaine were bringing me to Graceland so I could ride with him in the limousine to the airport. I told him that was the plan. After we arrived the teenagers went downstairs to shoot pool.

Then Elvis wanted a favor: "Ask Kissy and Elaine to meet me on the front porch."

When he got there, Elvis awarded each of my daughters with a special gift. Taking two treasured necklaces out of his wallet, he draped them over their heads and closed the ceremony with a kiss on the cheek. The long, rope-style chains were 14-carat gold with a shining Tender Loving Care (TLC) logo made to resemble the Taking Care of Business (TCB) necklaces his Memphis Mafia wore. The TLCs were usually given to his guys' wives or to Elvis's special women friends. The gifts were especially meaningful since they were usually reserved for those who had won Elvis's favor.

"Now you're members of my group," he told them. "When we get back from the tour, your dad can explain the rules to you."

Of course, spunky little Elaine just had to know right then about the rules for anything she was joining. Embarrassed, Kissy rolled her eyes and watched with a silent grin. Elvis caved in.

"You have to wear them *all* the time whenever we go somewhere," he told the girls with a smile. "If you don't, I'm taking them back."

Elvis did not have to worry about that. The pendants were displayed around their necks like badges of honor, providing them with plenty of chances to tell their friends about their exploits with the king. I am willing to bet my daughters wore their TLCs even in the shower and to bed at night.

OVER THE NEXT two months, Elvis had two tours and an engagement in Tahoe, where he had cut back to one show per day in an "Elvis in Concert" format, except for two shows on Friday and Saturday nights. Tish Henley had made the trip to Tahoe in my place. Before the end of the month, Elvis headed for his third ten-day tour of the year. He trudged along. Some shows were better than others, but Elvis was giving all he had.

Tish recalled the grueling twenty-four hours a day with no start time and no end time: "My schedule depended on his show schedules. It was hard work and a big responsibility. You had to always be around; you couldn't get out and sightsee. Many times I'd called my kids and not even known what city we were in; most of the time we are in a different city every day. You'd go to the show; they would load you on a bus and go to the airport. You fly; then you are picked up and taken to the next hotel, do another show, and repeat the process. It was hard, but it was the best time of my life—to have a true friend like Elvis.

"Toward the end we were doing only one show a night," Tish continued. "Around five o'clock in the afternoon, we'd start getting him up and get him to eat a little bit, since he didn't eat much before a performance.

"It was amazing. No matter how many times he'd done this, Elvis still got nervous. You could tell because he would start saying, 'It's getting about that time.'

"I have seen Joe Esposito have to *push* Elvis to get him onstage. Elvis would say, 'I'm not ready just yet. I'm not ready just yet.'

"Joe would say, 'It's time. They're waiting for you.' I can't count the times that Joe would say, 'You're going on *now*' and *push* him. But when Elvis finally walked out there, it was like an umbrella that you open and close."

AFTER THE FOURTH tour of the year came the bodyguard fiasco. Here is the story I was told: Elvis was fed up with the aggressive behavior a few of his bodyguards had continued to exhibit after being previously reprimanded about their handling of unruly fans at his concerts. Some of their actions had led to lawsuits, which were settled out of court. But it did not end there.

Vernon was upset about some of the bodyguards' unauthorized expenses, most of which were later explained away. Elvis had a problem with what he called "interference" from other jobs they worked that compromised the time he felt they needed to devote to their duties for him. Elvis decided that the employees needed some time off to reflect on their job performance, responsibilities, and dedication.

Elvis hated confrontation and instructed Vernon to deal with the problem. Vernon fired three of the bodyguards without notice and told them the firings were a move "to save money." There was some truth to that. Anybody could look at Elvis's schedule and see a steady reduction in the number of performances he was giving. The misunderstanding grew worse, however, when Elvis would not communicate with the guys, who were not just employees but longtime friends.

After the incident—a year or so later—one of the bodyguards claimed Elvis had them fired because they had confronted him about using drugs and had urged him to get help for his drug problem. I had heard nothing about the confrontation regarding drugs at the time it allegedly happened, and thought it strange that the bodyguards had never talked to me about their concerns or asked for my help with an intervention if they felt his pur-ported drug use was so dangerous.

Anyway, Elvis received word about a behind-the-scenes exposé they planned to write, and attempted to dissuade them, but by then it was too late. The bodyguards later said they wrote their book *Elvis: What Happened?* in an attempt to save Elvis from destroying himself with drugs. Elvis viewed their writing the book as a betrayal and was deeply hurt. He saw it as an attempt to ruin him both personally and professionally.

ELVIS WAS IN Palm Springs, avoiding the fired bodyguards, who were still working on the book, when one of his aides started feeding him false infor-mation about a business venture Elvis had become involved in with Joe Esposito, Mike McMahon (a bond salesman and developer), and me.

Joe and I had originally formed a corporation called Racquet Ball of Memphis, Inc., which was primarily an investment toward our retirement. We had broken ground a few months earlier for a couple of racquetball buildings and hoped to expand the business to a franchise. McMahon was brought in to handle day-to-day operations because Joe and I planned to be on the road frequently with Elvis.

We had an agreement with two developers, who were going to purchase the land and begin building facilities in Memphis and Nashville. We had one year to secure mortgage financing. During that time we talked to Elvis about our venture and asked if he would be interested in becoming a full partner for the right to use his name. We were not asking for any money but outlined how his name would be an advantage. It would be an endorsement of the sport; it would make it easier to attract investors to secure the loan on the property; and it would be a magnet for memberships, which was to be the venture's primary source of revenue.

Elvis said, "Give me a few days to think about it."

He liked our concept of a national chain of racquetball clubs that would be uniquely different, or hip, appealing to an adult clientele and raising the public's perception of racquetball from a game to a sport. Rather than just having three or four courts with gym-type locker rooms, our facilities would be like a private club with eight or ten courts, along with practice courts. They would include saunas and areas to relax and enjoy food and drinks. Racquetball was new to Memphis, and Elvis always got excited about intro-ducing people to anything new; plus, he was committed to physical fitness.

The more racquetball Elvis played, the more excited he became about participating in the business deal. I had gone to the National Racquetball Association when we were developing the original corporation and had figures supporting the projected growth of the sport internationally. I think Elvis believed he was getting in on the ground floor of a sport that could really make a difference. He had already offered to support two of his karate instructors in expanding their karate schools and had invested in a karate movie that one of his guys was developing. Elvis's goal was to help advance karate—to grow the art. I think Elvis looked on the racquetball courts as an extension of those ventures.

He decided to become a part of our corporation on the terms we had presented to him: the use of his name and no up-front money; full partnership, 25 percent. My feeling at the time was he wanted to help Joe and me succeed with our retirement plan as much as anything.

Until our financing was in place, we agreed to lease the properties, paying for the rent with membership fees and walk-ins. Elvis signed the purchase agreement as one of the four partners. If for some reason we were unable to get financing to buy the facilities, we had the option to sign a long-term lease. No one saw any problem with doing that.

Then one of Elvis's aides told him that "his money," none of which he had given to the venture, was being spent recklessly. He claimed McMahon had purchased a new car and hired a pricey secretary at a salary quoted to be more than twice the amount she was actually being paid.

Elvis exploded. He called McMahon and in an irate conversation told him he was pulling out of the deal; he wanted nothing to do with the racquetball courts and wanted his name taken off everything. When McMahon called me, I told him it would be okay: "When Elvis gets back to Memphis, we'll clear up the misunderstandings."

Elvis, however, was not willing to discuss the matter when he returned, so we had to comply with his instructions. By the time Elvis pulled out, we had already replaced the original Racquet Ball of Memphis, Inc., with the new Presley's Center Courts, Inc., name and logo, which was being used on business and merchandising materials. We had to change our name a second time and redesign and reproduce everything from signs to stationery to apparel.

The club was rocking along nevertheless, and we were meeting our obligations without Elvis investing any money in the cause. Interested investors cooled, however, after they learned Elvis had pulled his support from the project. The financing, for whatever reasons, was not in place by the deadline.

That left the three of us liable on the lease for coming up with the money to purchase the property. We opted for the long-term lease and began revising our projections and reviewing how to gain memberships without Elvis's endorsement. We fell behind on the notes.

The attorney for the corporation met with Elvis's attorney to discuss obtaining a loan for forty thousand dollars, amortized over three years with 7 percent interest, to enable us to meet our financial obligations so we would not default. Our attorney had told us we were entitled to twenty-five thousand dollars in damages because of expenses incurred in reorganization and redesigning the company that had resulted from Elvis's failing to honor his agreement.

Both the corporation's attorney and Elvis's attorney appeared to be in agreement over how to resolve the dispute, and the meeting ended amicably. Elvis's attorney, however, did not respond in writing to the proposal he had verbally accepted in the meeting. Either he was unable to talk with Elvis about it or Elvis refused to accept our offer. The corporation was advised to proceed with the lawsuit so Elvis would realize this was an important business and legal matter and not just an idea he could blow off when he got angry. Most of all, we wanted to engage him in a conversation where he would have to listen to the facts.

The conversation never happened, but eventually Elvis did pay the corporation the twenty-five thousand dollars we requested for damages. He also loaned us the forty thousand dollars we had asked for, which we repaid in 120 days. Joe and I found a way to retire the rest of the pressing debt from our personal resources, with Dean pitching in to help. Joe continued to work for Elvis, and I continued to be his physician.

Center Courts, Inc.—without Elvis—continued to operate successfully for about five years until we were bought out in 1981. The new owners kept the courts operational until about 2004 at the same locations. Today, of course, racquetball continues to be popular around the world, and international tournaments have elevated the status of the athletes who excel in the sport. Racquetball is now included in the Olympics; I am certain Elvis would have been proud of that.

Somehow various accounts of our business dealings have been erroneously reported, stating that Elvis invested large sums of money or had to pay vast amounts as a result of the legal entanglements resulting from our investment. Elvis, however, never paid any money out of pocket for his racquetball venture with Joe, McMahon, and me. One book claimed that "Elvis was supposed to contribute $1.3 million in exchange for 25 percent of the deal."

Actually the $1.3 million was the total price tag to purchase both locations from the contractors. This included the property for which all four of us would be obligated if we decided against a long-term lease.

The major problem since the beginning of the enterprise apparently was the exclusion of Vernon and Parker from Elvis's decision to participate. It was not a conscious attempt to circumvent them. Neither Joe nor I felt we needed their permission to approach Elvis about his interest, and we certainly did not feel it was our place to ask Elvis if he had cleared his decision with his father and manager before he proceeded.

As THE DATE to leave on the next tour approached, Elvis was still somewhat angry with me over the racquetball mess. One night he called and asked if I could come out to the house. After I arrived he started asking me for different medications I did not think were justified, so I just leveled with him. "Maybe it would just be helpful for you to get someone else to go on the tour because I don't think you would be very content with my going."

We talked about it off and on, and he said we did not need to do that, but I alerted Tish that she would need to go in my place.

The day before the tour, Elvis told me he had another doctor he had talked into going. Tish went along anyway. I sat out that tour and had planned to do the same when tour number six started. Tish called after the first show, however, concerned about the treatment Elvis was getting and the way he was reacting to his medications. The Hofheinz Pavilion in Houston, Texas, was the tour's second stop. It was a matinee performance, which was unusual when only one show was scheduled per day. Elvis bombed; people literally got up and walked out.

I was in a business meeting in my office with Mike McMahon, when Barbara Klein buzzed me and said decisively, "You need to take the call on line two."

It was Parker. He said, "Vernon and I have discussed it, and we would appreciate it if you would consider coming back on tour. We can't keep booking tours and canceling dates. At the rate we're going, we'll just have to give up the whole thing if you can't be on the tour."

They wanted me to meet them in Mobile, Alabama, to try and take control of what was going on.

I told Parker: "I won't come back unless Elvis apologizes for cussing and calling me names over the racquetball situation."

Elvis had not apologized much in his lifetime, so it was difficult for him to say, "I'm sorry."

After a partnership meeting with my associates at the Medical Group, I called Parker back and told him I would come; but I would have to charge them if I was going to travel with Elvis on a permanent basis. I could not take off from my practice without charging, as I had done before. My associates said they lost money when I was away, and they had to work overtime to take care of my patients.

We came up with a figure to bill Elvis to compensate the Medical Group for the problems my absence created. We took an average two months in the office, figured out what the income was from an average day, and charged a per diem for my time on tour. The money was to be paid directly to the Medical Group, rather than to me. I had never charged Elvis for house calls, and he had mentioned that to me on numerous occasions.

I had laughed and said, "How do you charge for an eighteen-hour day?"

People had witnessed the side effects from Elvis's medications during his performance in Houston. Elvis had taken Sparine (for depression), which contributed to muscle and speech problems. It knocked the bottom out of him—dropped his blood pressure. He couldn't do diddly-squat. Whenever Elvis took Sparine at night, he stayed lethargic all the next day because it was a long-acting drug. If he took a second dose, it could carry over for a longer period of time. I had noticed when monitoring Elvis's condition that whenever he had problems onstage with his balance and speech, his blood pressure was way below normal.

In addition to administering Sparine, the doctor attending Elvis may have also given him Donnatal, a combination drug used for people with irritable bowel syndrome and also for stomach ulcers before newer drugs became available. It has a barbiturate plus an antispasmodic in it. A doctor has to be careful when using that medicine because of the time it takes it to act. The drug always had a debilitating effect on Elvis's speech and motor functions when he performed, because of the relationship between the time he took the medication and the time he had to be onstage.

Many times Elvis had no choice whether or not to take certain medications in order to prevent having to leave the stage during a performance for what he termed "nature's call." It was a difficult balancing act for any doctor to time his medications where they would be the most effective in treating his chronic intestinal problems and not cause embarrassing side effects.

Slowly and painstakingly we made it through the next week of shows.

Elvis was really struggling, especially after Lakeland, Florida, and Huntsville, Alabama, where he performed a brutal five shows in two days. I knew of no other entertainer in the music business who had as rigorous a tour schedule as Elvis on a continuing basis.

Finally I told Parker in front of Elvis, "This is insane. I can't be a part of seeing what this kind of schedule is doing to him."

As a result, Huntsville was the last time Elvis ever performed two shows in one night on the road.

IN MID-OCTOBER WE began our seventh tour of '76 in Chicago Stadium with two sold-out shows. The next night, in Minneapolis, Elvis was really into his performance and worked the crowd into an absolute frenzy. By the end of the show, hysterical fans rushed the stage, and Elvis narrowly escaped into the safety of his waiting limousine. It seemed like old times.

Carese Rice Collection

Two days after the end of that tour, Felton Jarvis, Elvis's record producer from RCA, had everything set up at Graceland to finish recording the album Elvis had begun in January. But Elvis was not the least bit interested in recording. Nothing went as planned. He would cut a song, go upstairs for hours, come back down, and give away clothing—like he was cleaning out his closet.

The second night Elvis's behavior was even more outrageous. He emerged fortified with his submachine gun, scaring the life out of the musicians. Felton disbanded the session. Elvis was remorseful, saying he just could not concentrate on record-

The king on stage in Evansville, Indiana, October 24, 1976.

ing. Obviously! In true Elvis-style he made certain there were ample "I'm sorry" gifts. He gave J. D. Sumner his white Cadillac limousine to carry his Stamps Quartet back home to Nashville and to use for their road dates.

Dean described the episode in frightening detail and told me how grateful he was when the rock 'n' roll horror show was over. Elvis wanted "to get away from everything," so he took off for Vail with Lisa Marie and Linda. Elvis was in a particularly vulnerable point in his life emotionally, in addition to his usual stressors. Linda was focusing more on her acting career, and they had been spending more time apart from each other. I was not surprised when Linda did not return home with him, but it never occurred to me that their relationship was actually over.

IN MID-NOVEMBER ELVIS threw a party at Graceland. Everyone was having a good time listening to music and milling around in the den and patio area, enjoying the brisk fall weather. I noticed three young ladies who were new to the regular group: Ginger Alden and her two sisters. When Elvis came downstairs, he seemed to gravitate to Ginger right away. She did not look at all like Elvis's type to me, and she was a *very* young *twenty*-year-old. Ginger was incredibly shy, and no one except Elvis attempted to warm up to her. I noticed he talked to her a lot before she and her sisters went upstairs with him.

Carese Rice Collection

Anaheim, California, November 30, 1976.

When Dean told me a couple of nights later that he had accompanied Elvis and Ginger to Las Vegas on their first date, I didn't think much about it. I thought their courtship would be over in a month.

Two nights after playing in Anaheim, Elvis opened at the Vegas Hilton for fifteen shows. Ginger was there for every one of them. Elvis had slimmed down some and looked great. Priscilla brought Lisa Marie to surprise her daddy; they stayed for the weekend. I was always impressed that after their divorce Priscilla would bring Lisa Marie so often to be with her daddy and watch him perform. Priscilla seemed to like Vegas and was sort of the queen bee at the Hilton.

Ginger's parents also traveled to Vegas and stayed for several shows. Vernon was not shy about his disapproval of Elvis's attention to the Alden family. Elvis had bestowed an unprecedented amount of gifts on the Alden women during an unusually short time span. It was as if he had three girlfriends. He lavished exquisite furs and jewelry on them almost from the day they met. Elvis presented Ginger with a 1977 Lincoln Mark IV in Las Vegas, and when they returned to Memphis, he bought her a new Cadillac Seville to drive until her Mark IV arrived. She kept both automobiles.

Elvis was blind to the effect that his obsession with the Aldens had on Vernon and other people around him. In the midst of it all, Vernon had to be hospitalized again for chest pains.

Lisa Marie was the centerpiece of Elvis's Christmas that year. He gave her a personalized golf cart that she managed like a skilled race-car driver. When New Year's Eve arrived, he seemed grateful that Ginger had decided to accompany him to Pittsburgh, where he performed a spectacular show. He accompanied himself on piano during a couple of numbers, and the crowd was ecstatic. It was obvious at that point that Ginger's presence definitely affected his performance. He was once again at the top of his game.

Carese Rice Collection

New Year's Eve 1976, Pittsburgh, Pennsylvania.

IN THE PAST Elvis had always wanted me to talk to his date and find out what she thought about him and what her opinions were about things he had said or done. He wanted to know how he was progressing, so to speak. I counseled with Elvis a lot about his girlfriends because I had always thought that if Elvis could get the relationship part of his life worked out, everything else would fall into place.

Elvis felt Ginger was "the one" and that if he could work out his relationship with her, everything would be where he wanted it. The situation waxed and waned, but it never reached the point where he was comfortable with it. Ginger was not at all like other women Elvis had dated. It was obvious from her actions that she was not fixated on pleasing Elvis. She exercised her independence and would leave Elvis whenever she had somewhere else she wanted to be. Elvis didn't know what to make of Ginger; she presented quite a challenge to him.

Despite their turbulent relationship, Elvis had his jeweler take the eleven-and-a-half-carat diamond out of his TCB ring and put it into a new setting so he could place it on the finger of the reigning Miss Mid-South. On January 26, 1977, after a courtship of only nine weeks, Elvis reportedly asked Ginger to marry him.

I was stunned when I heard the news. I could not believe Elvis was setting himself up to continue to be run ragged in a relationship that was proving to be so highly stressful. I thought it extremely odd that Elvis never confirmed to me that he planned to marry Ginger, but that was what the ring indicated.

Elvis had expressed to me on many occasions that he would like to have another child, a son. Maybe he was just ready for marriage this time. The only thing he ever said to me that might explain why he was so wrapped up in Ginger was that there was something about Ginger's eyes that reminded him of his mother. He seemed to be drawn to her.

When the first tour of '77 began, Ginger refused to accompany Elvis even though she apparently had agreed to marry him. She reportedly told him she had too much to do to prepare for the wedding, although no date had been set. The only good thing about the ordeal was that critics continued to comment on Elvis's lost weight, and that pleased us both.

I don't know anybody who felt Ginger was right for Elvis—mainly because her actions did not show she cared enough about him or wanted to be at Graceland. Many nights after he would go to sleep, she would leave the house and be gone when he awoke. Elvis had his security watching Ginger's house and following her to see if she was dating somebody else. He was so insecure with Ginger that it was sad.

Carese Rice Collection

Johnson City, Tennessee, February 19, 1977.

112

DEAN HAD HEARD Elvis was taking Ginger to Hawaii—just the two of them on a romantic getaway—with a couple of aides, of course. But by March 3 my family and a party of about twenty were with Elvis aboard the *Lisa Marie*, headed to Waikiki Beach in Honolulu, Hawaii. Our original destination was the Rainbow Towers in the Hilton Hawaiian Village Hotel, with its breathtaking views of Waikiki Beach and Diamond Head. Elvis rented the penthouse and half of the thirty-first floor for his guests. Elvis would bring us all together in the late afternoon for drinks on the balcony, to watch the sunset, and to talk about what makes life worth living.

Don Ho, a Hawaiian entertainer, was performing on the island; Elvis had all his guests join him on a hotel shuttle bus so we could ride together to the show. Elvis really enjoyed showing people a good time. Not everybody on the bus was equally enthused, however. Some guests acted as though Elvis had lost his mind; they could not understand what the king of rock 'n' roll saw in Don Ho.

After staying at the Rainbow Towers for a couple of days, the beach house that the Grateful Dead had been renting in Kailua, Hawaii, on the other side of Oahu, became available. Edna and I left to stay there with Elvis, Ginger, Billy Smith, and Dick Grob. Kissy and Elaine stayed at the hotel but came to visit us in what Elaine called "the house that rained." It had a sprinkler system beneath the soffits all around the outside of the house, with water dripping gently from the sprinkler heads. From anywhere in the house we could look out and see "rain" falling and hear it slapping softly against the stone walkway. It was so restful that Elvis slid into a peaceful groove.

The rest of Elvis's group stayed across the mountain and traveled through Pali Pass to the beach house. Some of the guests preferred having their privacy; others seemed to resent being separated from Elvis. We would spend a lot of time together, however, lying on the sandy beach when the sun allowed, or by the pool at the house. We could not believe that with all the great food in Hawaii, Elvis would send Kissy and Elaine to McDonald's to buy him sandwiches—just another sign of Elvis's unpredictable nature. What he seemed to enjoy most was playing touch football with his guys.

He put a lot of time into planning activities for his group. Elvis enjoyed educating everyone about the native art and dances at the Polynesian Cultural Center and selecting spots where we could feast on native cuisine. Oddly enough, Elvis wanted to do his own shopping in the little stores on

Photo by Kissy Nichopoulos

At the beach in Hawaii, March 1977.

Photo by Kissy Nichopoulos

Hawaiian vacation, March 1977.
(standing: Dean Nichopoulos; left to
right seated: Dr. Nick and Al Strada)

the island. The special thought he put into the gifts he purchased was the best part about receiving them.

His gift to Edna and me was a gorgeous mother-of-pearl crucifix for the prayer room in our new home. For all his guests he personally picked out beautiful shell necklaces, a souvenir of our vacation, which was also his gift to all of us.

When he handed out the necklaces, Elvis could barely see. He had gotten sand in his right eye, and it was burning, irritated, and swollen almost shut. I treated his eye at his request. Then he received a call from Memphis telling him that Vernon was experiencing chest discomfort. Elvis decided to return home to be with his dad and to let Dr. David Meyer check his eye. Our dream vacation was cut short.

IT HAS BEEN widely written that Elvis was in bad physical condition when he left Memphis for Phoenix, Arizona, on March 22, 1977. It was reported that IVs were administered to Elvis on the six-minute drive to the airport. That is simply not true. Elvis's problem was more emotional than physical. He wanted Ginger to come along, and she had other plans. He was not ill; he was dejected and chose to be nonconversational en route to his plane.

After the tour actually began the next night in Tempe, the situation changed and worsened. The problem did not involve Ginger, however, at that point. It was another issue entirely. RCA had planned to record two shows on the tour; but with no announcement made of a change in plans, they recorded six shows in eight nights.

Everybody, especially Elvis and Felton Jarvis, was exhausted from the pressure and extra work involved. Tensions were high. Unless a person has been there, there is no way to understand what it is like to play as many as eight shows in ten nights in six different cities. It was a tremendous responsibility performing for thousands of people and recording an album simultaneously. The work involved was horrendous.

Ginger did join that tour. But by the time she arrived, Elvis was too tired to do anything but argue. She would get bored closed up in the hotel room and liked to browse in the hotel gift shops and boutiques. In Baton Rouge, Louisiana, Elvis was so upset when his guys could not find Ginger that he wanted to cancel the rest of the tour and go back to Graceland. When he was told he could not do that, he took matters into his own hands. By the time I arrived in his room, Elvis had ingested something and could not possibly go onstage.

We called Tom Hulett, president of Concerts West, the company that had booked the date. He came to Elvis's room and made the decision on the spot to cancel the show. Hulett told me to have Elvis fly back to Memphis and hospitalize him. I didn't believe it was really medically necessary, but I certainly didn't think it could hurt. I thought Elvis's behavior was a childish episode designed to make a point with Ginger about how much he needed her. Their relationship was taking a lot of adjustments, which he was trying to make, but he never really took command of it.

After we left Baton Rouge, Elvis insisted on going to Graceland for a while before checking into the hospital. We finally arrived at Baptist Hospital sometime after six o'clock in the morning. The effects of the drugs had worn off by then; I guess Elvis was stalling, hoping there would be no way to detect what he had taken. He did have what we believed was intestinal flu. His urine screen turned up contraband Demerol, however, which changed the entire complexion of the ordeal that had transpired some four hundred miles away.

The tour had been exceptionally stressful for Elvis, who had been fighting depression from the beginning. I was not surprised he had attempted to cope by returning to what he knew lifted his spirits. It is a familiar pattern among patients who must continuously struggle to conquer ever-present addictive tendencies.

While we had Elvis in the hospital, we ran tests on his colon and continued to do daily urine screens. The four days he was in the hospital, we never again found results that indicated Demerol. If he had a stash of the drug, he had not brought it to the hospital with him. We gave him placebos, which he took without complaining. There was no indication at that time that Elvis needed to detox. The Demerol in his system appeared to have been an isolated incident.

That incident did show, however, that drugs I had not prescribed were still available to Elvis if he decided to take them. One of the many things we learned from the cancellation in Baton Rouge was that confiscating contraband drugs would probably always be a work in progress.

Years later I was told that immediately after he was discharged from the hospital, Elvis flew to Las Vegas and then to his home in Palm Springs. Going along were Billy and Jo Smith and Alicia Kerwin, a bank teller Elvis had been dating. Alicia went in Ginger's place after Elvis claimed Ginger and he had a fuss and were breaking up for good.

The story goes that Elvis was asleep when he had an emergency situation necessitating treatment by doctors in Palm Springs. Then Dr. Ghanem, one of the doctors who treated Elvis when he was in Las Vegas, was contacted, and he flew out on his private jet to treat Elvis. Dr. Ghanem reportedly told those present that Elvis had suffered an overdose related to Placidyl, a sleep medication. Although I never discussed the episode with Dr. Ghanem, my opinion is the results, as they were described to me, more closely resembled a Demerol overdose.

While in the hospital, Elvis had been receiving Demerol placebos for four days before this event. He apparently judged the effects of the medication based on the amounts he had been receiving there. My guess is that Elvis did not realize the harm in continuing the medication he had been given in the hospital in what he thought was the same dosage. Giving a patient a false sense of tolerance is the real danger in using placebos.

APRIL 21, WHEN the next tour began, Ginger, not Alicia, accompanied him. His performances and the critics' reviews were extremely inconsistent. Fans were beginning to make more pointed comments about Elvis's health. RCA Records recorded a couple of songs live to add to the upcoming album he had cut at Graceland. That helped break the routine.

By the end of the month, things had unraveled. The *Nashville Banner* broke a story about Parker attempting to sell Elvis's management contract around town and being unable to find a buyer. Although Parker supposedly called the newspapers and denied the story, Elvis got really edgy. To make matters much worse, that article was followed a few days later by the lawsuit regarding Presley Center Courts.

Then the tabloids chimed in. Steve Dunleavy, who had penned the body-guards' tell-all book, *Elvis: What Happened?* was a writer for the *Star*, and the paper had awarded his inside information with a cover story to promote his new work. It appeared from the information it was printing that the *National Enquirer* had inside eyes and ears on Elvis both on tour and at Graceland. Elvis was really bothered about who could be "spying for the tabloids" and assigned Dick Grob to identify "the snitch." Also, by the end of the week marked by turmoil, Vernon had filed for a divorce from Dee Stanley Presley. Everything seemed to be unraveling. Thankfully, Elvis had a couple of weeks to rest in Memphis before his next tour.

The tour started in Knoxville at the Stokley Athletic Center on the University of Tennessee campus. It was unseasonably hot for the twentieth of May, and the gym was crammed. Metal folding chairs were placed on the hardwood floor, where fans were feeling the effects of the heat. Elvis came out to a receptive applause in the makeshift arena. Just minutes into the show, he was sweating profusely and working even harder to deliver over a substandard sound system.

This won't last long, I thought, sympathizing with how pale and lethargic Elvis looked in his heavy stage clothes.

Then things nose-dived. As Elvis began giving away his coveted scarves, some excited women down front surged forward, collapsing the first few rows of chairs as they stampeded toward the unusually high stage. There were a couple of injured fans who were swiftly led away as order was restored. Elvis stepped back to drink some water.

He thanked the crowd for coming "to sweat with me" and cautioned, "When the show's over, I'll only be three feet tall."

As always, the audience appreciated his wit, and the rest of the night sailed along good-naturedly.

Clarese Rice Collection

Elvis on stage in Rochester, New York, May 25, 1977.

Dean was often the aide working with Elvis to ready him for his performances. While backstage, Dean would wrap Elvis's fingers in Band-Aids to avoid their being scratched by women gathered around the stage reaching up for a scarf or just to touch him. Dean always placed Band-Aids around Elvis's rings to keep them from being pulled off or from sliding off when he slung out his hand to point his finger at the audience, which was one of his signature gestures.

Elvis's hands would swell so badly when his weight fluctuated that he would buy large rings and then adjust the size to fit with Band-Aids. After getting him all suited up in his heavy stage attire, Dean would run Elvis through athletic stretches and limbering exercises that would relax his muscles to avoid injuries during his onstage maneuvers.

By the time we got to Binghamton, New York, six days later, Elvis had reached the point of exasperation with Ginger. He could not understand why Ginger always wanted to take her sisters along on tour. Or if she went without her family, why she would get homesick and want to go home. He sounded like a broken record saying he was going to break off the relationship, but he could not keep himself from calling her back. Elvis finally decided to let Ginger have her way. He flew her home in the *Lisa Marie* and invited Kathy Westmoreland to keep him company.

The band and crew were excited that we had a layover in Binghamton—two nights in one city. It gave us time to spend the afternoon playing a relaxing game of softball and throwing Frisbees for exercise. Unfortunately, Elvis was unable to join us in the fun. Even at this stage of his career, when Elvis was on tour fans would lurk around the motel where he was staying, waiting for any opportunity that might lead to their getting up close and personal with the king of rock 'n' roll. The few times he had tried to venture outside, an unmanageable number of fans turned up in a matter of minutes, seeking autographs and photos. Elvis had learned to get inside and stay put. Or so I thought.

Nichopoulos Collection

Joe Esposito and Dr. Nick get some exercise during a rare layover on tour in New Haven.

Two nights later Elvis was not feeling well before the show in the Baltimore Civic Center. We were having difficulty getting the results we needed from his medical prep we used almost daily to treat his intestinal problems. His stomach was distended, and he was bloated more than usual. Not only did this situation cause discomfort, it also limited his ability to be as active as his show demanded. As would sometimes happen with his medical prep, we were not able to time things perfectly.

After being late going onstage, Elvis had to excuse himself. He was sweating profusely, trembling, and embarrassed when he came into the dressing room backstage, where he had to take a thirty-minute break necessitated by the medication he had taken earlier. I don't think I'll ever forget the hurt look on his face as he prepared to step back onstage before an impatient audience, who had come to see a performance he realized by that time he could not deliver.

IT WAS DURING a makeup show in Macon, Georgia, that one of Elvis's worst fears materialized. He developed a catch in his throat and was unable to sing two of his audience's favorite songs: "How Great Thou Art" and "Hurt." Elvis believed he had let the Macon crowd down for a second time. He was beginning to take it harder when his shows did not live up to his expectations.

Already dispirited, Elvis received word that in three weeks CBS would be taping his concerts in Omaha, Nebraska, and Rapid City, Iowa, for a television special that would air before the end of the summer. I wondered how Parker expected Elvis to get excited about taping two routine dates in ordinary cities, especially with the negative publicity surrounding the release of the bodyguards' book that was due in bookstores just weeks before the special's projected airdate.

There was nothing thematically interesting about the style in which the concerts were shot or their lackluster locations. The result was a sobering performance by a somewhat contemplative Elvis, who left audiences wondering just what he had intended to convey. That he was ill was evident; that he was not on drugs was also apparent to those willing to see the man and not the image others had recently drawn of him.

Elvis became a bit more daring by the end of the tour, as evidenced by his arrival in Madison, Wisconsin, shortly after midnight. Al Strada and Dean were in a car following Elvis to the motel when his limo suddenly stopped at a service station and Elvis jumped out and froze in a karate stance in front of two guys, who had apparently ganged up on the attendant.

Dean reported, "Elvis barked orders for them to back off. They recognized he was Elvis, but I think they were a *little* uncertain about his skill in the martial arts. They stood down."

The fight was averted, and Al and Dean stood by and watched as Elvis, the peacemaker, signed autographs and posed for photos.

The next night they checked into a warmer-than-normal Netherland Hotel in Cincinnati, Ohio. Dean recalled that Elvis kept saying he needed his room to be cooler; their pleas to the manager seemed to go unheeded. Dean walked back into the suite about three o'clock in the afternoon. No Elvis. He looked all around, even in the closet. Still, no Elvis. With nowhere else to look, Dean peered out the window.

Elvis was walking down the street as fast as his feet could carry him to find a cooler hotel. Dean took off running after him to guard the king of rock 'n' roll before fans learned Elvis was on the loose. After the show Elvis flew home to Graceland and his frosty bedroom to spend the night.

The following evening Elvis flew from Memphis to Indianapolis, Indiana. A CBS crew captured footage of him deplaning to add to the TV special they were developing from his concerts shot a week earlier. Executives from RCA Records met backstage with Elvis before the show and presented him with a plaque bearing a copy of his latest album, *Moody Blue*, and an inscription declaring it the billionth record pressed by RCA. Elvis flashed his famous crooked grin and shook his head in disbelief.

What an unbelievable ride! I thought.

Elvis successfully compensated for his lack of energy, and the show that followed was probably his best on the ten-day tour. I was grateful the saner, shorter tour itinerary was working so successfully and that no concerts had been scheduled in 1977 for Las Vegas or Lake Tahoe. Elvis was obviously tapping his reserves at this point.

Carese Rice Collection

Dean was concerned: "We saw the uncut version of the last concerts for the TV special, and they cut out so many great songs. Why do they want to do that? Do they want to make him look bad or something?" he asked me, shaking his head in disbelief. "He was on fire the whole week."

We were all grateful Elvis would be returning to Graceland, which was sort of his security blanket, for about two weeks before starting the next leg of his tour.

The king of rock 'n' roll says farewell in his final concert, Indianapolis, Indiana, June 26, 1977.

"IF HE WAS awake when I got home from working at the Medical Group, the first thing he would do was call me to come down there [to the mansion] because he was so dad-blame lonesome," Tish Henley recalled. "By the time I got there, his girlfriend would have gotten up and gone to get ready to go out clubbing. He'd be there alone. Of course in those days there wasn't cable, so you either bought a movie or you watched regular TV.

"He would do a lot of reading, and his favorite place to do his reading was in the bathroom. He would say, 'Hey, Tishanna. (That's what he called me.) Come on. Let's read this.'

"Sometimes he'd read and sometimes he would want me to read to him. Elvis would sit in that uncomfortable, black, plastic-looking chair in the bathroom. When we went in there to read together, somebody sat on the top of the commode and somebody sat in the uncomfortable chair."

Tish confirmed that it was difficult for anyone to know Elvis was as sick as he was: "He rarely complained. Actually, after that last tour he was so upset with himself. He had continued to eat and sit on his butt. He was concerned, like all of us; he had a mirror and he could see. His weight kept him from making the moves he wanted to onstage, his clothes were tight and uncomfortable; he tired easier.

"When it was time to tour, he always thought we could get him in shape in twenty-four to forty-eight hours. He would want me to play racquetball with him; he was a lot more aggressive playing before a tour than when he was just playing for fun.

"But his goal was always to do the very, very best he could to entertain his fans," Tish remembered sadly. "It didn't make any difference how he felt; he did the best he could."

ALTHOUGH *ELVIS: WHAT Happened?* had reached the stores and he knew many fans would undoubtedly have read it by the time he hit the stage, Elvis remained optimistic about his upcoming tour. He had not mentioned the book to Tish, Dean, or me but resolutely had said that the tour beginning in Portland, Maine, on August 17, 1977, was going to be "the best one yet." I knew he believed that in his heart. I think Elvis had come to terms with what he had told reporters in an effort to explain himself years before: "The man is one thing; the image is another. It's very hard to live up to an image."

I had always marveled that Elvis was a man who went through a metamorphosis when the spotlights found him. One wish of mine that forever will go unfulfilled is seeing what Elvis, a man who continually reinvented himself, had planned to do to delight his fans and win over skeptics on the tour that never materialized. Elvis's sudden, tragic death on the very day the tour was to begin put an end to whatever he might have done to exonerate himself.

FIVE

DIFFERENCE OF OPINION

Elvis Presley's final resting place in his beloved Meditation
Garden at Graceland.

In the days immediately following Elvis Presley's death, I was physically exhausted, mentally numb, and emotionally empty. Touching calls and letters from close friends poured in and were gratefully acknowledged. Some were from former patients who had changed physicians when I began spending so much time on tour with Elvis. They asked if I would be willing to take them back as patients. The sincerity of my friends' support was the best possible panacea during those painful times.

The day after Elvis's funeral, I received a letter written by Dr. Thomas Chesney on behalf of Baptist Memorial Hospital's pathology staff containing information from Elvis's gross autopsy. The letter listed the weight and condition of Elvis's enlarged organs. It recognized his mild fatty liver and noted left ventricular hypertrophy (hypertensive heart disease). It stated the presence of arteriosclerotic cardiovascular disease with coronary atherosclerosis (mild), and aortic atherosclerosis (minimal). It did *not* mention or reveal the results of Elvis's initial tox screens completed the day following his death. Dr. Chesney did state, however, that the letter was for my use, "pending the completion of our microscopic studies," which I never received.

Based on information from the Baptist Hospital gross autopsy that Dr. Chesney furnished for my use, I prepared Elvis Presley's death certificate and filed it with the Tennessee Department of Public Health, just as I had done for other patients after they passed away. Because the medical examiner had determined Elvis's death was due to natural causes and no one indicated to me that Elvis's death might be under investigation by the DA's office, I thought filing for the certificate was my responsibility. Dr. Jerry Francisco, speaking as the medical examiner, told me he was not certain who needed to sign the death certificate, so I took the initiative. I wanted Vernon to have a certified copy of Elvis's death certificate at the earliest possible date so he could be legally appointed the executor of his son's estate.

ABOUT SIX WEEKS later, the bodies of Elvis and his mother, Gladys, were moved from Forest Hill Cemetery and laid to rest in the Meditation Garden at Graceland. A serious attempt to steal Elvis's body had led to several arrests, and the estate was incurring expenses for extra security and maintenance at the cemetery. Dick Grob, working as Graceland's director of operations, had dealt successfully with zoning ordinances and logistical problems, allowing Elvis and his mother to come back home.

Vernon decided a flat bronze marker with an eternal flame would be the most suitable tombstone for Elvis, and Dr. George Nichopoulos and Dean Nichopoulos were two of the names included on the tribute. One evening after the marker arrived, we attended a small graveside memorial service that mostly included Elvis's family members.

"Has there been any more discussion about allowing fans to visit the Garden and pay their respects?" I asked.

"Dick is working on it," Dean responded. "Vernon is still pressuring Dick to complete his investigation into whether Elvis was murdered. Dick is trying to piece together why the Stanley boys were not on duty when Elvis died and who leaked confirmation of Elvis's death to the *National Enquirer* before he was pronounced dead. Dick has confirmed the *Enquirer* had reporters on a plane bound for Memphis before the press conference. Al and I are helping out to give Dick more time to investigate."

Al Strada and Dean were the only aides still employed by the estate after Elvis's death, and they were working security with Dick and Billy Smith.

A STORY PUBLISHED in the morning newspaper on October 23, 1977, made it clear that Elvis would not be allowed to rest in peace. *The Commercial Appeal* article entitled "Presley's Autopsy Broad" summarized the obvious reasons why the hospital took such precautions with Elvis's autopsy: the suspicions cast on Elvis by his bodyguards' recently published book; six hospitalizations in four years; an autopsy requested by his family; and conflicting stories about what happened when his body was discovered.

The article emphasized that almost the entire pathology department at Baptist had watched the autopsy, along with Dr. Jerry Francisco, and were puzzled when they found "no anatomical evidence that disease killed Elvis."

It confirmed that Dr. Francisco had agreed to announce that the autopsy was inconclusive, but instead he said death was due to cardiac arrhythmia from unknown causes that may never be determined. The article claimed, "The Baptist personnel and pathologists at other hospitals were reportedly embarrassed." It noted that Baptist personnel felt the reputation it had been building for years was on the line.

Dr. Eric Muirhead, identified as chief of pathology and an internationally recognized authority on hypertension, told the reporter he did not believe heart disease could possibly have been a cause of death since the disease in the left anterior descending coronary artery had only narrowed it 40 to 50 percent, rather than 70 percent, which medical journals cite is the point at which physicians should worry about obstruction. Dr. Muirhead focused instead on the seven drugs found in Elvis's autopsy urine screen.

His statement brought up another dispute regarding the separate tox reports conducted from the autopsy. The coroner's report failed to find Placidyl in Elvis's body, although Duckworth pathology, which Baptist used to analyze the results, found it present. Baptist said it was using Bio-Science Laboratory (BSL) in Van Nuys, California, for its pathology procedures, so they sent samples of Elvis's blood and tissues to that lab for another opinion.

BSL reported ten drugs found in Elvis's body at death: Ethinamate (Placidyl), Methaqualone (Quaalude), codeine, pentobarbital, butabarbital, phenobarbital, Valmid, Valium, morphine, and chlorpheniramine. The bottom line was BSL had discovered high concentrations of codeine, Quaalude, and three barbiturates in Elvis's system that they believed acted together to cause his death.

Baptist expressed concern that all the drugs were depressants and that their combination increased their potentiation (the effect each drug has when used alone). Among the highest concentrations were codeine and barbiturates. These drugs were said to be in "near *toxic* levels," which actually meant the high end of a therapeutic dose. If a drug is at a toxic level, that means it could make a person sick. Toxic is the level above therapeutic, the level used to treat a condition. The level above toxic is lethal; lethal is the level at which death has been reported. The levels were not clarified, and reporters consistently implied that toxic was a death level.

More speculation followed: "The final autopsy report prepared by Baptist Hospital listed Elvis's death as a drug-related death, commonly known as 'polypharmacy.' Of particular note is the combination of codeine, Placidyl and the barbiturates."

Although the newspaper did not acknowledge it, Baptist Hospital's conclusion came from a paragraph in the Bio-Science Laboratory report under "Toxicologic Studies." It read:

> In accordance with interpretations made by our consultants versed in therapeutic and toxic drug levels in body fluids and tissues, and in accordance with our interpretation of results on drug levels and their clinical significance as recorded in the literature, it is our view that death of Baptist Memorial Hospital A77-160 resulted from multiple drug ingestion [commonly known as *polypharmacy*]. Of particular note is the combination of codeine, ethchlorvynol and barbiturates detected in body fluids and tissues. The levels in the

body fluids and tissues exceed some other known identifiable multiple drug overdose cases where codeine has been implicated.

The BSL report went on to state: "Placidyl is listed in a number of articles in toxicology literature as being lethal when combined with codeine."

I had never seen or heard of any of those articles and wondered why their sources were not cited. There was no warning about the two drugs being used in combination in the *Physicians' Desk Reference*; pharmacists I consulted could not confirm it. Anyway, since UT had not found Placidyl in its report to the coroner, Dr. Francisco said he doubted it existed. If it did, the amount would be so small it would have had no effect.

A pivotal issue for me was that the toxicology information was part of the *privileged* autopsy. Baptist claimed they had "maintained the confidentiality of the report," but in my view they inappropriately continued to discuss its results publicly. I thought surely the estate would confront them, but to my knowledge they never did.

Who was the reporter's "source"? I wondered.

As I saw it, the Baptist report was leaked to advertise that the hospital's conclusion was different from the coroner's determination of cause of death. Maurice Elliott, speaking on behalf of Baptist, finally publicly denied the accusation that the hospital leaked the report. He claimed they gave a copy of the completed autopsy to the medical examiner's office only so the ME could review it to determine if there was nonprescribed drug use in Elvis's body that would make his death a coroner's case.

The hospital thought the ME needed to review their results before he made his final ruling. Baptist said they asked the coroner's office not to make a copy of the tox report, and his office agreed. That did not keep Elliott from speculating later in the newspaper that the reporter's source for the leaked material had been someone from the coroner's wing—not the hospital. I could not understand what motive anyone in the medical examiner's office would have for shooting the ME's own theory in the foot, but that didn't rule out that sinister motives might have been at work.

The Center of Human Toxicology at the University of Utah in Salt Lake City also conducted tox tests for Baptist Memorial. That tox center discovered an additional drug, "meperidine" (Demerol), that no other lab had found, increasing the number of drugs in Elvis's body to eleven. The Demerol was in a small amount in the tissue; it probably remained from Elvis's episode in the spring. The Utah tox center's conclusion did not confirm the

Toxicology Report from the University of Utah

The following article appeared in the Salt Lake City Tribune on January 29th, 1978.

Toxicologists based at the University of Utah have completed laboratory studies of autopsy specimens from the body of Elvis Presley and have found that 11 drugs were present in the singer's system at the time of his death, The Tribune has learned.

All of those drugs were consistent with medical treatment, said the director of the Center for Human Toxicology, Dr. Bryan S. Finkle. He spoke to The Tribune in an exclusive interview. The center had been called in to provide a third toxicological analysis of typical autopsy specimens from Presley's body. He reported, "We have not detected any drug in Elvis that doesn't have a medical rationale to it—only agents prescribed for perfectly normal, rational medical reasons."

Dr. Finkle said the singer had not been drinking prior to his sudden death, which reportedly was blamed on an erratic heartbeat, last Aug. 16.

Efforts by the Tribune to obtain a copy of the report by the Center for Human Toxicology have not been successful. The center received the first of the autopsy specimens on Oct. 4, and when The Tribune learned of this Dr. Finkle postponed requested interviews for professional reasons as he was acting in a consultant's role and in that, cannot talk in specifics. He spoke, when interviewed, in general that, yes, he had been involved in the case and that he found 11 drugs, all consistent with medical treatment.

Of course, that the entertainer did have prescription drugs in his system at the time of death has previously been reported. Most accounts mentioned from eight to 10 drugs.

The Center for Human Toxicology, which has an international reputation among toxicologists and forensic scientists, was the third organization called in in this phase of the Presley autopsy. The others were the Baptist Memorial Hospital in Memphis, Tenn.,and Bio-Science Laboratories, Van Nuys, Calif. Bio-Science requested the Center of Human Toxicology conduct the third examination, said Dr. Finkle. While certain agencies, including the center based at the University of Utah, and the Shelby County, Tennessee, Medical Examiner's Office, involved in this story receive public monies, it appears unlikely that there will be disclosure of specifics about the toxicological analysis.

The autopsy performed was done at the request of the Presley family. In a nutshell, rights of privacy prevail and the parties appear to have no legal duty and are not compelled to disclose certain documents, in particular the toxicological report of the Center for Human Toxicology.

Dr. Finkle, as a consultant in the Presley case, said he wrote a two-page report based on his findings at the request of Bio-Science. In it he lists the found drugs, their concentrations and he concludes with an opinion as to the potential or possible toxicological consequences of having this number of drugs in these concentrations in a body.

The laboratory results here apparently satisfied Shelby County Medical Examiner Dr. Jerry T. Francisco that Presley's death could not be attributed to drug overdose. However , it was learned that the death certificate was signed before the final Finkle report was mailed. Dr. Finkle's opinion was solicited earlier by a phone call, and dr. Francisco later said publicly that the prescriptions drugs found in the singer's system were not a contributing factor.

The Associated Press, reporting on a press conference Dr. Francisco called last Oct. 21, quoted the medical examiner as saying that four drugs were found in significant quantities in the entertainer's bloodstream. They are Ethinamate, Methaqualone, codeine and barbiturates. The first two are sedatives; codeine is a narcotic analgesic or milder, secondary pain killer, and barbiturates are "downers" or sedatives or depressants.

Dr. Francisco was quoted as saying that four other drugs—the antihistamine chlorpheniramine, meperidine, morphine and Valium—were found in what were said to be insignificant amounts.

Meperidine and morphine are pain killers and Valium is a tranquilizer.

Presley was not taking morphine per se; the morphine was a byproduct of the codeine.

University of Utah Toxicology Report Press Release

hospital's theory of a drug interaction death, so no more was mentioned about their findings.

The doctors involved in the autopsy had expressed the goal of doing the best job they could to avert criticism regarding what was indisputably at that time the world's most famous body, so I wondered why the only criticism being voiced about the autopsy ruling was coming from Baptist Memorial. That baffled me. What exactly were they attempting to do by continuing to break their pledged confidentiality?

I HAD ALWAYS received a copy of my patients' autopsies so I could discuss the findings with their families. Dr. Chesney's letter was insufficient for that purpose. I was annoyed I had to read information in the newspaper that the hospital should have given to me, particularly since I was the attending physician who had pronounced the patient dead in the ER. None of the normal courtesies afforded to a staff doctor were extended to me. Why was I not furnished copies of the tox screens? I could not think of a legitimate reason why, and that made me uncomfortable.

I accidentally learned that Dr. Francisco, Dr. Muirhead, and Maurice Elliott had made a visit to Graceland to confer with Vernon. I had never known members of a hospital staff to visit a patient's family. I could not imagine their doing it without the family's primary physician. In that meeting Dr. Muirhead and Maurice Elliott told Vernon that the results of the hospital's autopsy confirmed their belief that Elvis's death was drug related. However, Dr. Francisco told Vernon that he had not thoroughly reviewed the hospital's report at that time but would do so and announce his final ruling at a press conference in a couple of days.

When the time came for the decisive press conference, Baptist still had no idea what the coroner's reaction was to their final report or if it had influenced him to change his original decision. After reading the results of the hospital's report in the local newspapers, most people felt the coroner would have no other choice but to state that his provisional ruling had been incorrect.

Conversely, the embattled ME, not one to be intimidated by people expressing their opinions, stepped confidently up to the microphone and spoke his convictions. He stated that after evaluating all the autopsy findings, the official cause of death in the case of Elvis Presley was "hypertensive heart disease with coronary artery disease." He took issue with the Bio-Science Laboratory report. He said potentiation had not occurred. Since only one lab had found the

Placidyl and only one of the other labs had found Demerol located in Elvis's system, Dr. Francisco said the two drugs did not exist in a high enough quantity, if they even existed at all, to be included in the count.

He stated that only four of the ten drugs found were in "significant" levels, and they were all still in the therapeutic range. The drugs he named to be in significant amounts were codeine, a minor narcotic; the sedatives Methaqualone and Valmid; and the barbiturates. The other drugs were in trace amounts: chlorpheniramine, an over-the-counter antihistamine; morphine, a metabolite from the codeine; Valium, a tranquilizer; and Ethinamate (Placidyl), a sedative. His conclusion: there was no evidence of drug abuse at the levels found.

That was an important statement for the media. It meant that as a result of the completed autopsy, Dr. Francisco had ruled Elvis's death would not become the subject of an inquest; there were no suspicions on his part that a law had been broken. Dr. Francisco's words also made it final that the official autopsy would not be released to the media unless, of course, the Presley family chose to release it.

The release of the autopsy would have been a blessing for me. The media would have had solid information on which to base their opinions and make decisions; it would have eliminated their need for conjecture.

Opposing medical positions that the media interpreted as a cover-up kept the controversy raging. When hospital pathologists did not concur with his preliminary ruling, the medical examiner appeared to be withholding or hiding information. Journalists picked a side: they joined the hospital team's overdose theory rather than the coroner's heart attack verdict. The hospital could not release its autopsy report. It had a gag order, so to speak, due to the Presley family's private autopsy request. That made the hospital the underdog.

Dr. Francisco was the voice—the face on the case—since he was the coroner whose job it was to give the legal ruling on the cause of death. The way I saw it, the leaked toxicology portions of the autopsy were a desperate attempt on the part of dissenters to allow their opinion to surface and gain support.

As for the official death ruling, there was some coronary artery disease found, just as Dr. Francisco said. That did not prove, however, that Elvis suffered a heart attack. The pathologists had to ask themselves the question, was there enough coronary artery disease to cause death? In the pathologists' opinion, there was not. The medical examiner, on the other hand, believed the coronary artery disease was advanced enough to have caused death.

After all the evidence was carefully considered, there was nothing concrete in Elvis's body that anyone could point to and say, "This was unequivocally the cause of Elvis's death." That situation happens often. That is why Dr. Francisco said the cause of death "may never be determined." A lot of people die from electronic abnormalities of the heart that cannot be found at autopsy. Only an EKG conducted while a patient is living can diagnose electronic abnormalities. Even young high school and college athletes with no history of heart disease have dropped dead suddenly with no autopsy findings that reveal the cause of the death. Questions forever go unanswered.

Dan Warlick and I discussed the situation.

"[Dr.] Jerry Francisco never came to the same conclusion [as the Baptist pathologists] that it had to be a drug-induced death. However, that implied that anyone who disagreed with that position appeared to be trying to cover it up instead of simply holding a different theory," Warlick said. "What we had in the end were two sets of professionals, the clinical pathologists and the forensic pathologists, looking at the same set of facts and having different medical opinions. The difference of opinion was not the problem; the problem was their failure to recognize that a difference of opinion was all it was."

Then Warlick made an interesting point: "The Baptist Autopsy Protocol doesn't list 'Cause of Death.' It never has in the past." He knew this from having worked with the pathologists at Baptist. "For a medical autopsy it [the form] lists 'conditions found.' It's only when you get to the forensic side [medical examiner's office] that you list the 'Cause of Death' and the 'Manner of Death.' So they [Baptist Memorial] were not even used to signing anyone's death certificate over there and saying this is what we found. They tell the attending physician generally and get him to sign it.

"My point is," Warlick emphasized, "they [Baptist] took that extra step on this [Elvis's] case. Then they got into that fuss with Dr. Francisco. They don't usually sign those [death certificates] with *cause*. That wasn't their job. If a person was found dead, they would send them over to us [at the coroner's office where Warlick worked at the time]. They would not do an autopsy on anyone they didn't have to. They only wanted to do an autopsy on people who died in their hospital as a general rule to find out how well they are doing taking care of people.

"They [Baptist pathology] have some very smart people, for whom I have a great deal of respect. What they generally did was to describe their findings. Had they stopped at that, they could have just said they disagreed with Dr. Francisco's subjective interpretation of the objective findings," Warlick concluded. "Ultimately that is what they did. But they handled it in such a controversial way that it sounded like one side was lying and the other not."

FUELED WITH THAT information, I obtained a copy of the Bio-Science Laboratory report and began my own search in earnest. The term *polypharmacy* intrigued me as a cause of death. *Polypharmacy* simply means "more than one chemical." I had been practicing polypharmacy for years; so had every doctor who prescribed more than one medication at a time to one person.

I had only read newspaper comments regarding Baptist Hospital's autopsy analysis, but it appeared to me that they had omitted a number of important factors from their equation when attempting to determine if Elvis's death was drug-related. I believed the hospital's ruling had been premature, just as Dr. Francisco's provisional ruling had been. Baptist's evidence was too clinically based to suit me. I felt a forensic-based analysis could yield different results. Sure, there were a lot of drugs in Elvis's system, but were the levels deadly? No. Was there proof that in combination they had caused death? No.

Considering Elvis's actions on the night he died, that he had conducted business meetings, played racquetball, and then read while attempting to go to sleep, overdose just did not seem possible. Still, if there was even a possibility that drugs killed Elvis, I, more than anyone else, wanted to know. There was a lot to consider:

- The idea that *downers*, even in high numbers, could have killed Elvis was laughable to me. Elvis was not even asleep when the sudden event struck that caused his death. How could the sedatives have killed him if they could not even put him to sleep?
- For the most part, except for the codeine, the medications in his body were ones he had been taking over a period of time—nothing exceptional. He had been taking the same medications every day and walking around—alive—so that combination at those specific levels did not just happen to kill him on that particular day.
- The Demerol (meperidine) was only found by one laboratory, so it was undoubtedly a very small trace. I did not prescribe that Demerol to Elvis; he had been addicted to Demerol and detoxed from it. Contraband Demerol was found when he was hospitalized on April 1, 1977, and I still suspected it had led to his drug reaction in Palm Springs shortly after that. The Demerol could not have been influential in Elvis's death; it had been in his body for too long.
- Elvis had not taken the Dilaudid I had prescribed for him the night he died. There had already been questions raised about the role of that drug in his death. The answer is simple: either Elvis never got the

Dilaudid or he decided not to take it. Dilaudid was not in his blood, so it did not kill him. Some people claimed the Dilaudid was probably in his stomach contents that were not analyzed. That would not have mattered. If a substance is found only in the stomach, it cannot be the cause of death; it can only be a clue to the manner of death. If a drug existed in the blood in a sufficient amount at the time of death, and pills containing that same drug were found in the stomach, then the pills in the stomach were the source of the drug in the blood.

- The Ethinamate, or Valmid, found in his system was a medication I had never heard of before Elvis told me about it. It was given to him by a doctor in California and worked well to replace Placidyl for his insomnia. That is why his Placidyl level was low; he had replaced that medication with Valmid.

- Methaqualone and Valium were both tranquilizers and probably the best medications made for insomnia, anxiety, and panic disorders, all of which Elvis suffered from, especially when traveling or preparing for a tour. Unfortunately, during that time period the public abused the medications to the point where Quaaludes were discontinued and Valium severely restricted. It's a shame that happened, because they were really good medications when used for the purposes intended and in the proper doses. They created far fewer side effects than many of the drugs that replaced them.

- The codeine is a strange one. Elvis did not tolerate that medication well. It made him itch, so he did not like to take it. I had thought it was likely the dentist Elvis went to see the night he died gave him codeine; however, I never considered codeine in Elvis's death picture. A person does not die suddenly from a codeine overdose; he goes into a coma—it is a slow death.

It was quite interesting how Bio-Science Laboratory came to the conclusion they did regarding the codeine. They reported the concentrations in Elvis's blood to be 1.08 micrograms per 100 milliliters of blood. Then they cited a case in the Registry of Human Toxicology in 1976 where a patient had 1.20 micrograms of codeine per 100 milliliters and died. They assumed that since codeine was the only drug found in that patient's system, the patient's death was caused from a codeine overdose.

The point I guess they were trying to make was that even though Elvis had a much lesser amount of codeine in his system than in the comparative case, he had other drugs going on that hyped up their effect. Therefore, the other drugs in Elvis's system made up for the difference in the amount of codeine found in his body and the amount found in the body in the fatal case being cited; so Elvis, too, died of a drug overdose. That conclusion was a stretch at best. My guess was if the laboratory's pathologists could have found a better reference case, they would have used it. Its logic did not convince me.

The laboratory (since it did not have a history of the deceased) failed to take into consideration that Elvis may have had a tolerance to codeine, which meant he could take more of the drug and be less affected than most people. I did not prescribe codeine for Elvis; it was one of the medications prescribed by another doctor and mailed to him. Elvis took it for severe arthritic pain in his neck and back. I never had believed Elvis achieved a euphoric effect from the codeine; codeine is a minor narcotic, and many people do not get high from taking it.

No MATTER HOW I studied it, no matter whom I consulted, I could not make the conclusion of the Bio-Science Laboratory report work for me. The lab's message was clear: the drugs found in the body of Elvis Presley at the time of his death, in the levels and combinations in which they were found, had caused his death. Their research appeared to be well documented, and they had enough credibility as a laboratory to have their work respected; I just could not accept the report's analysis and final conclusion. Journalists and the public had no such problem.

The Associated Press (AP) and United Press International (UPI), two legitimate wire services, published the story about the Bio-Science Laboratory report. Following as it did his bodyguards' book *Elvis: What Happened?* and the leak of certain autopsy findings, it was damning information. It was the beginning of a process that led to Elvis Presley being wrongly outed as a medical drug addict who died from a drug overdose.

The coroner's official report and the cause of death listed on his death certificate were lost in the scuffle for headlines. The polypharmacy theory was juicy bait, causing a feeding frenzy in the tabloids.

As A RESULT of the controversy, I decided to review my own autopsy notes, thinking that since some time had passed, I could be more objective about what they would tell me.

When Elvis's chest was opened during autopsy, there was no evidence of food blocking his esophagus or blockage of the trachea. I had considered choking might be the cause of death because of several choking spells he had previously experienced while eating and trying to talk or laugh simultaneously. His lungs were examined; they were healthy—totally dry. There was no fluid buildup present in the lungs as there would have been in an overdose. The airways were open. There were no signs of lung disease.

Elvis's internal organs were enlarged, but that in itself did not mean anything, because enlarged organs would not be significant as a contributing factor in a death. Elvis's heart was probably one and a half times the size of a normal heart, but that was not surprising. An oversized heart is a normal finding in athletes, and Elvis was very athletic when he performed. Heart enlargement is also found in people with high blood pressure. The other findings regarding arteriosclerosis were noted in Dr. Chesney's letter. There was no evidence of a recent heart attack or other injury in the muscular walls of his heart.

One thing I had wanted to follow up on was the bone marrow samples. The doctor who collected them thought they looked like cancer cells, so initially he suspected Elvis might have had cancer in the bone marrow. I learned that, after he investigated this further with special stains for the studies, he felt that the cells were not cancer cells but normal cells going through the natural changes of dying cells.

Elvis's liver was found to have abnormal amounts of fat globules found in hepatic cells. We were aware of his fatty liver when he was hospitalized in 1975 and had a liver biopsy taken at that time in an attempt to discover the cause. We had been unsuccessful.

I realized during the autopsy how much more severe Elvis's discomfort must have been than I had realized. His megacolon had shown up on our X-rays, but not to the extent that we saw there. A normal colon is two to three inches in diameter and four to five feet in length; his colon was two to three times that size. If it gets to be that large, it acts like a reservoir, where contamination can occur with numerous bacteria-producing toxins that could lead to organ failure.

Barium was still in his colon from several months before when he drank the white, chalky substance during an office visit for X-rays of his intestines. Barium can actually set up to a concretelike consistency and block the passage of fluids or dejecta through the colon and require surgery. Many of his treating physicians thought drugs had caused Elvis's colon condition, but in reality the size of his megacolon seen at autopsy was much too severe for the problem to have been caused by drugs alone, if at all.

Elvis was in my care for more than ten years, and I was never able to determine the exact cause of his colon disease. When he moved back to Memphis and was evaluated for the problem, we thought he most likely had a poor functioning colon secondary to the medications he was using at that time. I tried many treatments that I knew about and the GI consultant recommended. A lot of the medicines would work for short periods; then he would build up a tolerance. We constantly changed his treatment regimen in an attempt to achieve a greater degree of function.

During his hospitalization in '75, I asked for a surgical consult with the idea of removing his colon partially or entirely. The surgeon would not consider the procedure as a cure at that time. He said the operation was not a medically appropriate or approved procedure. The idea might have sounded drastic for a problem that so many people experience on a regular basis, but Elvis's problem was chronic and severe, causing a tremendous inconvenience for him both professionally and personally.

Since Elvis's death, more information has become available on colon diseases as a result of new treatments through research. There are a couple of diseases that fit Elvis's possible medical diagnosis. One is Hirschsprung's, which may start at birth or in early childhood; the other is colon paralysis, more recently called "colonic inertia." The conditions occur either from an absence of nerves to the colon or from damaged nerves to the colon, which impede its ability to contract and thus move substances through the intestines and out of the body. Although normal transit time for food to travel through the colon after ingestion is twelve to seventy-two hours, slow transit time from a damaged or diseased colon may take weeks. This delay can cause abdominal swelling, lasting for two or three days before decreasing drastically or disappearing, accounting for his intermittent distension, thought to be weight gain.

After years of research, I found a solution. Dr. Chris Lahr and Dr. Thomas Abell, two specialists at the University of Mississippi in Jackson, have been treating colonic inertia for twenty years with good success. Their definitive treatment for the disease is partial or complete removal of the colon, which I advocated when Elvis was hospitalized in 1975. The doctors explained that colonic inertia can be either congenital (caused by a genetic disorder) or acquired (through viruses, bacteria, or a disease of the autonomic nervous system), I never gained access to the hospital's microscopic autopsy findings of the colon to confirm my suspicions.

"Elvis's condition was autonomic neuropathy," Dr. Lahr confirmed. "Drug addiction does not cause a dilated colon. Elvis had all the symptoms: sweating profusely, weakness, migraine headaches, rapid weight change, slow intestinal transit, toxic megacolon. When the colon gets distended, it causes abdominal pain, abdominal distension, and bloating. By 1977 Elvis was a walking time bomb."

With the disease progressing and no treatment available that we knew about at the time, something tragic could have happened at any time.

"Thing is, when the problems get to the point where Elvis's apparently were, those treatments you were using aren't really effective," Dr. Lahr said reassuring me. "The nerves down there are sort of paralyzed and won't open up. [Nerves are like wires that carry electricity, which stimulates the function of the bowels.] There's no medicine that would do it. Surgery would definitely have cured him. When you get to that stage, nothing else helps. I've operated on over three hundred people with the same thing (paralyzed colons) and they were not drug abusers. It's a disease, and we can see it now with an MRI, which you did not have at the time."

Drs. Abell and Lahr pointed out that Elvis's mother had ptosis (droopy eyelids) and migraine headaches, signs of mitochondrial disease, a genetic condition inherited through the cells of the mother. She gave birth to a still-born child (Elvis's twin brother), and she died at an early age, which would be consistent with that disease diagnosis. So, Elvis could have inherited the disease from his mother, however, he could not have passed it on. The doctors agreed if they had access to samples taken at autopsy, the condition could be confirmed. Unfortunately we were limited to the information we had.

AFTER REVIEWING MY personal autopsy notes, I settled on what I considered the most plausible theory of Elvis's death, one on which Dan Warlick and I agree. Because Warlick was the investigator for the coroner's office and also examined Elvis's body at autopsy, I had the highest regard for his opinion. We believe Elvis died from a normal physiological event brought into play called "Valsalva maneuver." This Valsalva maneuver caused the heart to stop when the body strained.

"When the body senses a vascular occlusion or blocked major artery—such as can occur in the lung, called a pulmonary embolus—the heart is signaled to stop creating the pressure in the vessel. When Elvis compressed his abdominal aorta by straining, his heart, in response, went into arrhythmia and quit working suddenly. All of the information from the scene investigation is completely consistent with this theory," Warlick told me.

I believe this in turn may have caused a drop in blood pressure, which resulted in a grand mal seizure; Elvis fell, and his face was buried in the plush carpet, where he suffocated. Warlick, however, doesn't agree with that part.

In either scenario, it is my opinion that if colonic surgery had been available to Elvis during his lifetime, it would have ended his chronic colon problems, giving him a better quality of life and removing the risk of a Valsalva maneuver.

"I hope I can make this clear for the last time," Warlick stated when we talked recently. "Elvis Presley did not die of a drug overdose . . . It makes a better story [for the media], but it's not true. That poor guy had issues with his physiology that were in large part genetic."

The truth was that at times Elvis had abused drugs recreationally, and those incidences led to judgment being heaped upon him. That is always the chance we take with our lifestyle choices: that someone will discover our sins and live to tell about them.

FINALLY ON NOVEMBER 27, 1977, Graceland opened its gates to welcome Elvis's fans.

"They can walk up the driveway to the Meditation Garden and visit with Elvis," Dean informed me, obviously pleased. "Access is limited, and so are the visitation hours, but there's no charge. Vernon feels like it's at least a start."

Fans from throughout the world send floral tributes daily, year-round, to Graceland's Meditation Garden to honor the life of Elvis Presley.

SIX

HOUND ON A HUNT

Nichopoulos Collection

Dr. Nick and Edna share a romantic moment remembering
their own wedding.

During the two years following Elvis's death, I settled back into the saner side of life, where I had missed my family, friends, patients, and church community more than I realized. I had another labor-intensive celebrity patient. The drama involved in caring for him kept my work from ever falling into the "routine" category.

Meanwhile Dick Grob completed the investigations Vernon Presley had requested about certain mysteries surrounding Elvis's death. The information wasn't pretty. A tip phoned into the office at Graceland alerted Dick to Jim Kirk, a Memphis man who was connected in a dubious way to the *National Enquirer*. Kirk had been discussing an interview with Ginger Alden regarding Elvis since before she had received her much-debated "engagement" ring.

Having talked with her on several occasions, Kirk recognized Ginger's "distinctive voice" when, according to Kirk, she called about 1:30 in the afternoon on August 16, 1977, telling him "to keep a watch on the mansion." Kirk called the tabloid's headquarters in Florida and told them he had a tip on a big Elvis story. Ginger called back about 2:30 p.m., Kirk claimed, and there was a lot of noise in the background: "This time she identified herself as being Ginger Alden. She said, 'I can't talk too long. Elvis is dead, ah, and I thought you might want to know.'"

The *National Enquirer* dispatched a crew to Memphis before the announcement of Elvis's death at four o'clock that afternoon, thus landing the lead on the nation's top story.

The most difficult part to accept was Kirk's version of a debate over the fee the *National Enquirer* agreed to pay Ginger for an exclusive interview the day after Elvis's funeral. The auctioning price was said to have risen to $110,000 but was knocked down to $35,000 when Ginger failed to honor their exclusivity agreement.

Jim Kirk had also supplied Dick with valuable information about David Stanley on the day he failed to show up on time for duty. Kirk said he tried to get David on the telephone at Graceland to verify Ginger's phone call about Elvis being dead, but he could not reach him. Kirk had unknowingly verified that David was not present at Graceland during the emergency, as he claimed he was. No one in the house was able to place David there during the critical time period.

Dick had a good relationship with David and persuaded him to give his account of the Stanley boys' whereabouts on August 16, 1977, the day Elvis died. Rick Stanley was supposed to be on duty until noon, when David would relieve him. Rick had asked Al and Dean to cover his shift so he could keep a date. Neither of them would do it; David finally agreed to relieve him.

David showed up after Rick left Graceland—sometime after 2:00 a.m. The maid confirmed the time, remembering that David had a guest with him, and they shot pool downstairs. Then David said he changed his mind about relieving Rick, because he did not want to get "tapped" into doing something and "trapped for the rest of the night at Graceland." David claimed he left Graceland about 4:15 a.m.

The night manager at the Howard Johnson motel down the street from Graceland said David arrived there before 4:30 a.m. David admitted spending the night with his date, drinking beer, dropping pills, having sex, and passing out. He awoke about noon on August 16, took a shower, messed around, and arrived at Graceland about 2:30 p.m. He drove up to the back of the house, where he heard Elvis was dead; then he took off in his car. Several people said David was crying, "I killed him; I killed him," which is what they relayed to Vernon that made him suspicious. David went straight to the motel to give his brother the news.

Rick was sound asleep at the HJ when David arrived. Rick had met his date after leaving Graceland, and by her admission, they spent the evening drinking and drugging until he passed out. His companion said Rick never left the room after he arrived; the night manager confirmed her statement. Rick's date said they woke up with David pounding on the door sometime after 2:30 p.m. When Rick answered, David told him Elvis was dead. She said they both looked scared, and Rick cautioned her to "forget all about the night, the drugs, and everything."

After I learned the details of Dick Grob's investigation, I knew the rumors I had heard about the possibility of David delivering a fatal karate blow to Elvis the morning he died was just another one of the wild tales that surfaced after the tragedy. No one at Graceland was ever able to place David in the bedroom suite where he claimed to have been, before, during, or after Elvis's death.

As time went by, the controversy over the cause of Elvis's death faded away. I thought everything that could be said about the way he died had been said. The fans still loved Elvis no matter what was said about him. They concentrated more on enjoying the fruits of his creative labors than on how he died. Many of Elvis's friends and extended family members began writing accounts of their life with Elvis. The fickle public seemed to be moving on to other concerns. The circumstances surrounding Elvis's death was old news by the summer of '79—or so I thought.

ELVIS'S FATHER, VERNON Presley, passed away on June 26, 1979, at Baptist Memorial Hospital from the heart condition that had plagued him for the final four years of his life. Graceland's living room and adjoining music room held his funeral; the Meditation Garden received his body. Those of us who knew him best understood he was where he wanted to be—with his son, Elvis, and his wife Gladys—the family circle was complete.

Vernon had been the executor of Elvis's estate, along with the National Bank of Commerce that took over as Elvis's will specified. Most people anticipated that the reading of Vernon's last will and testament would name Priscilla coexecutor with NBC bank, since she was Lisa Marie's mother. Elvis's only child and sole heir was only eleven years old at the time.

The City of Memphis was still discussing various ways they could memorialize Elvis. It had expressed an interest in buying Graceland and converting it into a museum. The estate was worth more than a half million dollars, a considerably large sum at that time, and the city calculated they could make the museum self-sustaining by charging an entrance fee and selling memorabilia. Two months after Elvis's autopsy, talks slowed when local newspapers implied his death was drug related. The major concern after Vernon passed away was, what's going to happen to Graceland?

ON AUGUST 10, 1979, the ABC-News network sued Dr. Jerry Francisco, Shelby County medical examiner, and Hugh W. Stanton Jr., Shelby County district attorney, seeking the release of Elvis's autopsy report on grounds it was a public record. Seemingly acting as an advocate for the public's right to know, ABC had become a hound on a hunt. An ABC producer had previously contacted me requesting an interview regarding Elvis's death, but I declined because I had no official authority to speak on anyone's behalf.

ABC had gone to Dr. Francisco and requested that he release Elvis's autopsy report to them. When he told them he did not have it, they pulled the legal play. The notice blindsided me. I thought the controversy over Elvis's autopsy report had long since been settled. Not so! That lawsuit deposed me and required that I bring to the deposition all documents in my possession that related to Elvis's death. ABC must have thought I had a copy of Elvis's

Artist, John Robinette / Photo by Frederick Toma

"KING OF THE WHOLE WIDE WORLD"

Elvis Presley saw his fame and fortune as a means for helping others. What he really loved was seeing people's reactions to his lavish gifts and making dreams come true. The tales of his unconditional generosity are legendary.

A family portrait taken at the wedding Elvis gave as a gift to one of his bodyguards. (*Left to right:* Elvis, Edna Nichopoulos, Dr. Nick. *Seated:* Priscilla Presley with little Lisa Marie)

Elvis's father and friends, including his Memphis Mafia, proudly display Shelby County Deputy Sheriff badges, earned so they can legally carry the guns he gave them. (Kneeling left to right: Dr. Nick, Elvis (seated), and Red West. Standing left to right: Billy Smith, Bill Morris, Larry Fife, Jerry Schilling, Roy Nixon, Vernon Presley, Charlie Hodge, Sonny West, George Klein, Marty Lacker)

Edna Nichopoulos's extraordinary multicolored diamond ring Elvis gave her as a thank you for sharing one of her recipes.

Kissy Nichopoulos's TLC necklace that Elvis presented to her on the front steps of Graceland.

"GOOD ROCKIN' TONIGHT"

"Presley is in good voice, looks fairly trim and seems to be having a ball,"
Variety said of his festival opener in Las Vegas. His two-hour closing show
was rated among the best he ever gave.

Elvis performing in his American Eagle jumpsuit sans cape in Montgomery,
Alabama, March 6, 1974.

Elvis appearing at the University of Dayton for an afternoon show on October 6, 1974. The evening show matched its attendance record of 13,500.

"FOLLOW THAT DREAM"

"Wherever that dream may take you…" required a lot of stops. When Elvis said, "The worst part is the touring," he meant the travel hassle to be on stage for only an hour.

Carese Rice Collection

On stage, Nashville, Tennessee, July 1, 1972.

Carese Rice Collection

Elvis in Evansville, Indiana, October 24, 1976, during a routine he would suffer for later.

Elvis and Dr. Nick preparing to board the *Lisa Marie.*

Dean Nichopoulos leading the way for the king in Binghamton, New York, May 26, 1977.

"LOVING YOU"

Performing on stage was Elvis's goal in life and what ultimately made him happiest—being with his fans. Now fans travel to Memphis to experience Elvis in their own special way.

Elvis opening his seventh tour of 1976 in Chicago Stadium in October. One fan following the tour described that show as: "Incredible. Over the top, even for Elvis."

Elvis delights fans while wearing his Inca Gold jumpsuit during another stop on the 1976 tour.

Elvis singing his heart out in his career closing performance: Indianapolis, Indiana, June 26, 1977.

Graceland's wall of love holds messages from fans around the world.

"Blue Hawaii"

Hawaii was Elvis's favorite getaway spot for R&R, as in rest and refresh. The time zone shift allowed him to become a day person and enjoy the natural beauty of the islands.

Edna and Dr. Nick

Photo by Kissy Nichopoulos

Edna Nichopoulos with her hair in rollers is preparing for a night on the town with Elvis, Dr. Nick, and Ginger Alden.

Photo by Kissy Nichopoulos

Elvis refusing to yield to coaxing from Dean, Dr. Nick, and Edna, who want him to put on his swimsuit.

Courtesy of Joe Esposito

Elvis making the catch in a friendly game of touch football.

"I GOT LUCKY"

There is no way to fully explain how people close to Elvis felt about sharing time with him. His extraordinary magic made regular people feel special—including his fans.

Nichopoulos Collection

Elaine Nichopoulos, Dr. Nick, Edna and Kissy Nichopoulos, shown here at a picnic in Memphis, spent many of their family vacations with Elvis.

Nichopoulos Collection

Former Aide Dean Nichopoulos at Graceland working for "the boss" as fans visited the Memorial Garden to pay tribute to Elvis.

Courtesy of Tish Henley

Dr. Nick's Nurse Tish Henley treated Elvis on tour and cared for him at Graceland, where she also lived.

Elvis in great spirits before a playful audience in Johnson City, Tennessee, February 19, 1977.

"MEMORIES"

Each year in August Elvis's fans and friends gather in Memphis to celebrate his life, his legacy, and the friendships formed by their mutual love and respect for the king of rock 'n' roll.

Photo by Claudia Knos

Photo by Claudia Knos

George Klein hosting a charity event at the Peabody. Elvis's friend from their high school days also hosts a weekly Elvis show on Sirius/XM Satellite radio.

Songwriter Mark James penned "Moody Blue," title of the last album Elvis recorded, and "Suspicious Minds," voted by fans in a Graceland poll as their all-time favorite Elvis record.

Photo by Jud Phillips

Dr. Nick visits with a friend from Oklahoma at Marlowe's, the famous restaurant on Elvis Presley Boulevard, which has been a favorite hangout for Elvis's friends and fans since 1974.

Dr. Nick and longtime friend and legendary photographer William Eggleston stand at the famous Graceland gates, passageway to Elvis's world.

Good friends of Dr. Nick and Elvis wearing diamond rings the king gave to them. (*left to right:* JoCathy Brownlee Elkington and Barbara Klein Bauer)

autopsy. Since I did not, they had to settle for what I had: the simple letter from Dr. Thomas Chesney, written on behalf of the Baptist pathologists. ABC's staff interpreted that letter as "proof" that Elvis had not died of a heart attack. It proved nothing of the sort as far as I was concerned.

The lawsuit allowed ABC to depose Dr. Eric Muirhead, Baptist's pathology chief, and Dr. Harold Sexton, one of his assistants, in addition to Dr. Francisco and me. At last I was included in the discussion. We were all told by the court that we were free to discuss the events of Elvis's death but were not allowed to reveal any of the medical or technical information included in the autopsy. That information, of course, was what ABC was attempting to obtain. Despite its lawsuit, all ABC had acquired was my letter from Dr. Chesney and the newspaper article with the leaked autopsy results contained in the Bio-Science Laboratory toxicology report.

It was clear the network's lawsuit was not going to yield the information the network was seeking; it was even clearer that the Presley estate, which owned the report, was not going to make it available to them. Another avenue had to be found for obtaining the prized autopsy report. Maybe somehow enough suspicion could be cast on the manner in which Elvis died that the release of the information detailing his death would have to surface. That appeared to be their best shot.

If ABC could force the coroner into changing his ruling of death by natural causes or create enough suspicion that the coroner's ruling was wrong and the pathologists' conclusion was right, then the coveted autopsy would have to surface so the conflict could be resolved. The "truth," as they considered it, would be known. The autopsy report *had* to be made public.

ABC plunged into the death investigation at Graceland, deposing Dan Warlick, the chief investigator at the death scene. Warlick shared that he had tried to give both Dr. Francisco and Dr. Muirhead his report on the crime scene before the autopsy began but that neither one of them was "all that interested" in what he had found, guessing each was intent on the job before him at the time. ABC apparently took Warlick's remark to mean that Dr. Francisco had ignored the information, rather than possibly meaning he had heard as much of it as he needed to know.

BY NATURE AND by profession, an internist who is a diagnostician works like the lens of a camera. We view patients in extreme close-ups—zooming in on little signs they may not have noticed about themselves—to give us a fresh perspective on their health. Patients' actions and reactions often provide vital clues to a mysterious ailment hidden within. Diagnosticians are also critically attuned to mental and emotional traits: signs of apprehension, irritability, hysteria, egocentric behavior, etc. Diagnosis is the investigative mystery that I love.

When I was a student at Vanderbilt Medical School, I took a class in physical diagnosis under Dr. Rudolph Kampmier, one of the most respected teachers in his field. He would "read" people in the classroom—up and down—and come up with all kinds of diagnoses just by observation. He would give us assignments such as picking out a person riding with us in an elevator, diagnosing him, and then reporting to the class how we had arrived at our diagnosis. Even to this day I continue to practice the art. It is a good way to utilize time rather than worrying over things one cannot control. Sometimes my honed instincts automatically shift into overdrive.

That was the case one September day in 1979 when I unsuspectingly opened a door from a patient examination room in the middle of a busy morning rife with ailing patients. A scuffling crew of men with lights blazing came tearing down the hallway to confront me. The crew was obviously accustomed to ambushing unsuspecting citizens and shooting on the fly. Earlier I had told the reporter that I was busy with patients and had no time to talk; the impertinent man now leading the pack had darted outside to get his crew and then made his way through the door that Barbara Klein, my trusted receptionist, had used to locate me.

The bushy-headed man, with a confusing name Barbara had forgotten in the middle of the unnerving situation, told me that we could either sit down and discuss what he had to say, or he would continue to question me on the spot. Barbara remembered plainly his saying "there will be no surprises" and you "can approve what you say if we do a sit-down."

In an effort to restore the office to sanity and so other doctors could care for their patients, I led the crew into my small office—about the size of a walk-in closet in a contemporary home. There were two producer-types, the correspondent with a bushy mustache, and two embarrassed-looking technicians—all wilted from the sticky Memphis heat. Introductions were brief, just long enough so I could hear their impressive ABC-TV 20/20 titles and that some of them were from "out of New York." I concluded that these were the guys who had filed the lawsuit against Dr. Francisco for which I had been deposed. I'd had my say there and had not planned on giving them any more of my time.

I had dodged these guys successfully for weeks and was perturbed with myself that I was in this predicament. The crew had been hanging around the parking lot behind our office building like car salesmen flipping coins for the next vulnerable customer. It was either let the situation drift or have them arrested for loitering on private property. I should have exercised the latter option.

The audio tech slumped to the floor, slipping the strap of his heavy recorder off his shoulder, clipped a microphone onto my tie, and adjusted the knobs on his audio deck to suit his earphones. The anxious cameraman nodded he was ready to roll tape. The skinny young correspondent flopped into the chair across the desk from me, while each of his associates hunkered down on the floor on either side of him. Professional courtesy being absent, I was not told the purpose of the interview.

"May I call you Dr. Nick?" the correspondent asked.

Such a humble beginning, I thought, *for a man who seemed to bow to no one.*

Next, he asked how Elvis and I met. The producers smiled. From where I sat, it was obviously five against one. I felt like a trapped animal about to be poked into a cage. He asked a few more questions; then in no time we were there: "At what point in your relationship did the singer begin to have a drug problem?"

I did not feel I had to answer that question and told him so: "I won't discuss that for obvious reasons; it's confidential and personal."

The team facing me keenly watched my reactions. It seemed as though they regarded each question as a point scored for their team. They were obviously focusing on my reactions more than my answers.

"Did you ever counsel Elvis against taking drugs?" he asked.

How insulting! I thought. The reporter's attitude was too combative for me, and I did not appreciate the direction the interview was taking.

After all, I thought, *what right do these people have to challenge me like this on camera?*

When the reporter saw I was about to end the interview, he shifted questions and asked nicely about my relationship with Elvis. The question was appropriate; I answered it.

Then the ABC reporter asked if my financial dependence on Elvis had ever affected my medical judgment.

I thought, *What the heck is he talking about? What financial dependence?*

"I was *never* financially dependent on Elvis," I retorted.

"Isn't it true you owed Elvis over two hundred thousand dollars on your home and several tens of thousands of dollars more than that in various other loans?"

CONSTRUCTION LOAN AGREEMENT

WITNESS this agreement this 29th day of July, 1975, by and between GEORGE C. NICHOPOULOS and wife, EDNA S. NICHOPOULOS (Parties of the First Part) and ELVIS PRESLEY (Party of the Second Part).

WHEREAS, Parties of the First Part are desirous of securing temporary financing for the construction of a personal residence on a lot in Memphis, Tennessee, owned by them and further described as being Lot 40, Section A, Eastwood Manor Subdivision, as recorded in Plat Book 23, at Page 29 in the Register's Office of Shelby County, Tennessee; and

WHEREAS, Party of the Second Part is willing to lend Parties of the First Part such amount as may be necessary to construct said residence up to a maximum amount of TWO HUNDRED THOUSAND DOLLARS ($200,000.00).

NOW, THEREFORE, IT IS AGREED as follows:

Party of the Second Part hereby agrees to lend Parties of the First Part a sufficient amount, up to a maximum of TWO HUNDRED THOUSAND DOLLARS ($200,000.00), as a construction loan for the purpose of building a residence on the lot as above-described, said loan to be evidenced by a Promissory Note signed by Parties of the First Part, secured by a Deed of Trust on all of said property. Said Note shall become payable in full on July 29, 1976, and shall be non-interest bearing until maturity, after which said Note shall bear interest at the rate of ten percent (10%) per annum until paid. The provisions of said Promissory Note and the Deed of Trust, executed concurrently with this contract, are hereby made a part of this agreement.

It is understood and agreed that the principal amount on this construction loan to be repaid by Parties of the First Part to Party of the Second Part (exclusive of penalty, interest and other proper charges) shall be dependent upon the total actual amount of

Dr. Nick's controversial home construction loan financed by his friend Elvis.

- 2 -

funds advanced from time to time to Parties of the First Part
for completion of said residence, whether or not such total amount
shall be less than TWO HUNDRED THOUSAND DOLLARS ($200,000.00) or
shall exceed TWO HUNDRED THOUSAND DOLLARS ($200,000.00).

It is further understood and agreed that payment of the costs
of building said residence shall be made directly by Party of the
Second Part to the contractor building said residence upon receipt
of invoices submitted from time to time by the contractor as construction progresses, accompanied by the written request of Parties
of the First Part to advance such amounts.

Parties of the First Part warrant that they have good
title to the aforesaid Lot 40 and that same is unencumbered except
for 1975 realty taxes not yet due and payable.

Said Parties of the First Part agree that they shall
bear the expense of securing a mortgagee's title guaranty insurance
policy in the amount of TWO HUNDRED THOUSAND DOLLARS ($200,000.00)
for the protection of Party of the Second Part.

IN WITNESS WHEREOF, the Parties hereto have executed this
agreement the day and year first above-stated.

GEORGE C. NICHOPOULOS

EDNA S. NICHOPOULOS
Parties of the First Part

ELVIS PRESLEY

By
(per power of attorney)
Party of the Second Part

"No." I started to clarify the statement by explaining the house loan was a business deal with Elvis that I was repaying monthly. Then I stopped. How I financed my home was not a subject for discussion on national television. I had no idea about the other loans he was talking about.

This is a ridiculous waste of my time, I thought, preparing to pull the plug on the crew's nonsense.

Then the reporter held up a legal-size manila folder like a courtroom attorney preparing for his "Aha" moment, and said: "The records indicate that especially in the last year of his life, you prescribed certain medications to Elvis Presley in quite extraordinary large amounts. Why?"

My answer was as direct and honest as I could make it at the time: "I can't comment on that, and I don't believe it's true."

I was wondering, *What is he talking about? Certain medications . . . extraordinary large amounts . . . the last year of his life?*

If anything, I was prescribing *far less* medication for Elvis at that time.

Then, in his best "It's showtime" manner, the correspondent enthusiastically announced, "Well, the records we have, Doctor, and I will say this as gently as I possibly can, indicate that from January 20, 1977, until August 16, 1977, the day he died, you prescribed to Elvis Presley—and the prescriptions are all signed by you—over five thousand Schedule II narcotics and/or amphetamines. It comes out to be something like *twenty-five* per day."

I expected him to rise up from his seat at any moment for a victory dance.

"I don't believe that," I answered.

He asked if I needed to refresh my memory or if I denied it.

"I deny it."

Then he paused dramatically, and in the tone of an authoritative judge said, "Make a statement as unequivocal as you can, then, Doctor."

I thought I was doing just that.

"I don't have anything else to say," I said.

"Do you deny that you prescribed large amounts of narcotics to Elvis Presley in the last year of his life? To wit . . ."

What's this "to wit" business? I wondered as he started running pill numbers again.

"I don't have any comment," I said.

Then he began rolling through a list of drug names and just kept on, talking faster and louder—like a gun rapid firing a round of deadly ammo. He asked if I remembered writing a Dilaudid prescription for Elvis on the day he died. What was the rationale for that? he wanted to know. Wasn't Dilaudid an extremely strong narcotic analgesic?

Apparently some research had been done. I could have handed him the *Physicians' Desk Reference* and shown him that Dilaudid is for "moderate to severe pain" . . . that the 4mg pills I had prescribed may be taken every four to six hours . . . that Dilaudid also comes in 8 mg pills, which I chose not to prescribe.

Finally the dapper correspondent admitted he was not a doctor but that his opinion was that I could have prescribed from a whole range of analgesics, beginning with aspirin, for a more appropriate treatment for the toothache Elvis said he had.

By that time the reporter was completely worked up. It was time to quit, but he just would not let go. He was like a bulldog pulling on a rope. Relentlessly he continued and asked about the six hundred pills he said I had prescribed for Elvis the day before he died.

"That's not true," I shot back.

He continued pressing on harder and harder. I guessed he was going for the big Perry Mason finale, where the accused stands up and shouts, "Yes, I did it! I killed him!"

"Let me make a statement," I said. "I've got a lot of work yet to do. And as far as I'm concerned, the interview is closed."

He wanted one final answer as I was removing my microphone.

"Do you have any regrets?"

"No regrets," I answered.

No regrets about being Elvis Presley's doctor and friend, if that's what he meant. I had plenty of regrets about talking to the team from *20/20* and their cocky front man.

That interview would prove to be my baptism by fire for the future hot seats I would occupy. My efforts to accommodate the correspondent became the basis for a story, which would christen me a "public figure," stripping away my Sixth Amendment rights as a private citizen. The media, I learned, could have catapulted me into that role even without my permission, but at least I would not have supplied the rope that choked me.

SHORTLY AFTERWARD, TWO suits and ties walked into the Medical Group reception area and demanded to see Dr. George Nichopoulos. It was apparent they did not plan to have a seat and wait their turn.

The gentlemen were from the state Healing Arts Board, which was responsible for licensing physicians. They presented a legal indictment to me with the formality of an invitation to a presidential inauguration. I signed as I would have done for a gift delivered by any other courier. I even had to note the time when I was officially served: 12:55 p.m., September 7, 1979.

Joseph Dughman, a young Nashville attorney for the state public health department, and Steve Bilsky, a recent law graduate who was one of five investigators for the Health Related Board working as its Memphis field representative, had officially served the papers. I later learned Dughman filed the document in Nashville and drove directly to Memphis for his interview with ABC and to serve papers on me—in that order—hoping to keep a lid on the story until ABC News aired its scoop on *20/20*. I was stunned.

Thanks to UPI, the story hit locally via the *Memphis Press-Scimitar* on September 11, 1979, giving me a heads-up about what was happening. Although ABC's scoop was blown, the print news actually worked as publicity for their program. The article, "Elvis' Doctor Target of Medical Probe," reported the conflict over the cause of death between the medical examiner's office and "sources at Baptist Hospital."

It also listed the state's charges against me: "The complaint against Nichopoulas [my name was misspelled] said he had 'dispensed, prescribed or distributed drugs or controlled substances in an unprofessional manner by failing to determine whether or not the amounts were excessive or being abused by the individuals.'"

The article also stated that the complaint said, "An examination of records indicates that said drugs were either not prescribed for legitimate medical reasons or prescribed in excessive amounts or were not prescribed in good faith to relieve illness or infirmity."

Two days later *The Commercial Appeal* ran a piece entitled "Nichopoulos Under Probe for $1^1/4$ Years," where I could finally read details regarding the investigation. Bilsky told reporter Lawrence Buser that he had been picking up "rumors and little tidbits" about me since early 1978. He claimed that "no one pharmacist" had tipped him, that the investigation was as "routine as getting up in the morning." Then he stated that when the investigation picked up steam "over the past *fifteen* months" (italics mine), they brought in more auditors to help.

The origins of Bilsky's "rumors and little tidbits" later surfaced. One of my patients, who worked as a freelance reporter for the national media, informed us that after ABC interviewed me, they drove across the street and barged in on Jack Kirsch at the Prescription House, a pharmacy where I had filled most of my prescriptions for Elvis. Kirsch, a tall, frail man who looked like an underfed character in a Charles Dickens novel, had apparently given the television crew leads about medications written for Elvis, because they accused him of generating zero results. They claimed Kirsch's wild goose chase had caused ABC to give bum leads to the Healing Arts Board investigators, who had also struck out in finding prescriptions written and filled in Elvis Presley's name.

Dr. Nick and his friend William Eggleston rest during a photo shoot outside the Medical Group office building. The Prescription House in the background is directly across Madison Avenue.

That team eventually discovered that most of my prescriptions had been filled right there at the Prescription House. I think Kirsch was afraid he would be fingered in something illegal, and he pointed investigators in other directions so that his pharmacy would be excluded from their search "to get Nichopoulos." When caught in his deception, Kirsch inevitably confessed on camera that he had filled prescriptions for me—as if doing that were some crime. Even though he added that either my nurse or I always picked up the medications (Elvis had never picked up drugs himself), that did not seem to derail anyone's predetermined plotline.

After receiving the indictment, which followed an investigation I was totally unaware of before or while I was being interviewed by the *20/20* correspondent, the Medical Group's attorney, Ken Masterson, called ABC-TV

News in New York City. He proposed to the *20/20* producer that he conduct another interview, a civil exchange that would allow me to answer questions properly and both of us to get across the points we wanted to make—something fair and balanced.

ABC seemed appalled that we would propose such a thing. They acted as if it were bribery—an attempt to censor the press by replacing their "news" with a fluffy public-relations piece. Both the producer and the correspondent would have nothing to do with our offer. I was not surprised. Apparently they were happy with the frightened, deer-in-the-headlights look their cameraman had shot of me the first time. Trusting *20/20* to keep their word was one mistake I would never make again. Since they denied our request to hold another interview in a civil tone where their allegations could be properly addressed, it was clear they were not interested in the truth.

Neither my attorneys nor I knew the goal of the story ABC was chasing. With the help of my reporter/patient, we learned that Charles Thompson's sister was married to James Cole. Her husband, also a former newspaper reporter, had joined his brother-in-law in the enterprise after the producer arrived from New York City to find a story that would allow his family to spend the summer with relatives near Memphis while he worked here. As fate would have it, Thompson's sister (Cole's wife) was a law professor. One of her former students, Jack Fosbinder, happened to be the chief investigator for the Healing Arts Board. Thompson had let it be known that CBS's newsmagazine program *60 Minutes* had been killing *20/20* in the ratings, and he was looking for an investigative story that might skyrocket their ratings.

That is when Jack Kirsch gave the ABC crew the tip that the Healing Arts Board, with some new computers they had recently acquired, was conducting an audit of Schedule II drugs distributed between May 1978 and October 1978. Kirsch surmised that the board might be able to help them "snag Nichopoulos" by extending the dates they were investigating to include 1977. It was learned that after a brief phone call, the two organizations made a pact: ABC needed a paper trail to link the "vast amounts" of drugs prescribed for Elvis Presley back to me. They would give the Healing Arts Board information and contact names to use in their investigation in exchange for a jump on the story when charges were eventually filed. Then ABC could scoop the rest of the press and watch their *20/20* ratings soar.

After I received their indictment, my attorney and I approached the Health Related Board about their relationship with the ABC News team. They waltzed around the issue, denying any complicity between the two groups. Bilsky said that the board's concern was not what Elvis did with the drugs or whether he took the drugs, but whether I had written prescriptions "in an indiscriminate matter without legitimate medical reasons."

Well, if that is honestly what this is all about, I thought, *why hasn't the Health Related Board notified me that I am under investigation?* Then I could have shown them my "legitimate medical reasons" for writing the prescriptions, since they had never seen my patients' records. We could have saved time, money, and a lot of aggravation.

A court date was set. I had four months to prepare my defense before the medical board hearing. I was feeling pretty confident about what I needed to do to resolve the issue. Then the bombs began to drop.

DIRECTLY BENEATH *THE Commercial Appeal* article about the probe ran another news story. "20/20 Concludes Drug Dose Fatal" was scheduled to air that evening, September 13, 1979. The article stated that the program had "reache[d] an inescapable conclusion that Elvis Presley died a drug-related death."

In the article *20/20* proudly pointed to "Presley's stepbrothers," the Stanley brothers, as its key interviews and stated that they, actually Rick, had picked up a Class "A" narcotic for Elvis in the early hours of the morning on the day he died. Since the news story said that the program had "authenticated toxicology reports," surely they knew that the Class "A" narcotic they were boasting about discovering was not found anywhere in Elvis's body at autopsy.

The story would also feature "a very candid interview" with Elvis's girlfriend, whom they admitted had taken a drug that fateful day. But, the article added, "she certainly wasn't a drug addict." I noticed no one had made that disclaimer earlier when referring to the Stanley brothers. The title of the story, "The Elvis Cover-Up," had me curious. There were a lot of directions that story could go. Unfortunately, it went in the worst direction possible— straight after me.

Correspondent Geraldo Rivera, the "investigative" reporter who had entrapped me for the interview in my office, began the *20/20* segment by confirming that the autopsy revealed no clear cause of death. He promptly dismissed Dr. Francisco's determination of heart disease, saying it was still years away from being fatal to Elvis. Geraldo inaccurately reported that Elvis Presley's case was a medical examiner's case (an assumption they made erroneously, possibly based on Dr. Francisco's presence at the autopsy as a consultant). He stated that ABC had filed suit to get the autopsy report made public. Dr. Francisco was accused of keeping "the evidence" off the public record. I guess what they meant by "the evidence" was the Baptist autopsy report Geraldo must have thought contained the *real* cause of Elvis's death.

There was no mention of the fact that the Presley family, at my insistence, had requested the autopsy and therefore it was private; or that the hospital's pathologists had conducted the autopsy, so only the Presley family had the authority to provide or release its results—not Dr. Francisco.

ABC's theory was that the cover-up started at Graceland before Elvis's body was moved, not at the autopsy, as I had suspected they would claim. They had interviewed the ambulance driver, who said he was shocked that the people in Elvis's bathroom (one of whom was a nurse) were attempting to revive an "obviously very dead" body. The paramedic said someone told them, "We think he's OD'd." The paramedic claimed the medication (on which Elvis supposedly overdosed) was never turned over to him by anybody at Graceland, including me, implying that someone or everyone had withheld it. The EMT also told how the bathroom was cleaned up and no drugs were found.

From their interview with the paramedics, ABC surmised that I had intentionally misled the police when they questioned me about the drugs during the investigation, which means ABC agreed there *was* an investigation. ABC was accusing me of taking an active part in the cover-up by claiming that I had not handed over the Dilaudid pills to the paramedic or to Dan Warlick, the coroner's investigator, or to the hospital pathologists.

I did not hand over Dilaudid pills, because I did not have any. That did not make any sense anyway. If I'd had the Dilaudid pills in my possession, then those could not have been the pills that killed Elvis. The autopsy had already disclosed that Dilaudid was not in Elvis's bloodstream, so why were they still talking about that drug? The allegations, accusations, and suppositions were so illogical that I thought every viewer would see the program as I did: a flimsy exercise in investigative reporting—nothing more.

ABC said that when Dr. Eric Muirhead "heard the evidence" (that they had gathered against me), he had wondered what part I might have played in the missing stomach contents. As chief of pathology, Dr. Muirhead certainly should have known how stomach contents are handled when a patient is Harvey-teamed (cared for by the specialized trauma team). I thought that in his heart he must have known nothing irregular had taken place. To imply that it had and that I had been a party to it was slanderous.

If I were still a private citizen and not in the process of being outed as a public figure, I would be suing some of these people, I thought.

ABC did not present a single expert witness who could discuss Dr. Francisco's ruling of cardiac arrhythmia and coronary heart disease. They did not interview family members, who might disclose that heart disease was prevalent on both sides of Elvis's family tree.

Since ABC had not claimed they were unable to find witnesses to give balance to the coroner's theory, my conclusion was that they had not tried. Maybe balance just did not fit into their interpretation of accurate news reporting.

Dick Grob

ABC's *20/20* crew talks to Dick Grob (in sunglasses) at an event honoring Elvis in Tupelo, Mississippi. Geraldo (with microphone) has his cameraman capturing video for their upcoming special.

Geraldo continued, stating that "based on the evidence" viewers were about to see, they (ABC) believed there had been a cover-up involved in Elvis's death. Their "evidence" included:

- the disagreement between the coroner and the pathologist over cause of death, revealed by a member of the Baptist Memorial autopsy team;

THE KING AND DR. NICK

- the Bio-Science Laboratory toxicology report and its list of drugs;
- clips from Dr. Francisco's press conference and sound bites from experts giving their opinions as to why the coroner's decision was inaccurate;
- the Stanley brothers' (whose own drug histories ABC failed to reveal) version of Elvis's history of abuse, based on the intake of drugs they furnished to him;
- Dr. W. S. Nash, the Baptist pharmacist who had filled the final prescription for Dilaudid;
- John O'Grady, the PI who had investigated the various doctors whom he said had provided Elvis with numerous and various drugs;
- Rick Stanley, chiming back in to verify who these doctors were and how they fit into the drug scene;
- a clip from Dr. Elias Ghanem in Las Vegas on the day Elvis died, denying Elvis was a drug abuser—in his professional opinion;
- me speaking my denials (totally taken out of context) while a list of drugs scrolled over my shocked face; and
- Marty Lacker telling how he was now drug free, although he had once taken drugs prescribed by me.

Then Geraldo returned to the video of me. He talked about my list of debts and entangled finances (that bore little resemblance to the truth). They showed a frightened Jack Kirsch explaining why he had filled my prescriptions, which they called "questionable," without having any criteria for judging that. Then two politicians weighed in, making convoluted statements open to various interpretations—as is a politician's way.

That was not the end. There was a long shot of Geraldo descending the steps of the Shelby County Courthouse, punctuating his conclusions to *20/20*'s investigation into the *real* cause and circumstances of Elvis's death that they had labeled "The Elvis Cover-Up."

"Consider, if you will, the following points," Geraldo said in the tone of a college philosophy professor.

There were eight. (I guessed they were his "to wits.")

Item: No *real* police investigation was ever made.

(*Where did he get that idea?* I wondered. The homicide division of the Memphis Police Department is a legitimate law enforcement agency.

They were there with an assistant district attorney and a member of the sheriff's department at the death scene in Elvis's bedroom suite. The investigative team's report was the basis for Elvis's death being ruled a death by natural causes; therefore, there was no reason for further investigation. There was no murder to investigate.)

Item: Dan Warlick, the investigator for the medical examiner's office, never searched the house trailer where Graceland's resident nurse kept "all the drugs."

(If Warlick *had* searched and found drugs in the house trailer where the nurse lived, that would have shown that Elvis did *not* have access to an unlimited drug supply; his medications were responsibly withheld from him.)

Item: Elvis's stomach contents were destroyed without ever being analyzed.

(There was nothing meaningful to keep in the pumped stomach contents; he had been fasting for days. There were no pills clanking around in a pan, as David Stanley, who wasn't present at the autopsy, had claimed.)

Item: There has never been a coroner's inquest.

(The coroner does not order an inquest if a death is not ruled foul play. No homicide—no inquest.)

Item: The Shelby County DA was never officially notified and asked to determine if there were any violations of criminal law.

(Certainly the DA read the report his assistant at the scene filed. There were two assistants at the hospital. I imagine the DA simply concluded that if there were no crime, then no criminal law had been violated.)

Item: No attempts were made—even after the toxicology report—to discover where Elvis got "all those drugs."

(The drugs were medications, obtained from a drugstore and administered by a nurse following the instructions of the doctor who had been treating Elvis for a decade—except for the codeine that could have come from a dentist, whom no one to my knowledge had interviewed. Had ABC's investigative team not taken the time to connect the drugs in the toxicology report to the medical reasons for which they were administered? None of the drugs in Elvis's system were illegal. Why did they keep trying to make it look as though they were?)

Item: Reports were missing from the coroner's file—photographs of the death scene, investigative reports from the ME's office, and the "alleged" toxicology report prepared *by* [actually *for*] the medical examiner were missing from the file.

(Just because they were "missing from the file" did not mean they were "hidden." Why should the coroner give the state's records to ABC? What made ABC think they had a legal right to see the coroner's records and use them to augment their television story?)

Item: Officers of the county government believed there had been a cover-up.

(ABC had found someone to concur with their theory, but not for the reason they thought. As we'd discover later, there was a different dirty-politics agenda going on here that would make city officials and the national TV network compatible bedfellows.)

Finally, the conclusion of the show was a dispirited Geraldo explaining that he had hoped his story would not be true. He concluded he had once been angry with people who had told stories about Elvis being a "medical addict."

If Geraldo really felt that way, I thought, *why has he not spent some time working to see if there is another side of the story?*

Why has Geraldo not found some credible witnesses, who could have told him how Elvis was the sole support for a large number of family members, providing a couple of hundred jobs that required a huge payroll, and running a highly functioning business operation up to the day he died?

Why has there not been someone included on the program to present a picture of Elvis as a dedicated, hardworking man, who was overcoming some serious medical challenges to entertain thousands of people on a horrendous schedule that kept him physically depleted?

The answer was obvious to me. That story might not have boosted ratings. Celebrity sleaze disguised as news is a winner every time.

FALLOUT FROM "THE Elvis Cover-Up" was swift, intense, and nasty—like a mafia hit. The first bullet was delivered on September 14, 1979, the day after the *20/20* program aired, via the city's morning newspaper, the *Commercial Appeal*. Their headline read: "Nichopoulos' Practice Review Is Ordered By Baptist Hospital."

Why does Baptist keep catering to this bunch from ABC-TV? I thought. *Or am I just getting paranoid?*

The more of the article I read, the madder I became. The hospital's spokesperson, Maurice Elliott, announced that the Baptist emergency room would conduct a review of overdose cases treated in its ER "to investigate reports that Nichopoulos was the physician listed as treating a significant number of the patients." Baptist knew that was ridiculous. Elliott admitted in that newspaper article that my charges by the state Board of Medical Examiners had instigated their decision to probe into my cases to see if there were problems with my treatment of patients. Elliott made the disclaimer in that same article that Baptist Memorial had never before had cause to review my treatment of patients.

If Elliott could give a long story like the one I had read to the newspaper, surely he could have called me so I could have mentally and emotionally prepared myself before walking into the hospital to make my daily rounds. I could not understand the medical profession's obsession with taking their case to the media.

That same day, another huge headline in *The Commercial Appeal* announced, "Nichopoulos Target Of Criminal Inquiry In Death Of Elvis." ABC had proudly claimed at the end of "The Elvis Cover-Up" that it had "lit a bonfire" under District Attorney General Hugh Stanton Jr. As a result of the *20/20* "investigative story," the DA's office said it was now investigating whether "Elvis Presley's physician might be criminally liable for his death."

Stanton claimed in the morning news article that he had earlier "ruled out the possibility of a homicide investigation" because of conflicting medical opinions in the autopsy reports. He had realized that a difference in professional opinions was all it was. Now, since *20/20* had shown there *might* be "probable cause," Stanton related that he was going to explore the "drug angle" first.

According to that same article, executive assistant attorney general Jewett Miller said their office began investigating my case after the Medical Board of Examiners, who had indicted me, notified them that "the Nichopoulos case might involve items of a criminal nature."

Miller admitted, "What we read—in the newspapers—produces smoke in sufficient quantity that we are going to take a look at it. We're looking into those allegations, that in addition to being civilly responsible," as charged by the state Board of Medical Examiners, Nichopoulos "might be criminally responsible."

What a coincidence, I thought.

They made that decision on September 13, 1979, the very day *The Commercial Appeal* published its article "20/20 Concludes Drug Dose Fatal," a news story that promoted "The Elvis Cover-Up." Miller even admitted that their decision came just hours before the program aired. It was made in enough time for correspondent Rivera and host Hugh Downs to announce it at the end of their show.

In the article on "The Elvis Cover-Up," its producer, Charles Thompson, said the program "reaches an inescapable conclusion that Elvis Presley died a drug-related death."

I was sick over what was happening to Elvis's legacy. I was even sicker realizing that my career and my livelihood were at stake. No one had proven conclusively that drugs killed Elvis. Until they could do that, why were they filing criminal charges against me? The proverbial cart was before the horse.

For the first time I began to realize that having truth on one's side is not enough. How could I defend myself against a television news network? It seemed hopeless.

The collusion between ABC and the DA's office was not over. By the ABC producer's own admission, investigators from the DA's office contacted ABC's list of Elvis insiders, just as the medical board had done, and interviewed them. I would not know this until years later when I read *The Death of Elvis: What Really Happened*, written by Thompson, the ABC producer. Using their power of subpoena as a government agency, the DA called witnesses to testify. After the interviews were completed, the DA's investigators shared their information with ABC for its next Elvis story.

The way my attorneys and I saw it, ABC had cleverly obtained aid for their investigative efforts by convincing the state board to join forces with them to build a case against me, cleverly called "Operation Nick." ABC needed to generate a paper trail that would connect the drugs to the doctor whom they were determined to prove killed Elvis Presley. In their minds ABC had created motive and opportunity; they needed to solidify the means by which Elvis's doctor had perpetrated the crime. Apparently, the network's representatives needed to sucker the state into utilizing its manpower to engineer the construction of their witch hunt and to fund much of the labor cost involved.

The small crew who had verbally assaulted me in my office, under the guise of an interview, had craftily directed their crusade for television ratings into a pursuit of a story disguised as a quest for truth. ABC had used the Healing Arts Board, the Medical Board of Examiners, and the DA's office to pull the drawstring bit by bit until they had me tightly shut up in their bag.

There was never a pretense of fairness as far as I could see. Everybody, it seemed, was jumping on ABC's bandwagon. State attorney general William Leech revealed in *The Commercial Appeal* article "Elvis Autopsy Report May Be Subpoenaed," which ran on September 20, 1979, a week after the ABC story aired, that there was a possibility he would subpoena the "secreted autopsy report on Elvis Presley" as the state "builds its case against . . . Dr. George Nichopoulos." Leech even said that exhuming the body of the deceased was possible, though unlikely.

My legal team kept telling me that the brouhaha would soon be over. They said that this was not about whether I killed Elvis. It certainly looked that way to me. My attorneys insisted that "after ABC gets the autopsy report and satisfies its curiosity," my case would be stale news. I could only hope.

It was one thing to be forced into using all the resources available to me to finance my own legal defense. It was another for the presentation of my case to be weighed against a glitzy, prime-time television show with investigative pieces funded by three powerful organizations. Few would be reviewing my records in the courtroom; seventeen million households had seen the initial airing of "The Elvis Cover-Up." An hour-long follow-up version was slated for broadcast on December 27, 1979, shortly before my medical board hearing. It kept the media feverishly tracking the pill numbers and the damage done.

"The Elvis Cover-Up" was leading the charge for what the broadcast media seemed to consider justice, which in the public's eyes meant capturing the doctor who wrote the prescriptions that killed Elvis Presley. The public was emotionally and morally outraged by the television program's content, concluding that I had overprescribed drugs in a reckless manner, causing Elvis's death. Newspapers published editorials about the need for professional organizations to police themselves and the need for government to create laws to protect patients against addictive drugs and the doctors who prescribe them.

Anonymous hate mail, as well as death threats, arrived daily in my family's mailbox and at the office. My wife and receptionist intercepted as many letters as possible, hoping to spare me the hurt of looking at the address scribbled by angry fingers on the envelopes.

It was the newspaper's policy in those years to give location information on the subject of an article, so both my home and office addresses accompanied many of the stories written about me. Almost everyone knew by now that I conducted daily office visits to patients at both Baptist and Doctors Hospital. The Memphis Police Department took the responsibility of safeguarding my family and me. They provided on-again, off-again security whenever they determined the situation warranted it, helping to ease my anxiety more than they could have realized.

Despite the negative publicity in the local and national media and the increasingly hostile public sentiment, I tried to focus on giving my family and patients the best care I could. I did not want other innocent people suffering from the emotional havoc impacting my life. As humiliating and personally painful as matters were, I realized it would not be getting better anytime soon for Elvis or for me.

SEVEN

SWINGING PENDULUM

Special Collections, University of Memphis Libraries

Dr. George Nichopoulos enters the courtroom to answer his charges before the Tennessee Board of Medical Examiners. (left to right: Attorney John Thomason, Dr. Nick, and Attorney Ken Masterson)

The judge ruled that my appearance before the Tennessee Board of Medical Examiners on January 14, 1980, would be an open hearing as compelled by the state's sunshine law. That law states that any meeting that consists of two or more members of a governing body empowered to deliberation toward a

163

decision affecting the public or making recommendations to a governing body must be open to the public. That ruling sent the media scurrying to have field crews in Memphis in a couple of weeks. I had greater concerns.

Photo by Rose Clayton Phillips

Media from across the nation cover the "World's Most Famous Medical Board Hearing."

At that time Tennessee had a limited doctor-patient confidentiality statute, so any of my subpoenaed patients would have to either testify before the cameras or go to jail. I was gravely distressed that presenting patient records for my defense would expose confidential information—trusted conversations that could break up a marriage or cause someone to lose a job.

A seven-page complaint had originally charged me with "indiscriminately" prescribing drugs to entertainer Elvis Presley and fifteen others, including singer Jerry Lee Lewis and Arthur Baldwin, a nightclub-owner-turned-FBI-informant in the state's "pay for pardon" scandal. Those portrayed as victims of my "indiscriminate overprescribing" were colorful enough to magnetize network and syndicated video crews to join the traditional and tabloid press at the scene of the hearing.

An amended fifty-nine-page complaint had followed three months after the first one. After the state accommodated ABC by compiling a seven-page official report to serve on me, Joseph Dughman had to complete his formal charges. He addressed this in "Suit Against Nichopoulos Is Amended," an article that ran in *The Commercial Appeal* on December 18, 1979.

The article stated that Dughman said, "The charges against Nichopoulos were expanded after a routine fifteen-month audit of Memphis-area pharmacies that found irregularities lengthened to include almost all of 1976."

Dughman claimed the amended complaint was "only a matter of getting it [the complaint] complete, in its final form." He said that no new pharmacies had been audited.

The final complaint, however, was extended to twenty months (from January 10, 1976 to August 15, 1977) after *20/20* suggested to the state that they expand the auditing period to include the last eighteen months of Elvis's life. The additional months increased the numbers to "196 prescriptions of 17 different drugs to Presley," and it lengthened the list of patients I was accused of harming to twenty people, including my daughter and me.

The new indictment charged me with overprescribing the following drugs: the depressants Quaalude, Leritine, Parest, Amytal, Tuinal, Placidyl, and Percodan; the tranquilizer Valium; the stimulants Dexedrine, Biphetamine, Carbrital; Dexamyl, which was a stimulant that also had a sedative in it; Lomotil, a synthetic classified as a narcotic and used for diarrhea; and Hycomine Compound tablets, a synthetic narcotic-type drug used as a cough suppressant. The complaint noted that some medications were in liquid form, including injectables. The only drug on the list that I had given Elvis by injection was Valium, for when he was vomiting and could not keep down the medication in pill form.

Unfortunately, the list of pharmaceuticals made Elvis look like a walking drugstore. These were legitimate medications, however, used for specific purposes and situations. Plus, Elvis did not have the drugs in his possession; they were administered according to his needs by either a nurse or me. My charges kept focusing on Elvis's drug intake, yet officials insisted "the cause of Presley's death would not be at issue."

While the original complaint had Elvis's name simply on a list with other patients, it was clear in the expanded complaint that it was medications written in his name that they were concentrating on identifying. The new complaint charged:

The quantity of said drugs prescribed to Elvis Presley was in excess of that amount, if any, which was medically appropriate for the treatment of Elvis

Presley. It is further alleged that the combination of various drugs prescribed *to* Elvis Presley was not medically appropriate for Elvis Presley.

"How can they determine what's 'medically appropriate' when they haven't seen Elvis's medical records?" I asked my attorney.

"The sheer volume of the prescriptions written in Elvis's name," he replied.

Dr. Nick and Attorney Ken Masterson pause for a moment of good news, January 1980.

"This hearing is primarily about the numbers. But it's also an effort to obtain Elvis's medical records—to get them into court testimony as you will be compelled to do when presenting your defense."

The agenda seemed clear. Get Elvis's doctor—get Elvis's medical records.

ABC was still working to get a copy of the autopsy results that they had contended in "The Elvis Cover-Up" should be available to the public because the autopsy was conducted by Shelby County medical examiner Dr. Jerry Francisco.

He had repeatedly said he was acting as a consultant, not as the medical examiner, when he attended the Elvis Presley autopsy performed by Baptist's chief of pathology, Dr. Eric Muirhead, and analyzed its results. Dr. Francisco reiterated that the Presley family, rather than the attorney general, had ordered the autopsy, and the report was not a public record. The national media continued to ignore him. It was my best guess that ABC thought the only chance left at obtaining the autopsy report was to get Elvis's death ruling changed to homicide; then the autopsy report would have to be released. Releasing the autopsy would have helped me tremendously; having the death ruled a homicide would have been devastating to my fight for justice.

One of my attorneys, John S. Thomason, thought I was entitled to see the autopsy report in order to prepare my defense. The problem with getting to see the autopsy was that its confidentiality was the subject of a chancery court lawsuit previously filed by ABC, and a hearing was still pending. Until the hearing, a chancellor had ordered that the autopsy report and other medical test results on Elvis be locked in a safety deposit box in an undisclosed location. As it turned out, the attorney for the Elvis Presley estate had a copy of the autopsy results, and he allowed us to read it, but only after he was compelled to do so by the circuit court.

MY LEGAL DEFENSE team filed an answer, my denial of charges, to the Board of Medical Examiners. Jim Balentine, staff writer for the *Memphis Press-Scimitar*, accurately reported the answer on December 31, 1979.

In addition to Ken Masterson and John S. Thomason, my team of attorneys also included Frank W. Crawford. Each of them signed the document that was quoted in the newspaper. Our answer to the charges said I was "in direct contrast to physicians the courts had found guilty of violating drug laws by overprescribing." Those doctors gave drugs to patients without examining them and made "a substantial charge for issuing a prescription."

"In contrast, Dr. Nichopoulos, before prescribing Schedule II substances to the relatively few patients of his to whom such prescriptions are given, obtains a medical history, and conducts a complete physical examination, then prescribes suitable drugs to the patients, one prescription at a time," our answer continued. "He does not charge for refilling the prescription, unless other medical services are performed at that time, and does not prescribe controlled substances to patients with whom he is not medically familiar."

As the newspaper cited, we had attempted earlier to have my charges dropped by contesting the indictment, due to the convoluted circumstances on which it was based. "The original charges made against Dr. Nichopoulos by Joseph K. Dughman, for the Health Related Boards, were instigated by and made to accommodate the American Broadcasting Company (ABC) in connection with a television program broadcast on September 13, 1979, entitled *20/20*."

One of the most difficult issues to address in my defense came next: "The charges against Dr. Nichopoulos subject him to ever-changing standards to which he and other physicians practicing their profession in this country are unreasonably held accountable," the document contended. Although interpretations are "constantly changing," I had made every legitimate effort to comply with them.

My answer also declared that state law "even permits a physician to prescribe a controlled substance to a person who is addicted to the habit of using such controlled substances if the physician is making a *bona fide* effort to cure the habit of such patient."

I felt certain that when the board members studied my records, they would find the patients in question had not received refills early and that the amounts of their prescribed medications had decreased, rather than increased. Moreover, some of the patients named had been drug dependent when they came to me, and were now drug free. Surely the board would find value in the results of my treatment.

The next charge, termed "special cases," was personally painful for me because it dealt with my overprescribing drugs to my daughter Chrissy and me. At that time there were no written guidelines stating that doctors should not treat members of their families or themselves. Doctors routinely wrote prescriptions in their own names to replenish medications used in their medical bags for immediate treatment of patients. After legitimate causes were established for the "special cases," they were both dropped before being debated by the board.

The conclusion of my defense document summarized my treatment of Elvis Presley from early 1967 until mid-1977:

> At that time Elvis Presley suffered from chronic insomnia and a propensity to gain weight. Although he avoided the use of some drugs upon which many persons are dependent, for example, alcohol, caffeine, and nicotine, he did exhibit a need for drugs for sleep and to control his appetite.

I knew the State of Tennessee was not interested in what Elvis's other doctors had done. They were only interested in whether *I* had violated its laws; however, I felt compelled to add the following in my defense document, on which the newspaper was reporting:

> Although Dr. Nichopoulos was not the only source of drugs available to Elvis Presley, Nichopoulos did undertake, as best he could, from the time he became Elvis Presley's personal physician, to look after him as a patient, to control his substances, and to keep him in good health and physically able to perform for his millions of admirers.

Then the newspaper article made our most important point:

> By no means were all the drugs prescribed under the name of Elvis Presley dispensed to him. The contents of many were discarded and placebo substances were substituted; some were apparently stolen by persons who had access to the Presley home so that security measures became necessary.

There was a time when a couple of Elvis's guys had informed me that a few volunteers making placebos were dipping into the meds, not only for their own use, but also to sell pills for extra cash. That is another reason we devised the envelope system for dispensing medications. It made it easy to identify the guilty parties scavenging the drugs. Once eager to welcome me on the scene, they later exited upon my arrival as if I'd been skunked. Naturally they had been first to give the media their quotes about the "drug scene" at Graceland, in which they had willfully participated and later piously condemned.

Our defense document was honest and straightforward. I was confident truth was on my side. I believed the doctors sitting in judgment of my actions would be open and objective concerning the number of prescriptions I had written and my reasons for doing so. My hope was that the medical board could separate the issue of the number of prescriptions I had written from the death of Elvis Presley. I was not so sure about the broadcast media that lived for sound bites; my decision about their openness and objectivity was still pending. I felt the traditional press was fulfilling its mission as best it could under the impassioned circumstances. I did not know how to categorize the emerging celebrity news media as they joined in the preparations for my upcoming hearing.

THE MEDICAL BOARD of Examiners is basically a peer review body—the regulatory and enforcement arm of the Tennessee Department of Health. Its hearings are designed much like a trial, although the board is not bound by criminal courtroom procedures. Instead of a judge, there is a hearing officer from the secretary of state's office. In my case Mike Bramham acted as court administrator.

The governor-appointed board acts like a jury. They hear evidence from both sides before delivering a verdict; but unlike the jury in a criminal trial, the board deliberates publicly. Board members are all physicians. Those serving at my hearing included: Dr. John H. Burkhart, the board's president, from Knoxville; Dr. Howard Foreman from Nashville; Dr. Charles E. Allen from Johnson City; Dr. Edgar Akin from Chattanooga; and Dr. Charles Dowling of Memphis.

The day before the medical board hearing, I learned of a grassroots effort to help me. Dr. Varna P. Love, a radiologist with the Medical Group, wrote and mailed a letter to a thousand physicians in Memphis, encouraging them to write letters of support to Dr. Dowling, the local member of the medical board. She had also sought donations on my behalf. Although Dr. Love took some heat for her brave actions on my behalf, she explained unapologetically, "This is just as proper as the news media crucifying him before he even gets up there [before the board]."

Years later I would continue to gratefully read the letters from people who put aside their own concerns to come to my aid.

At the same time I discovered that my pastor, Father Nicholas Vieron, had implored members of Annunciation Greek Orthodox Church and others in the Memphis Greek community to support me spiritually and financially as they felt led to do. His prayers and sincere consultations had been a major source of encouragement over the years.

Father V had talked with Elvis many times, patiently answering questions of a religious and spiritual nature. Father V had counseled me about spending too much time with Elvis—especially on tour. He was concerned I was not giving my own family and other patients the attention they needed and deserved. Although I had failed to heed his advice, Father V never judged me. Now he was stepping out in faith to manifest physically what he knew to be an immediate need.

That night I knelt in the small prayer room of my home before the inlaid crucifix Elvis had given to Edna and me. I expressed my gratitude for the gift of faith and how it continued to reveal itself visibly in the love and loyalty of my family and friends. I begged for strength to bear my burden. I prayed for courage for my loved ones to withstand the ordeal with dignity, mindful of the pain it had caused them. I asked for a change of heart for those bent on persecuting rather than understanding human frailty and for wisdom for those involved in the proceedings ahead.

FINALLY THE FATEFUL day arrived like a swinging pendulum—a dreaded yet anticipated time—which held in its balance my sentence or my release. A caption under a photo of the event in the *Memphis Press-Scimitar* on January 14, 1980, read: "The World's Most Famous Medical Board Hearing." It was a distinction I had tried my best to avoid.

The five-hundred-seat city council chambers provided the space for the historic event. Due to the unprecedented publicity, a large group was expected to turn out to "see the doctor swing," as one tabloid reported the focus of the proceedings. Less than a quarter of the auditorium was filled, however, peopled only with visitors involved enough in the outcome to ignore the cold and customarily wet Memphis winter weather.

Our tedious schedule called for a projected five-day hearing, extending to Saturday if necessary. The sessions were scheduled to begin at 8:30 each morning and end ten hours later, with only two short breaks. Since the hearing was not intended to be a spectator sport, no one was particularly concerned about the convenience of its viewers.

When I entered the room, I could not see the public section for the bright lights; yet I knew they were there—my entourage—present for moral support and because they really cared.

I said to myself, *Yeah, Elvis. I get it now. This is like your Las Vegas debut.* I was just as scared as I knew he had been.

I was seated with the other hearing participants in sort of a lion's den behind a curved, wooden rail that separated us from a swarm of media, buzzing around the barrier like flies on dead meat. Blinded by their glaring pole lights and incessant flashbulbs, I was unable to distinguish the crew from *20/20*. I was told they were there, strutting around like show dogs on awards day.

Plainclothes officers discreetly patrolled the public viewing area; security officers and sheriff's deputies were more visible around the hearing area, where a violent attack would be more likely. Unfortunately, in recent weeks several members of the board had received death threats by phone and by mail, apparently from the same people who had accused me of killing Elvis. Police provided heavy security for the board members, the witnesses compelled to testify, and my family and me.

As anxious as we all were to begin, the opening was delayed by a half hour while Officer Bramham coaxed the media into moving their barricade formed by photographers, videographers, lights, and cameras. Attorney Thomason objected to the press corps blocking the public's view and turning the hearing into a media event. I felt the media's presence was a needless distraction and could only hope their presence did not intimidate my patients.

Among those testifying were a record promoter, a singer/guitarist in an all-girl rock band, an investment broker, twin brothers, a gardener, a former rock star bodyguard, an antique dealer, a restaurant cashier, a receptionist, the owner of a topless nightclub, a former heroin addict, and, of course, a doctor and his daughter.

What could be crueler than asking a person to confess to total strangers what they had withheld from loved ones for fear of judgment or rejection— alcoholism, cocaine and heroin addiction, abortions, anxiety neuroses, eating disorders, phobias, insomnia? Dark secrets and weak moments would now be paraded on videotape—just another day's work for the media, collecting the exploits of the seventies generation's crash landings. I thought that if my patients could make it through this humiliating ordeal, I could certainly survive it.

On the hearing's first day, the prosecution called half of the witnesses. When Alan Fortas took the stand, my mind flashed back to the good old years when I had first met him in Hollywood while he was working for Elvis. The nephew of Abe Fortas, the former Supreme Court justice, Alan was one of those lovable guys people refer to as a "teddy bear." All the women wanted to hug him. Short in stature, Alan was obese, which led to problems with his legs and back due to extra weight. He also had debilitating migraine headaches, chronic neck pain, and insomnia, probably from sleep apnea.

Over a sixteen-month period, Alan had received a total of twenty-five prescriptions for three medications: Quaaludes and Placidyl, sedatives, and Eskatrol, an appetite suppressant—not twenty-five prescriptions for each drug, as had been implied. My habit was to write a prescription for only one drug at a time on one sheet of the prescription pad, not multiple prescriptions on one sheet. The medications in question had not been prescribed concurrently; they were alternated. Experience had proven to me that the medications I was giving him were the best drugs to administer at that time—in the way I had prescribed them—for his specific problems.

"I've been going to him for twenty years, and to my knowledge, I have to call him one of the finest doctors I've ever known," Alan said, while emotionally battling a speech impediment to release his heartfelt words.

The board showed no reaction to his emotional outpouring.

The prosecution continued to call its witnesses one by one; it coupled the prescriptions with the reasons for which they were prescribed. As my patients told their stories, they simultaneously told mine, hoping to prove in the process that we had not intentionally broken any laws.

Then, in a startling move, the prosecution called *me* to the witness stand.

Wait one minute! How can the prosecution call me to testify against myself? That's got to be illegal.

My attorneys had already jumped to their feet. An argument ensued over my testifying at that time.

Neither side was getting anywhere with Officer Bramham; he was officiating the hearing with a firm hand. My attorneys asked for time to seek a ruling on the issue in chancery court. After learning that the ruling would delay the trial for an indefinite period, my defense team decided I should return the next day and roll with the flow.

ON DAY TWO I raised my right hand and swore to tell the truth as a witness for the prosecution. I discussed my prescribing practices and talked about each patient listed in the charges. When I got to count number fifteen, "Elvis Presley," a media scuffling ensued; lights brightened.

I went through the entire Elvis saga, describing the progression of our doctor/patient relationship. I was interrupted occasionally by questions from the state's attorneys or a board member; they were no longer taking intermittent naps as they had done when previous witnesses testified.

My testimony told how I began treating Elvis while he was making movies, traveled on the road with him when he performed, and continued to treat him when he was in Memphis. Elvis had other doctors who also treated him in different cities. After his near-fatal illness in 1973, I became his personal physician in Memphis. Elvis had undergone a nontraditional treatment from a Los Angeles doctor that resulted in my having to hospitalize him and call in two drug abuse specialists to detox him from drugs that had been administered to him during that procedure. Elvis continued to experience illnesses related to that unfortunate incident until his death.

Dr. Nick testifying before the Tennessee Board of Medical Examiners, January 16, 1980.

Prosecuting Attorney Joseph Dughman wanted to know if Elvis was "subsequently hospitalized for drug abuse or addiction."

"Elvis was admitted to the Baptist Hospital in August of 1975. He was not admitted specifically for drug abuse," I answered, remembering that I chose to detox him at that time simply because he was there.

I testified, under prompting, that Elvis also received medications from other doctors, which was a continuing problem. I attempted to consult with these other doctors who saw Elvis, "trying to get some continuity in his treatment," but received no cooperation from them. By 1975 a nurse lived at Graceland, so we maintained better control over the dispensing of his medications. In 1976 he seemed to respond better to efforts to keep him active, and his health improved.

The board seemed to be most interested in when exactly Elvis was known to be addicted.

"I thought he was addicted when I first got him in 1973. I do not think he was an addict," I answered. "He had a history of psychological dependence on certain medications, especially sleep medications. He had sleep disturbances; he would sleepwalk; he had serious nightmares and anxiety problems.

"I was successful in using placebos extensively in treating Elvis, but he had a lot of chronic pain problems, like degenerative changes in his back and in his neck from arthritis that I could not treat with placebos. There were times when he was home at Graceland that Elvis took no medication at all for pain or insomnia. His drug use while I was treating him seemed to accelerate with his stressors, and that was almost exclusively when he was touring."

Carese Rice Collection

After giving twenty-nine concerts in fifteen days in Vegas, Elvis performs his fifth concert in five nights in the Auburn University Coliseum on March 5, 1974.

Then the prosecutors brought up the large number of prescriptions written in Elvis's name, which they had misunderstood as being written for Elvis to take individually. I explained as best I could that the drug doses were not for Elvis alone, but for his entire company of as many as a hundred people who worked for him on tour and in Las Vegas and at Lake Tahoe. The drugs were purchased in Elvis's name because his father, who paid Elvis's bills, would not have paid for the pills if Elvis's name had not been on the prescriptions.

My testimony included accounts of how "I carried three suitcases full of equipment. I had different types of medications for people who were allergic to penicillin and other antibiotics and decongestants. I had expectorants . . . I had just what you could imagine you'd use every day in your office. I carried a laryngoscope. I carried some long forceps in case he aspirated. I carried these little bags for breathing. I carried suture material, adhesive tapes, splints, everything that you would expect a first-aid stand to have, plus what a physician would have."

One of the reasons, I added, that there were so many different prescriptions was because there were various allergies and viruses in the different parts of the country where we traveled. I called ahead to the health department in cities where we would be going to see what types of illnesses Elvis's people might encounter.

I explained that there were times when Elvis made four hundred thousand dollars for two shows a night. Rich as he was, he could not afford for any member of his key rhythm section to get sick and not be able to make the show. So many of his numbers keyed off of visual cues, and only his regular band members would know those.

Then I tried to emphasize that drugs were not dispensed freely to Elvis: "Prescriptions *written* in his name were prescriptions I *ordered* in his name. I kept the prescriptions, so I could issue the medications depending on his needs or his problems at any one time."

Elvis never had possession of his prescriptions when I treated him; they were administered to him in doses (in envelopes) at the required time.

Finally I admitted to one of my biggest mistakes: being sloppy in my record keeping regarding the drugs I dispensed in Elvis Presley's name. "The reason some of these things [Elvis's records] were not kept in the office and some of them were not written down someplace else was that people were always perusing his charts, and confidentiality would be broken. This occurred in the hospital as well, when other doctors and nurses would come in unauthorized and look at his charts. This was a constant and serious problem.

"I think that if he hadn't died, the end result as far as his improvement during this period of time would be an answer in itself," I told them. "Even though he was using substances, he was much better; he was much healthier [in the last twenty months] than he was prior to that time. I think we made a lot of strides in helping him, except for his colon problems."

Reviewing my relationship with Elvis for the board frustrated me.

"You can't imagine what a nightmare it was for me," I said. "I encouraged him to get psychiatric help. I tried to get him to go to sleep clinics. I tried to get him help from other sources. It was always, 'I'll do better' or some excuse. He just wouldn't do it."

This board was not interested in good intentions. They had tunnel vision. They focused on their duty: to examine the number of prescriptions written and for what purpose.

"He required more drugs than normal people," I concluded.

I did not mean to imply that Elvis was not "normal," but I did not know exactly how to explain Elvis to the board, who in their appearance amazingly resembled the original censors of rock 'n' roll that I had seen in the newsreels.

AFTER I COMPLETED my testimony that day, my defense team broke into action. It was late in the afternoon, so we only had time for two witnesses: the "California girls." First was Sheila Ryan, who had dated Elvis during '74 and '75 and later married actor James Caan. She told about the sleep problems he "always" had and how I administered medicine to Elvis.

"He was given a certain amount by Dr. Nichopoulos when he needed them. He didn't have them himself. I mean, he didn't have them in bottles of whatever he needed. Dr. Nichopoulos would come in at night and give him what he needed. And that was it," Sheila told them.

"In his dressing room? Elvis did not have a supply of drugs?" my attorney asked.

"Not that I can recall."

"So he could get any medications that he wanted also, wouldn't he?" my attorney asked.

"Not always," Sheila replied. "I remember a lot of controversy about medications he wanted and what he wasn't getting [from Dr. Nichopoulos]."

"Do you know of any activity on the part of Dr. Nichopoulos, or those working closely with Elvis, to control the taking of medications?"

"Yes. I remember there were times when Elvis would receive his medication for sleep. And then awake again. And he would want something more, and he would call Dr. Nichopoulos. And then there would sometimes be arguments as to what he should and should not have."

"Who advised you that placebos were being used? Dr. Nichopoulos?"

"I was not advised; I was witness to it," Sheila explained. "I saw it happen. I mean, I saw him."

"What did you see?"

"Well, one time I saw him [Dr. Nichopoulos] empty a capsule and put something [else] in it. And I don't believe he knew that I saw him do it."

"Did you see him give Mr. Presley that pill?"

"Yes, I did."

Next was Shirley Dieu, a former girlfriend of Elvis's road manager, who, like Sheila, had traveled on many tours and vacations with Elvis's entourage "90 percent of the time . . . for the last three years of his life . . . since I was about twenty [years of age]. I'm twenty-six now."

"Did you see Dr. Nichopoulos on these tours with Elvis Presley?" Shirley was asked.

"I saw him on most of the tours," she replied. "I know when we toured Las Vegas, usually Elvis had a different doctor taking care of him."

"I'd like to ask you some questions about the use of medications, or drugs, regarding the tours. Did he [Elvis] use alcohol or marijuana?"

"Never. He didn't allow any alcohol or marijuana around. If he found out about it, he would be really upset . . . The guys would have lost their jobs."

"What about using other kinds of drugs for recreational purposes?"

"I know that he was on medication, but I never felt or got the impression that he was getting 'high,' so to speak. Normally if he would take medication, he would go right to bed and it was for that reason. As far as recreation purposes, I never recalled anyone sitting around, smoking marijuana or taking any type of drugs or pills. If it were done, it was done because they were ill. Even then, I didn't know about it. I wasn't around to watch when people went to bed, what pills they took, or if they brushed their teeth or not."

"Were you aware of any efforts made by Dr. Nichopoulos to control the quantity of prescription drugs?"

"I know when Joe and I stayed in Las Vegas, there were little, tiny envelopes that were for each day. I don't know if Dr. Nick gave them to Elvis, but I know that they were gone through by Dr. Nick and [things were] replaced. When I asked, 'What are you doing?' they said, 'We're replacing these with sugar pills.'"

"Was Elvis Presley a generous person with respect to the people who went on tour with him and were his friends?"

"Well, I think that goes without saying. Elvis was a very generous person, not just materialistically but with his feelings also . . . he made everybody feel special."

"Are you aware of the fact that Elvis Presley loaned money and gave people gifts?"

"Everybody. He was generous with everybody. Even people off the street."

Before descending the stand, Shirley said, "Might I add that I loved Elvis very much? If I felt Dr. Nick did anything to hurt him, I wouldn't be here. I really wouldn't."

The media loved the pretty girls; the board smiled a lot and seemed to appreciate their sweetness and the distraction their appearance provided.

THE NEXT DAY the Medical Group coordinator explained that our practice had fifteen thousand patients, and about thirty-five hundred were considered to be my patients. The twenty patients listed in my indictment represented half of 1 percent of my patients. By choosing patients randomly and taking into account patients seen during six full working days at the Medical Group, only one out of every twenty patients received a prescription for a controlled substance.

Next, Tish Henley took the stand. Tish still worked at the Medical Group during the day and had been Elvis's private nurse after work. Since she had small children, she was accustomed to saying no when necessary. I had never doubted she would do that where Elvis was concerned.

She confirmed to the board that she and her family lived in a trailer behind Elvis's house and that she had supervised medications given to Elvis, his father, and his grandmother since 1975. She described how she kept Elvis's medications in a locked overnight bag in her trailer. Tish told how she or I "went along on Elvis's concert tours to see to the medical needs of his . . . musicians, equipment managers, singers, band, security team, and aides.

"I never gave any medications without Dr. Nick's orders," Tish said with the same confidence that had let me know I could always count on her to do the right thing. "I dispensed medications [on tours] for gastritis, sinusitis, flu symptoms; one man had had a gastric bypass; another man had had a kidney transplant; we also had diabetics on the tour."

Attorney Thomason then brought a visual into evidence, to the delight of the photographers. It was a chart showing the tours Elvis took in 1977 prior to his death. Then he introduced a second chart, which was transparent and used as an overlay, with jagged vertical lines indicating that the increase in the amount of drugs ordered in Elvis's name corresponded exactly with preparation for tours.

Despite the enthusiasm from the flashing bulbs, I never saw a photograph of the charts anywhere in the media, nor did I see an explanation of the amount of prescriptions I wrote in Elvis's name directly corresponding with the dates Elvis toured. It was as though none of that testimony had ever taken place.

Next, Felton Jarvis took to the stage, so to speak. Felton was diabetic, and Elvis had used his clout to obtain a donor kidney for him because he was in renal failure. In addition to producing Elvis's studio recording sessions, Felton accompanied Elvis on tour for eleven years, recording many of those tours for live albums. Despite his poor health, Felton had accompanied Elvis for seventy concerts plus sixty-eight Las Vegas shows in 1974; seventy-five concerts and fifty-one Las Vegas shows in 1975; ninety-seven concerts and thirty Las Vegas shows in 1976; and fifty-five concerts in 1977. (And people disputed that Elvis suffered from fatigue when I hospitalized him!)

Elvis's band was Felton's responsibility, so I dealt with him daily on the road regarding whether Elvis was show-worthy or had a condition that might impair him during a concert. He also was the liaison for other band members who might need medical care. Felton told the board how I had "doctored everybody" on the tour.

"When would you see Mr. Presley before a concert?" he was asked.

"I would usually go backstage just before a concert and brief him on how the stage was set up, how the sound would be . . . Usually Dr. Nichopoulos would be putting eyedrops in his [Elvis's] eyes."

"And that's all you saw?"

"Yes, sir."

ONE OF MY most satisfying moments during the entire hearing took place when Joseph Dughman, the trial counsel for the Health Board's investigators, finally had to admit that they had met and exchanged information with the *20/20* team before delivering my indictment to me. His associate, Steve Bilsky, the Tennessee Healing Arts Board's field investigator for Memphis, testified that they had not consulted even one licensed physician before recommending that the state file charges against me.

Dughman had stated earlier that he had given an interview to the crew from *20/20* while working as an investigator for the Tennessee Department of Public Health, but he denied that ABC News had prompted the filing of charges against me. James Cole, the freelance researcher for "The Elvis Cover-Up," confessed under oath that he was the one who gave the investigators at the Health Board the "tip" that Elvis had died a "drug death" in the first place. That was enough evidence of collusion for me, yet it was not enough to make the national media or to affect my case.

DR. WALTER HOFFMAN, founder of the Medical Group, had known me since I was a graduate student. He testified that I had "a unique quality of being more empathetic than any practitioner he had ever known." Coming from a peer whom I highly respected, the remark brought tears to my eyes; I was so grateful my family was present.

Dr. Hoffman accepted much of the responsibility for my poor record keeping. He explained how he was in charge of the personnel responsible for entering the information and that office construction had hampered the employees' ability to find some of the charts at the appropriate time.

"We don't always get everything into our charts," Dr. Hoffman confessed, adding, "There is no legal requirement to do so. It's just to remind ourselves."

The specialist I had consulted regarding Elvis's gastrointestinal problems, Dr. Lawrence Wruble, took the stand. I had called him as a consultant regarding Elvis's abnormal abdominal swelling and edema in 1973. Dr. Wruble explained to the board that we determined the swelling to be from "rather massive amounts of cortisone."

He said, "I knew he was being overtreated by physicians out in the West. He [Nichopoulos] was as concerned about it as I was."

Dr. Wruble disclosed how we "had a session" with Elvis while he was hospitalized about his level of drug use, which at the time I knew to be for his sleeping problem and before he went onstage.

"Have you seen me perform?" Elvis had asked him intently, as if it were one of the Seven Wonders of the World.

Dr. Wruble, who is a good-natured guy, was caught in a trap. He was too embarrassed to tell Elvis he had not seen him, but he did not want to hurt Elvis's feelings, which were fragile at that point.

Elvis continued, excited about his newly found audience of one: "There's no way to go to sleep after performing a second show without taking drugs."

Carese Rice Collection

The Hilton Las Vegas September Concert
Series, 1972.

Well, Dr. Wruble was unconvinced. He explained firmly that if performing did that to him, then he would "either have to cut back to one show" or we would "stop treating him."

Without putting up any argument, Elvis got it. We were able to convince his manager to cut down the number of his shows. Elvis's condition improved greatly, Dr. Wruble won Elvis's respect, and Elvis never complained about Dr. Wruble's treatment after that. The board of doctors seemed impressed by the Elvis success story.

Some other doctors who had seen Elvis through my referrals testified that he had shown "no signs of narcotic or hypnotic abuse" when they examined him. They testified that I showed "remarkable interest in the patients I referred to other doctors." Their sincerity was gratifying.

ON THE HEARING'S final scheduled day, after fourteen state witnesses and twenty-five defense witnesses completed their testimonies, a heated argument erupted.

It was not unexpected on my part. The state prosecutors wanted to know if the cause of Elvis Presley's death should be brought before the board. Deputy attorney general Hayes Cooney's point was that I was being charged with "unprofessional conduct" as it related to Elvis Presley's death. Then he added as a caveat, "Dr. Nichopoulos was not charged with murdering Elvis Presley."

"Yes, he was charged with murdering Elvis Presley!" John J. Thomason, my attorney, shouted as he stood up, convinced that statement should not go unchallenged.

Cooney wanted Dr. Eric Muirhead, who had been in charge of Elvis's autopsy for Baptist Hospital, called to testify. He claimed Dr. Muirhead's testimony was essential to the state's case. The attorney for Dr. Muirhead, however, said the doctor would not be allowed to testify publicly regarding information contained in the autopsy because he was under a chancery court order not to discuss any information contained in the report until the resolution of a pending lawsuit.

There was a rustling in the media pool. Hearing officer Bramham had to call for quiet. My reporter friends, content to take their notes from the public section close to my family, told me later that Geraldo Rivera pitched a mini-fit. It seemed ABC-TV's efforts to force the autopsy into public record as testimony during my medical hearing, incited by their television special, had backfired.

As a result of the lawsuit ABC News had filed against Dr. Francisco and district attorney Hugh S. Stanton the previous fall to force the release of Elvis's autopsy report, Chancellor D. J. Alissandratos had ordered all records pertinent to the autopsy sealed tight. Now it could not be brought forth.

Cooney and assistant attorney general Frank Scanlon had hoped to use Dr. Muirhead to rebut Dr. Francisco's testimony that Elvis's death was the result of heart disease and not drugs. Officer Bramham's ruling was that since Dr. Muirhead's only knowledge came from his discovery at autopsy, he could not be compelled to testify. The state tried to make an end run around the issue by having Dr. Muirhead testify in private. Officer Bramham again refused their request, stating Chancellor Alissandratos's ruling applied to that as well.

After a lot of thunder, but no lightning, the board agreed to hear the coroner's testimony about what he had found at autopsy, the results of which were not sealed.

Dr. Jerry Francisco was sworn in, introducing himself as the Shelby County medical examiner. He repeated what he had said for more than two years: "Elvis Presley died of cardiac arrhythmia brought on by high blood pressure and hardening of the arteries. Elvis's heart had been twice the normal size for a man of his age and weight, his coronary arteries had been occluded, and he had a long history of hypertension."

He went on to say that the drugs in the reported tox screen and the amounts found in Elvis's blood did not, even in combination, indicate the likelihood of a drug overdose. "The circumstances of Presley's death also indicated that drugs were not at fault."

If he had taken an oral overdose of drugs shortly after eight o'clock the morning he died, he might have been in a coma by 2:30 that afternoon, the time he was found; but he would hardly have been stiff and blue. The typical victim of an oral drug overdose dies a lingering death in a comfortable position.

"His [Presley's] death was quite sudden, and something catastrophic happened and he fell forward. In drug-related deaths," Francisco continued, "a victim is often found in a bed or on a couch, since a progressive coma usually precedes death."

Dughman, whom we now knew by his own admission was complicit with *20/20* in creating the allegations against me, was not willing to let Dr. Francisco go unchallenged.

Q: And aren't you aware, Doctor, that the conclusions listed on the autopsy are different from yours?

A: As far as the factual items are concerned, I have no problem. The opinions listed are the result of the preparer of the report. I can't determine what the others have found.

Q: But aren't the opinions in that report different from your own?

A: I'm not real clear exactly what opinion is in that report. [This answer was consistent with there not being a place on the Baptist Hospital report for a cause of death, only for *findings*, since that was what they are commissioned to discover.]

Since the autopsy report was not permitted into evidence, the defense attorneys introduced the now-infamous newspaper article with the leaked information from the toxicology report by the Bio-Sciences Laboratories in Van Nuys, California. Dr. Francisco confirmed the presence of those drugs.

He said, however, "The drugs listed in the article were the same drugs I considered in reaching my determination of heart disease as the cause of Presley's death."

Our next defense witness was Dr. Bryan Finkle, an English toxicologist and director of the University of Utah Center for Human Toxicology, one of the three independent laboratories that analyzed Elvis's autopsy specimens for Baptist Memorial. Dr. Finkle had worked in forensic toxicology for the New Scotland Yard. He testified that *none* of the individual drugs he found "can be regarded as toxic or life threatening." He added, however, that he did not have enough "medical information about Presley to determine whether the combined effects of the drugs could have played a role in the singer's death." He testified "that the concentration of drugs found in Presley's body was not sufficient to affect the oxyhemoglobin [respiration] of a hypertensive individual."

Dr. Finkle added that although he was quoted on "The Elvis Cover-Up" program as saying drugs *may* have made "a significant contribution to Presley's death," he was not informed when a member of the *20/20* staff telephoned him that he was being interviewed or that his statements "would be construed in such a fashion."

Dr. David Stafford, a toxicologist at the University of Tennessee Center for the Health Sciences, which analyzed the tox screen for Dr. Francisco, said that he had tested Elvis's autopsy samples for thirty or forty drugs and had found nothing consistent with the diagnosis of a toxic drug dose. He said the codeine "was certainly at a level that was *borderline* toxic at best."

I hoped members of the media were taking copious notes so that the public would be forced to take another look at the death they claimed was drug induced. I did not read or hear any of that information in newspaper or television reports that evening. Instead the media made it appear that if Dr. Muirhead had been able to simply give his opinion regarding polypharmacy, then they could rest their case. The testimony of our expert witnesses pleading Elvis's case had fallen on deaf ears. Apparently the media's minds were made up.

The Commercial Appeal - Photographer Tom Busler

The appearance of Dr. Nick and his attorney Ken Masterson would soon be broadcast to a worldwide audience.

AFTER A SHORT lunch break, the state showed portions of "The Elvis Cover-Up" to the medical board. I had to sit silently and watch while the hour-long television special added insult to injury. I stared at the hazy pictures on the courtroom monitor. To tell the truth, it sickened me to watch the career I had worked so hard to build implode in full view of the world. I was extremely disheartened over my inability to redeem Elvis's image. I wondered if ABC News would ever feel an ethical obligation to present our story in an open, honest way.

Finally it was time for my lawyers to make their closing arguments. Co-counsel Frank Crawford argued on my behalf: "Nichopoulos had a never-ending battle in trying to oversee the medications Presley was taking."

He summarized the witnesses' testimonies about how the treatment of my patients had worked, and reiterated, "He is a highly competent physician who rarely denied his service to even the most difficult patients."

Attorney Crawford pointed out that I had not profited from the drug dependence of my patients. In the end some of them had withdrawn from drugs, although it may have taken a longer time period than recommended by the *PDR* to accomplish that goal.

He acknowledged that even though I had rectified my faulty record keeping before the charges were filed against me, the fact that I did not keep accurate records when I should have was irresponsible.

Crawford summed up my defense by saying, "Dr. Nichopoulos is a fine, compassionate, sensitive physician, who said to his patients, 'I'm going to help you. Remember I'm not perfect, but I'm going to exercise my judgment,' and that's what he did."

That was our summation.

Prosecutor Frank Scanlon urged board members "to keep in mind the exact charges against Nichopoulos" and not to consider whether "Nichopoulos was a good man" or had "good intentions" in practicing medicine. He claimed the state had gone through the charges page by page with experts who said prescriptions were too great over a period too long and in combinations not appropriate to standards of good medical practice.

There had been nothing stopping Dughman or Bilsky from coming to see me in an official capacity before the day they dramatically served papers on me with TV cameras rolling. During a civil inquiry they could have simply *asked* why I was selecting certain drugs in certain quantities and certain combinations.

After I had followed the same procedure for two years with no complaints, *20/20* popped up, and everybody took off on a witch hunt. Apparently the board investigators were not doing their job at the time since they had let "vast amounts" of "dangerous combinations" go unchecked. As I tried to sleep the night before the rendering of my verdict, I kept thinking there had to have been a better way for the medical board to address its concerns regarding my prescription-writing practices.

Utilizing the extended day to complete their task, the Board of Medical Examiners met on Saturday morning, January 19, 1980, to vote on the charges against me. The five board members deliberated publicly for an hour before pausing ten minutes while they "weighed the evidence" and announced their decision.

Dr. Howard R. Foreman, secretary for the board, made a statement that was a mixed bag: "Mr. Chairman, I believe a brief period of suspension would be in order—and I do mean a brief period. I think this would give Dr. Nichopoulos an opportunity to reflect on his office practice and on his outpatient practice away from the office, as well, and to reflect on his manner of record keeping."

He continued, however, with better news: "At the same time, I feel very strongly that in no way can this man's license be revoked."

Without a doubt I breathed my biggest sigh of relief—ever.

"This man's too valuable to his community, to his family, and to his patients," Dr. Foreman concluded.

Dr. John Burkhart, president, delivered the ruling. On the first two charges of "gross incompetence," "gross ignorance," or "gross negligence," and "unprofessional, dishonorable or unethical conduct," the board unanimously found me innocent. The board confirmed that I was not found "guilty of negligence in the care of a patient."

They did, however, find there were certain regulations that I had violated: "dispensing, prescribing or otherwise distributing any controlled substance or any other drug not in the course of professional practice, or not in good faith to relieve pain and suffering, or not to cure an ailment, physical infirmity or disease."

I knew by what the board considered "medical standards of the community" that I had, in their opinion, prescribed "dangerous doses" to certain patients "over too long a period of time."

When it was all said and done, the biggest problem the medical board had was that I had selected an "upper" and a "downer" on the same day. They insinuated that if a person is obese and has insomnia, then the doctor has to choose which of the problems he wants to treat. He cannot use an upper to treat the patient's obesity and a downer to treat his insomnia on the same day. They suggested possibly treating each problem on alter-nating days.

The reality was that the only time we used a Dexedrine-type drug was when we were trying to control Elvis's obesity. The downers were used with or without the Dexedrine because Elvis had a chronic problem with insomnia, complicated with sleepwalking. I never felt I had the chance to explain that fully. All the board wanted during the hearing was for me to answer the questions I was asked in a word or two and not take any time to explain why I did what I did. They just wanted to get on with the hearing.

Dr. Dowling, Memphis's seated representative, said he based his vote on poor record keeping as well, adding, "But, I think we have to consider the extraordinary circumstances under which he was operating. He was under the gun. I think he exercised considerable restraint in trying to control the medication . . . I think there were very extenuating circumstances."

There were ten charges for which I was ultimately found guilty, which all dealt with overprescribing. That group included entertainers Elvis Presley and Jerry Lee Lewis, investment banker and Elvis aide Alan Fortas, the singer/guitarist in the all-girl rock band, the twin brothers, the gardener, the antique dealer, and myself. (All the charges were based largely on my not keeping better records of how I dispensed the medications.)

In the other cases it had not mattered whether the patients had withdrawn from the pills without symptoms, ultimately withdrawn on their own, or simply shown encouraging progress in their healing. The board believed the end did not justify the means.

Acquitted charges included: the owner of the topless nightclub, the record promoter and the executive, the restaurant cashier, the receptionist, the student, the salesclerk, and my daughter. They also ruled that I was not guilty in my treatment of the twenty-three-year-old ex–heroin addict. The board felt her testimony that I had helped her stop using heroin represented "the extraordinary qualities of this man."

When the board asked if I had a comment, I shook my head; I had none. I was drowning in an emotional undertow. When the prosecution and the defense teams were asked for comments, they were silent as well. It had been a hard-fought battle. Both sides had lost; both sides had won.

In the final analysis the medical board suspended my medical license for three months and placed me on three-year probation. At the end of that time, my license was to be renewed automatically. I was fifty-two years old; I had been a physician for twenty years.

As I left the courtroom after what felt more like a week at hard labor, I remembered Dr. Dowling's remark: "I certainly agree there was no evidence to indicate that there was any involvement by Dr. Nichopoulos in any way in the death of Elvis Presley."

Maybe that will be the end of it all, I thought with a sigh.

THE BEST
IN THE BUSINESS

Dr. Nick returning to his office at the Medical Group.

I t was one thing to face a medical board hearing that would decide whether I would ever again be allowed to practice medicine; it was quite another to be facing criminal charges. Jail time was an entirely new and different concept.

191

Each day I anxiously searched the newspapers for any news about my impending indictment. Finally James Chisum's article "Nichopoulos Grand Jury Findings Scrutinized," written for *The Commercial Appeal* on April 17, 1980, outlined the status of the state's case against me. It talked about what Jewell H. Miller, executive assistant to Attorney General Hugh W. Stanton Jr., called "one of the most extensive investigations ever conducted by a grand jury in Shelby County."

The magnitude of the project baffled me. My case was not the crime of the century. The state's investigation of me was more intense than when James Earl Ray was believed to have assassinated Dr. Martin Luther King Jr. That alleged murder was said to be a cover-up involving both the FBI and CIA, yet it did not attract the media coverage my case was getting. Still, representatives from the attorney general's office kept saying that despite the *20/20* claim, the state was *not* looking at me for the murder of Elvis Presley—then what *were* they doing?

The state was obviously out to get me for something. My attorneys explained the charge as "a Tennessee law prohibiting prescriptions of controlled substances in a manner inconsistent with legitimate medical practice." That was a euphemism for having "criminally prescribed drugs."

State prosecutors and investigators told reporter Chisum that the case they were building against me was "all inclusive" and intensely thorough from various sources: 30 witness interviews, reports from 25 other witnesses, prescription files from 124 pharmacies, videos from the medical board hearing, and a number of books written by Elvis's associates. It seemed to me the purpose of the publicity the state was giving my case at this point was to resurrect more "victims" of Dr. George C. Nichopoulos to testify.

I was amazed at what Miller told Chisum in his article. He said that District Attorney Stanton initially had planned a general investigation of drug prescribing by Memphis physicians but had been advised to concentrate on Nichopoulos because of the complexity of such an investigation.

"We hear rumbles about other doctors. But it's a very small percentage of the entire medical profession," Miller said. "I don't want to say anything that could be remotely construed as critical of the medical profession as a whole."

Then he added, "Memphis physicians contacted during the investigation have been unusually cooperative and helpful." I bet they had.

Miller told Chisum his interest grew as he learned of the impact of legally prescribed drugs. He said the widespread investigation had sharply reduced the amount of drugs going to drug abusers in the city. (I wondered how they measured that.)

"To me, that makes the investigation worthwhile, if nothing else comes of it," Miller said, confirming my thoughts.

So, it's not about Elvis, and it's not about me. It's all about drugs and proving a point.

Word traveled back to me that the state was talking to local pharmacists and physicians about "acceptable medical practices" and "community standards." I knew in large part those "standards" would depend on whom they asked, and what. There was nothing to stop investigators from selectively agreeing with the doctors whose opinions would allow them to bring my case to trial and discarding those whose opinions did not. With the rules that were already in place, there was no way to escape being charged by the state. How could I *prove* my innocence?

One day Father Nicholas Vieron dropped by my house, bearing a heartwarming message: my legal defense fund was willing to continue helping. This group, comprised of members from Annunciation Greek Orthodox Church and community supporters, had raised monies for attorney fees and witness travel expenses related to my hearing and had brought me more comfort than they could have known. A great friend, who owned one of the city's landmark barbecue-ribs houses, had committed to my project. Father V advised me to focus on my defense; they would assist with finances if a trial became necessary. It did.

THE SHELBY COUNTY grand jury indicted me on May 16, 1980, charging me with overprescribing drugs to eleven patients, including Elvis Presley, Jerry Lee Lewis, and myself. After posting a one-thousand-dollar bond, I was free on bail.

"I'm aghast!" Edna remarked, glancing at the *Memphis Press-Scimitar* photo of me with a sergeant from the Sheriff's Fugitive Squad.

"What?" I asked, knowing I must have embarrassed her.

"That's not the look I would have been going for," she said with a sigh. Edna pointed to my image wearing a white lab coat over hip plaid seventies trousers above the caption "Dr. Nichopoulos Surrenders."

I knew that the accompanying article, "Nichopoulos Turns Himself in on 11 Counts," had disturbed her, just as it had me. If convicted, I would face a maximum sentence of two to ten years on each of the eleven counts and/or a fine of twenty thousand dollars. Edna, as always, wanted to avert my attention from the impending catastrophic consequences so I would concentrate instead on what I could do to prevent them.

THE INDICTMENT MADE it official. I was accused of violating TCA 52-1435; I remember the number to this day. It "requires physicians to prescribe controlled substances for purposes consistent with their medical licenses." The indictment alleged that I had prescribed drugs "not in good faith to relieve pain and suffering and not to cure a physical infirmity or disease." Two other indictments alleged that I had dispensed drugs to Elvis Presley and Jerry Lee Lewis with the knowledge that they were addicted to them and without making an effort to cure that addiction.

That was the bad news. The good news was, the keepers of my legal defense fund, realizing the severity of my situation, decided we needed to get as aggressive with my case as the state was being. They wanted to draft a "heavy hitter" to help level the legal playing field. Grand jury clout and publicity from *20/20* had portrayed me as a villain in the eyes of the public.

"We want people to see you as the competent and compassionate physician we know you are," my supporters confidently told me.

The next day I went to court to dismiss my legal team—the first step in my new strategy. The media saw my brief court visit as a photo op. They snapped my "No comment" moment and displayed it above a caption that read, " 'Dr. Nick' Fires His Attorneys." It was the first time the press had used my moniker, but I knew it did not mean they had decided to "make nice."

WHEN DECISION TIME for a new attorney arrived, my defense fund point persons presented me with only one name. It was a done deal pending our meeting and agreeing that we trusted each other and were compatible enough to work together. When I heard the name, I did not need to read his vitae. As attorneys go, he was "top gun." Talk about high profile! He had convicted Teamsters' boss Jimmy Hoffa of jury tampering in 1964; in the midseventies he was a special prosecutor in the Watergate trials, placing John Ehrlichman, John Mitchell, and H. R. Haldeman behind bars. Yes, James Neal was *the man*!

Edna and I could hardly wait to meet the celebrity attorney. He was coming from Nashville to visit in our home—a gracious gesture. James Neal made as powerful a first impression as any individual we had ever met. He exuded confidence, no ego. That was instantly reassuring to us. His pleasant, good-natured manner quickly set us at ease. He was a little taller than I am—perhaps five foot eight. His Marine-proud chest strengthened his athletic frame, while my chest rested on the stout legs of a running back. His complexion was dark olive like my own, but his hair was straight and light brown, in contrast to my snowy-white waves. He had deep, penetrating eyes, as opposed to mine, which my patients said "sparkled."

Neal had a sharp, chiseled jaw that he would occasionally stretch upward when he wanted to emphasize a point. He had another trademark quirk: he would playfully roll an unlit cigar in his fingertips, place it in the corner of his mouth, and chew on the end while he listened. His maneuver had an unusual calming effect, yet it kept me constantly engaged. It took only minutes for me to decide that putting my freedom in James Neal's hands was the right thing to do. Neal decided, however, that we should learn more about each other—me first.

"I was born the son of Greek immigrants—kind, decent people," I began. "My father, Gus, believed in helping people. He owned the most popular café in town, and I worked there from the time I was old enough to see over the counter. I watched my dad treat everyone with dignity; he was never one to judge others. He had an enviable moral code and work ethic that I've attempted to emulate all my life.

"When I was growing up, my mother could read and write only in Greek and could speak only a few words of very broken English. My sister—who is eight years younger—and I mean everything to her. She still lives in Anniston, Alabama, where I grew up and was a high school jock and Eagle Scout who camped out a lot.

"My life dilemma after graduation was whether to be a minister or a doctor," I continued. "My buddies and I joined the army to get in on the GI Bill. I spent two years in the Army Medical Corps in Munich, Germany. I played football in the army, so I enjoyed those years.

"After I was discharged, I entered the University of the South, an Episcopal school of ministry, where I played football and earned my BS degree in premed. Then I went to the University of Tennessee in Memphis and completed my postgraduate work for a doctorate in clinical physiology. I was fortunate enough to gain admission to the Vanderbilt University Medical School in Nashville earlier than I had thought; but it took me a while to get my medical degree—eight years—because I was married with children. My field was nephrology—kidney disease. Eventually I performed the first kidney dialysis in the South.

Nichopoulos Collection

Dr. Nick's (#33 in backfield) high school football team, Anniston, Alabama, 1946.

Nichopoulos Collection

Dr. Nick and Edna in the early days, 1954.

Nichopoulos Collection

Dr. Nick with his kids during his residency in Nashville at Vanderbilt
University, 1962.

Nichopoulos Collection.

George C. Nichopoulos and family celebrating his Doctor
of Medicine degree from Vanderbilt University Medical
School, 1959. (left to right: his mother, Persiphoni
Nichopoulos; the graduate; his wife, Edna; his mother-in-
law, Christine Sanidas)

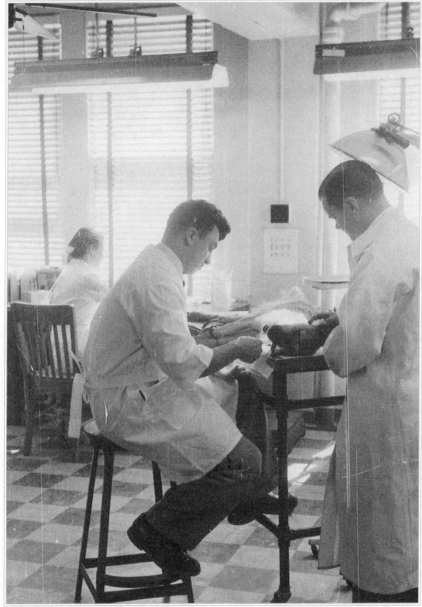

Dr. Nick and colleague during their training at the University of Tennessee Medical School, Memphis, 1954.

"I've been an instructor of clinical medicine at the University of Tennessee College of Medicine in Memphis, and I'm on staff at Baptist Memorial Hospital and Doctors Hospital," I said, winding down my résumé. "I'm currently an internist at the Medical Group. My love is diagnosis because of my background in physiology. Finding a medical problem that's difficult to pinpoint is what really intrigues me. I'm also drawn to *fragile* patients—those other doctors might not have time to treat—the marginalized segment in society who seem to always be suffering. I guess that's what got me into trouble."

Neal was a good listener. By the end of the night, I did not just have a lawyer; I had a teammate in the run for my life.

WITH THE LAW firm of Neal & Harwell aboard, there was more work to do than I had imagined. Neal had two efficient associates. Tom Dunden was a tall, slim twenty-something. He had all the patience that persistence requires, yet was quick as a switch in effecting necessary change. Donna Phillips was a balance of meticulous detail and creative application—the quintessential purpose-driven professional. Tom and Donna could accurately and precisely read their leader's mind from eye cues he shot over the tiny reading glasses propped toward the end of his nose. I was impressed with the efficiency of the team and determined to keep pace with them.

"The media was saying that Dr. Nick killed Elvis Presley; the state is try-ing to make this a death case," Neal said, recalling the "horrible publicity" from "The Elvis Cover-Up."

"I remember Geraldo Rivera piling pills up on the table and saying that this would be the volume of pills that Dr. Nichopoulos prescribed for Elvis personally," Neal said.

If Neal could still see it, I wondered how we would ever be able to over-come the damaging visual, but Neal had a plan.

"I decided to move for a change of venue because of local press prejudice," he said. "I hired a Memphis consultant to do a 'community attitude survey.' I assumed the results would say that the majority would be unable to be impar-tial. It turned out just the opposite. It proved out that the people of Memphis did not blame Dr. Nick for Elvis Presley's death. The majority blamed Elvis Presley. When the survey came back, what I was told is you do *not* want to take the trial out of Memphis."

The survey findings were clear. The people of Memphis believed that if Elvis did take too many drugs and if it led to his death, he was the one responsible—not his father, not his manager, not his doctor.

With that information in our arsenal, we proceeded to the jury selection process. The prosecutors were assistant district attorneys Jewett Miller and James Wilson. Miller was older and lead counsel. He had an extremely intense persona that could cover only temporarily a chain smoker's persistent anxiety. His habit kept him in a hypervigilant state—ready to pounce. Wilson, probably some twenty years Miller's junior, hung back, content to carry out designated assignments. It was Wilson who quizzed prospective jurors. They were informed that they could be sequestered four to six weeks; then they had to disclose whether they were members of an Elvis Presley or Jerry Lee Lewis fan club.

Then Miller chatted up the jurors regarding what they thought about drugs and the doctors who prescribed them. He presented questions jurors would be asked to answer, such as, was Dr. Nichopoulos prescribing drugs in good faith, or was he pushing pills? The prosecution's job would be persuading jurors that I had deliberately ignored the health of my patients and given them prescriptions just because they asked for them.

When his turn came, Neal had a kinder, gentler touch, which he delivered in a slow, deep Southern drawl. He asked potential jurors how they felt a doctor should treat a patient who had problems with drugs. He actually tested the theme for my defense over and over in front of the prosecutors, who—as far as we could tell—never caught on to his tactic. Neal told the group it would be up to them to decide if my heart had been in the right place when I wrote the prescriptions.

Then, just as he would later do at trial, Neal delivered what would be his closing argument: "Proof will probably show he didn't do absolutely right and he didn't do absolutely wrong. The question: Did he do the best he could?"

Neal's modest approach yielded a dynamic result. I could see it on the faces of the people willing to accept the responsibility of seeing that justice prevailed in the *State of Tennessee vs. Dr. George C. Nichopoulos*. The selected jury was comprised of a housewife and an aide at a nursing home; a secretary and a hardware store manager; an advertising company musician/composer and a player piano repairman; a nurse's aide and a retired hospital worker; an auto parts handyman and a grocery store cashier; a waitress and an interior designer. These were the six women and six men who would decide if the eleven counts before me would translate into 110 years in prison.

Pleased with the jury, Neal explained his approach. "I like to have a theme for the defense," he told me, expounding on the survey's guiltless view of me. "The doctor should *not* have turned Elvis away," Neal quoted the survey as stating. Then he added, "He *should* have been a good Samaritan."

The good Samaritan in the biblical story—the man who stopped to treat an injured stranger whom others had left to die—would be the symbol of my innocence.

Next, Neal shared his strategy for dealing with citizen judges: "Juries, particularly in complicated cases, will *remember* only about 50 percent of what they hear . . . They will *understand* about half of what they hear, and remember about half of what they understand . . . We need to make sure they go into that jury room remembering and understanding *your* 25 percent of the case."

It made sense to me.

Our defense needs "to be simple, clear, and straightforward," Neal instructed. No talking in circles or explaining anything that's not a major point we've decided needs to be made—keep on target.

"The jury is a key factor," Neal emphasized, "but so is the defendant's ability to testify."

I would be taking the witness stand to defend myself. I would need to do better than I had done at my hearing, my legal team cautioned. It would be their job to train me; my job to get into shape. The road to keeping my freedom would be a long, hard battle with little sleep for the duration, an anticipated month to six weeks. We would be in the courtroom all day and work on strategy in the evenings.

Neal and his team had an infectious energy that kept me so caught up in the process and what I could do that I had little time to worry.

Neal's theory: "Trial law is a lot like playing football or war; the team that makes the fewest mistakes wins."

So we planned my trial like a football game, understanding that preparation allows the defense to convert mistakes into points. Neal acted as quarterback. He selected the plays we would run against the prosecution and the defense we would use to thwart their advances. Neal was a former prosecutor, and he thought like one. He had a firm grasp of the fundamental attack the prosecution would use in their attempt to overpower us; so did I by the time the trial started.

WE WERE RESIDING in Judge Bernie Weinman's court in the new Shelby County Criminal Justice Center. It was designed as a theater in the round, with a circular, soft-white center light mounted overhead to resemble a spaceship. Deep-chocolate, nubby carpet spilled over everything in the arena: the walls, the floor, even the padding of the swivel chairs that also echoed the intended spaceship theme. Hippie van–style carpet covered the low barrier over which the spectators stared into the ring.

Prosecutor Miller began. He delivered his opening arguments in a rigid stance, reading from a long legal pad. His statement shocked me: "Heroin is not the big problem in Memphis. Dilaudid is."

I didn't know that, I thought. There was no medical literature I was aware of that informed physicians which drugs were being abused—what street drugs were the favorite flavors of the month.

Miller said the state would prove I continued to prescribe large amounts of drugs to the patients named in the indictment even after some had undergone hospital detoxification. Then he said, "Presley had very few medical problems, except those caused by excessive use of drugs."

Here comes the Elvis issue again, I thought.

Miller told the jury that the state was going to present "medical experts," who would tell them that George C. Nichopoulos was not prescribing these drugs (in the indictment) "for any accepted medical reason."

When it came his turn, James Neal stepped forward, holding a few index cards unobtrusively cupped in his hand. In a conversational tone and searching each juror's face, he shared his opener: "You will learn that Elvis Presley would have died ten years earlier without Dr. Nichopoulos. Presley suffered from high blood pressure, a bad colon, insomnia, ulcers, liver problems, glaucoma, obesity, and depression."

Shuffling the cards ever so slightly, Neal gave the jurors a footnote version of my life. Then he proceeded to describe my affinity for problem patients: how I had succeeded in reducing the amounts of drugs my dependent patients were using, and that now some were no longer addicted; how I helped Elvis Presley and Jerry Lee Lewis detox and become drug free, but they would return to me worse than before; how the huge number of prescriptions the prosecution alluded to were for members of Presley's entourage, but charged to Presley because he paid the bills; how I tricked Presley with placebos to decrease his drug intake.

Neal told the criminal court jury that the situation required me to make a choice. I could either "quit Elvis Presley and stay away from him, or continue to give him medication."

Next came a roll of witnesses. E. L. Hutchison, chief investigator for District Attorney General Hugh W. Stanton Jr., told of checking 150 pharmacies in Shelby County and Southaven, Mississippi, for prescriptions written by me from January 1975 to October 1979. It was the pill numbers game again, but this time the stakes were raised. Hutchison had obtained a sample of my handwriting, and an expert would verify that the signatures on the prescriptions were mine.

In line with his strategy that things be kept simple, Neal did not contest that I had written the prescriptions, although I did not believe I had written all of them. For one thing some of the prescriptions in the exhibit had three and four medications listed on a single sheet, and I always wrote only one prescription per page. The names of some of the drugs were typed, which was something I never did. We conceded, however, that I had written all of the prescriptions presented.

The prosecutors scored a major victory with the prescription numbers, even gaining the judge's approval to show the jury prescriptions not covered by the indictment. Neal showed his fiery side by vehemently objecting. He said prosecutors were broadening the charges against me after the fact.

Judge Weinman responded that "intent and knowledge of a patient's condition prior to the indictment would make the prescriptions not listed in the indictment relevant."

Round one was not looking good. It got worse.

Prosecutors brought in Robert Muehlberger, a handwriting expert, to verify that my hand had penned the *George C. Nichopoulos* at the bottom of the scripts. On cross-examination, however, Neal did get Muehlberger to confirm that numbers on twenty of the prescriptions had been altered substantially.

Then came prosecution witness Jack Kirsch, a man I had once considered a longtime friend. Since he was the one who had originally told the *20/20* producers about the state's audit and had contributed sound bites for "The Elvis Cover-Up," I did not know what to expect from him. Kirsch answered questions I had anticipated.

Under Neal's skillful cross, Kirsch flipped to a defense witness. He said he could not verify that I had actually prescribed those prescriptions phoned in to the pharmacy because he did not take all the pharmacy's calls. Neal also led Kirsch to tell the court that when I picked up the unusually large amount of drugs from his shop, I had told Kirsch that I would be using them to treat Elvis's entourage.

Next Kirsch said that I had asked him to help me locate pharmaceutical companies that would make placebos for me. Kirsch even told the jury I'd told him Elvis was getting drugs from "everywhere under the sun" and that some were even being flown in from out of town. I was definitely glad the prosecution had called Jack Kirsch to come to court. His testimony certainly helped me.

Then came a revisit to my sloppy record keeping. Prosecution witness Laura Domagala, chief of medical records for the Medical Group, stated that I actually compared "fairly well" to some of the other doctors. She said the state was only worried about the medications for eleven of the twenty-five hundred patients I treated annually.

D. Beecher Smith II, the attorney for the Elvis Presley estate, confirmed for the prosecution that I had received loans before Elvis Presley's death. Under cross-examination Neal had Smith explain further that a large portion of the loan had already been repaid and that the loan from Elvis was secured by the deed to my house in his estate's name. Smith also stated that monthly notes were current.

Marty Lacker, a member of Elvis's Memphis Mafia, testified after his wife, Patsy. He spoke honestly in "The Elvis Cover-Up" about surviving his own withdrawal from addictive sleeping medication. Neal had previously met with Marty, who agreed to testify on my behalf, but the prosecution called him as their witness first. Marty told his story about how I had advised him of the dangers of Placidyl, the sleeping pills he was taking, and warned him to stay within the prescribed dosage. I had respected Marty for his ability to do that and had never seen symptoms of drug abuse when I examined him. I also never considered Marty a drug addict or medically addicted. I had evaluated him to be smart and successful—a highly functional individual who was managing his life well.

The day finally came when the state would attempt to slide in the Elvis autopsy report. I could not understand why Dr. Eric Muirhead was so insistent that Elvis had died a drug-related death. What was worse, I could not understand why he kept trying to connect me to Elvis's death. Dr. Muirhead knew I had not prescribed the only medication close to toxic level that even had a chance of causing the alleged "drug overdose." Dr. Muirhead related to the criminal court how he had examined Elvis Presley's body when he conducted the autopsy as chief of pathology for Baptist Memorial. He went into detail about the body's organs and fluids. Then he just had to say one more time that the specimens did not include stomach contents; they were pumped out in the ER.

Miller asked, "Did you and the other doctors have any conversations during the autopsy?"

Where does Miller think he's going with this? I wondered.

Dr. Muirhead began his answer: "We had some discussion in terms of whether the death may have been due to—"

"Sidebar, Your Honor," Neal said, jumping to his feet.

The judge had already ruled earlier in the day that the prosecution could question Dr. Muirhead about drugs found in Elvis's body, but not about the cause of death. Here they were, trying to sneak it in again.

Judge Weinman declared, "The court will recess."

The soundproof walls in the courtroom muffled the attorneys' slightly modulated voices. That and the dim lighting had made it difficult for many in the press corps to stay awake, unless, of course, Elvis Presley's name was mentioned. At this point members of the international press corps, properly seated on the front few rows, began stirring and had to be shushed by an official. Unlike my medical board hearing, there was a "no cameras" policy at the jury trial, yet the number of reporters covering the event had increased.

In a civil agreement with the media, Neal had arranged for us "to come to a certain spot and answer questions after court recessed each day in exchange for not following us up and down the street and sticking those . . . poles in our faces."

Photo by Rose Clayton Phillips

Facing reporters after a day in court. (left to right: James Neal, Dr. Nick, and Elaine Nichopoulos)

That included ABC-TV, the crew who was now milling about the hallway, lobbying for the autopsy to be admitted.

"This case has become totally an Elvis Presley thing," Neal told Judge Weinman. "The state has already taken the position that there was no question of ill play [in Elvis's death], that there was no criminal conduct by Dr. Nichopoulos."

My defense team had discovered that the office of District Attorney General Hugh W. Stanton Jr. had taken the position in the suit filed in chancery court by ABC News that no foul play was involved. Neal asked the judge to "bar any testimony regarding the drugs found in Presley's body or testimony on the cause of his death."

Prosecutor Miller surprisingly agreed, stating that the cause of death was not being contemplated in this trial. He had certainly fooled me.

"What's going on?" I asked Neal, wanting to hear the bottom line.

"What the judge did was 'to split the baby,'" Neal explained. The judge ruled that the drugs found in Elvis's body after death were pertinent, but the cause of death would be irrelevant to the charges against me.

On cross-examination Neal was able to ask Dr. Muirhead about a previous conversation we'd had. Dr. Muirhead was compelled to admit under oath what I had told him: "drugs were always available" and I'd had "difficulty controlling the drugs available to this individual." I would "find drugs on the bedside table and remove them . . . then go back out there a few days later and find them back on the bedside table again."

Was Dr. Muirhead using my remarks to spark his "drug overdose by polypharmacy" theory of Elvis's death? I wondered.

Total silence came with the arrival of the next witness for the prosecution: Dr. Norman Weissman, a California biochemist from Bio-Science Laboratory. Everyone wanted to hear his testimony—especially me. But not Neal, who already seemed to know exactly what the doctor would say.

"I've never seen the number of drugs we found in this case in any other specimen," Weissman said of the Elvis Presley autopsy samples. He not only listed the drugs, but where they had been found:

- codeine appearing as Percodan, a narcotic in blood, urine, liver, and kidneys
- ethchlorvynol as Placidyl, a sedative in the blood
- diazepam as Valium, a sedative in the blood and urine

- ethinamate as Valmid, a sedative in the blood and the liver
- amobarbital as Amytal, a sedative in the liver and urine
- phenobarbital as Nembutal, phenobarbital as Carbrital, and methaqualone as Quaalude, all sedatives in the blood, liver, and kidneys
- phenyltoloxamine (Sinutab), a decongestant; amitriptyline in the form of Elavil, a sedative; and meperidine as Demerol, a narcotic, all in the liver and kidneys
- Three other drugs—diazepam metabolite (which have come from the Valium); the morphine (may have been a derivative of the codeine); and nortriptyline—were created when other drugs entered the body.

When he stood to cross-examine, Neal was quick to calculate that three of the drugs found might have been created by chemical interactions among the other drugs, thus reducing the number of drugs found at death from fourteen to eleven different compounds, just in case the jurors had not done that. Then he reminded them that "Presley obtained codeine from a dentist he visited the night before he died," just in case the jurors had forgotten.

"Isn't it true that of the drugs found in Mr. Presley's body, all were at therapeutic levels except codeine?" Neal asked Weissman.

"Methaqualone, I believe, was above the level of toxicity," he answered. Later, however, Weissman would recant, saying the methaqualone, which was earlier reported to be at toxic level, was "questionable" and actually on the borderline between toxic and therapeutic levels.

Weissman was forced to admit that there was no way to prove I had prescribed *any* of the drugs found in Elvis's body. Finally, Weissman concurred that I had prescribed only eight of the forty-four drugs submitted by the prosecution, some of them prescribed months before Elvis's death.

"I would not be of the opinion that if the drugs were taken in January, they would be found in August," Weissman stated conclusively, explaining that most drugs carry an average half-life of three or four days and some lose half their strength in fewer than thirty minutes. (The half-life is the time it takes a drug to lose half of its strength.)

Then, as a final remark, Neal asked Weissman to check the prescriptions already in evidence.

Weissman replied, "The Dilaudid, Dexedrine, and Biphetamine, which were prescribed for Presley on August 15, 1977, were not found in the body."

THE FOLLOWING DAY it was Jerry Lee Lewis's reputation placed on the chopping block. The prosecution wanted to show I had continued to prescribe amphetamines to Jerry Lee after I knew he was addicted, and did nothing to cure him of his addiction. I was interested in seeing what type of motive the prosecution would manufacture, since Jerry Lee had never given me cars or jewelry or loaned me money to build a house.

Dr. David Knott, identified with the Memphis Mental Health Institute, a drug and alcohol center, testified under court order. He told how I had asked him to treat Jerry Lee during his '76 hospitalization because I was worried he might be addicted.

Then the conversation turned to Elvis. Dr. Knott told how he was called in on a consult regarding Elvis during hospitalizations in '73, '75, and '77. On three other occasions Dr. Knott went to Graceland.

When Elvis was brought into the hospital in '73, "he appeared obese, somewhat lethargic," Dr. Knott said. "He was bloated from steroid injections and suffered from a number of physical problems."

Then he confirmed that Elvis was detoxed at that time.

"Did you conclude that Dr. Nichopoulos was trying to help his patients?" Neal asked.

"Yes, I did," Dr. Knott replied. "He [Nichopoulos] repeatedly sought my help for them [Presley and Lewis]. I believe he was trying to help them get off drugs."

He told the court that I had asked him to develop a regimen that would withdraw Elvis from drug use. Using a combination of phenobarbital, a relatively weak barbiturate, and methadone, a narcotic, Elvis was withdrawn from other drugs. He was drug free after eleven days.

"Did you then have a conversation with Dr. Nichopoulos regarding drugs and the interaction of drugs?" Neal asked.

"Yes," Dr. Knott answered. "We discussed the issues of narcotics and the additive effect on the central nervous system. If a sedative were to be used . . . it should be phenobarbital."

As Neal concluded his cross, he turned to where both the jury and Dr. Knott could see his face.

"Do doctors have doctors?" he asked.

"Yes, they do," Dr. Knott replied.

"Would you tell us who your doctor is?"

"I have two doctors," he answered. "One is Dr. [Lawrence] Wruble, and the other is Dr. Nichopoulos."

The jurors smiled.

THE TESTIMONY GREW more intense, with five expert witnesses lined up to take the stand for the prosecution. Dr. Alvin J. Cummins was back after testifying at my medical board hearing. He thought my prescribing practices were "outrageous" and "dangerous." He stated that narcotics, amphetamines, and sedatives are rarely justified—that they lose their effectiveness after two or three weeks. He explained it was "irrational" to use narcotics and sleeping pills at the same time with one patient because of the effect of the combination of the medications on the central nervous system.

Dr. Steward L. Nunn, chief of cardiology at the Veterans Administration Center, talked about how physicians "are turning away" from the use of amphetamines for weight control. He also was against using amphetamines to prevent weight gain. After a few questions by James Neal, he admitted that although he did "not approve of amphetamines being used to treat obesity, there probably are some doctors still using the drug for weight control."

After the two experts testified, Neal met with the prosecutors and the judge and said he stipulated that the prosecution's witnesses would all essentially tell the jury the same thing: Dr. Nichopoulos violated standards set by these five doctors who represented the medical profession in Memphis. Neal relieved the jurors from hearing additional testimonies condemning my prescription practices, and three doctors got to go home. There were whispers throughout the courtroom; even the spectators knew the prosecution had fumbled the ball. They could have continued to gain ground by having doctor after doctor carry on about how I violated their view of "professional standards."

Probably the most memorable prosecution witness was Dr. William Lerner, who traveled from the Medical College of Virginia. His talk was a boring two-hour discourse about drug abuse in general and what he considered the best approach to treating patients. He outlined a three-step approach to withdraw an addict from drugs: detoxification, gradually decreasing a patient's intake of drugs by substituting other drugs, and control of outside drug sources.

Well, I thought, *that's exactly what I was doing.*

In a way I felt sorry for the gentleman testifying; people were restless while he was talking, and he was obviously uncomfortable. Neal would lower his head and peer over his glasses when Dr. Lerner read from his notes. By the time Neal finished pacing and walked over to question him, Dr. Lerner was a nervous wreck.

Neal shifted into an interrogation stance, asking the doctor about an article he'd told Miller he had written. The good doctor was unable to recall where it was published. One by one, Neal delivered a litany of twenty probable medical journals, asking, "Was it in . . ."

"No. No, it wasn't in that one," Dr. Lerner repeatedly replied. He was unable to verify his written article had ever made it into print.

"*Placidyl.*" Neal delivered the word like a death knell. (It was one of the Schedule II controlled substances I was accused of overprescribing.)

"Placidyl," Neal repeated, after an effective silence. "What is the category of Placidyl now?"

Dr. Lerner, acting as though he was afraid to answer, explained: "It *had* been a Schedule III drug, meaning 'moderately addictive.'"

"Placidyl was a Schedule IV drug for five years. A drug with low potential for abuse," Neal said with a powerful punch. Neal looked down, walked slowly toward the jurors, then spun around to look directly at Dr. Lerner.

"*Narcotics.*" Neal spouted the word with the same emphasis as before.

Before he knew what he had said, Dr. Lerner, visibly shaken, described *narcotic* abusers as "usually" being "low-income street addicts."

"Are you putting Elvis Presley and Jerry Lee Lewis in that category?" Neal asked.

Dr. Lerner, clearly rattled, scrutinized Jerry Lee's and Elvis's prescriptions and medical records in front of him, supplied by the prosecution. He looked up, pleased, like a schoolboy with the correct answer: "They weren't addicted to narcotics." Then he glanced back hurriedly at the papers to make certain he was not mistaken.

During his testimony, Dr. Lerner kept intimating that a physician with a patient abusing drugs should probably find another doctor to treat the patient. Finally, as his cross-examination drew to a close, Neal called him on it.

Neal set up three hypothetical situations: "Let's say you have a man . . ." Neal went through each scenario.

After following the story with interest, Dr. Lerner answered: "I would seek another doctor for the patient."

Thus he confirmed Neal's "good Samaritan" analogy that I was treating the patients in the indictment because they could not find another doctor who would.

"Thank you, Dr. Lerner," James Neal said wholeheartedly. The defense could not have asked for a better witness.

The prosecution finally made it to the other patients listed in my indictment for whom I allegedly wrote "unnecessary" amounts of narcotics, sedatives, and amphetamines. There appeared to be little interest in the noncelebrity clients; these patients were just other chances for the prosecution to label me a "pill pusher."

THE MOMENT I'D been waiting for finally arrived: the opportunity for the defense team to present my case.

Dr. Walter K. Hoffman, a partner in the Medical Group, took the stand. It was great to see a friendly face shining back at me. He testified that the twelve doctors at the office frequently referred drug abusers to me.

Dr. Hoffman explained: "It was our consensus that Dr. Nichopoulos was best at handling those patients . . . These patients are not particularly nice folks, and they just kept coming back. They are demanding, and they are insensitive. I would not have had a private line in my office as Nichopoulos did, where those people could call me for help.

"These people are a very small segment of the population. They are nighttime people in a daytime world. He [Nichopoulos] did not promise any success. We accepted that and let him treat those people."

"Would Dr. Nichopoulos treat those people whether or not they could pay?" Neal asked.

"Yes, sir—to our dismay—sometimes."

Prosecutor Miller appeared frustrated on his cross-examination. He told the jury it was impossible to "dissect Dr. Nichopoulos's brain" to explain why "immense quantities of drugs" were prescribed. They had to look at the "available facts" to determine whether "Dr. Nichopoulos acted in 'good faith' when he prescribed those drugs."

The prosecution had again stated their case clearly. At that moment I gained a deeper understanding of the jurors' plight. Asking them to reach a conclusion based on "immense quantities of drugs" was like asking me to make a critical diagnosis based solely on a patient's body temperature. How could they use "available facts" to determine "good faith" when faith is "belief without proof"? The only way I knew a person could prove faith was to act upon it. That is what

I had done. I believed in my patients and trusted their desire to heal. My actions would have to speak for my intentions and find a compassionate place in the heart of judgment.

My mind flashed back to "The Elvis Cover-Up." The producers had created a compelling story built around Elvis's death. Elvis was the victim, his death a crime; drugs were the weapons. All they needed was the perpetrator—the murderer—the person who had furnished the drugs that killed the king. The producers' apparent goal was to show I had committed a malicious, willful crime for personal gain and needed to be brought to justice. They contended that due to the city's inept law enforcement officials and a negligent state government, the crime had gone unpunished.

Apparently, in an effort to protect itself against the network's allegations, the state had conducted its own investigation and was presenting its case against me. So here we all sat in the Criminal Justice Center with a jury deciding my fate and, in a sense, the state's innocence as well. I could only pray that the judicial system, having a higher standard of accountability than the media, would be able to replace assorted information with facts and grant me justice.

THE TIME ARRIVED for what I had anticipated would be the most difficult part of my defense. In order to plead my innocence, we would need to reflect intensely on Elvis Presley's life—the promises, the trust, the progress, and my failed efforts. In order to explain what I had attempted to achieve with Elvis, we would have to reveal the depth of his needs.

Al Strada told the court he had worked for a security company at Elvis's home before Elvis hired him as his wardrobe assistant. He admitted he had begun discarding medications to reduce Elvis's intake before the two of us ever discussed it. Al described a small, black bag that contained vials of saline solution that I had given him to replace the injectable fluids that arrived at Graceland via mail in unmarked packages postmarked from Las Vegas and Los Angeles. The packages were assumed to be from other doctors and were addressed to Elvis personally, but it was unclear whether or not Elvis had ordered or solicited the packages.

For a while Al had been the keeper of the meds I had prescribed to Elvis, to prevent my having to go to Graceland in the middle of the night to give Elvis additional sleeping medication if the situation warranted it. Al told me his duties had led to a confrontation between him and his boss, and he could

THE BEST IN THE BUSINESS

no longer handle Elvis's meds. That's when the resident nurse took over that responsibility.

Explaining the secretive jaunts in Elvis's plane to Las Vegas, Los Angeles, or Palm Springs, Al said, "Most of our trips started abruptly because Dr. Nick would not give him what he wanted in Memphis. We'd stay in one of the cities for about a week."

Elvis's cousin Billy Smith echoed Al's testimony regarding the placebo-making sessions, thus verifying that Elvis had not received as much of the medications as had been implied. Road manager Joe Esposito revealed how other doctors left various medications with Elvis, allowing him to administer them on his own, which occasionally led to problems.

Tish Henley explained how she followed a protocol I gave her for administering Elvis's medications and how that protocol changed depending on what illnesses Elvis had. Then she shared how she treated the minor illnesses of approximately one hundred people working on tour with Elvis and afterward brought home and destroyed piles of leftover drugs.

Dr. Lawrence Wruble, one of the city's leading gastroenterologists, detailed Elvis's medical problems that the prosecution had contended were only problems created by drugs.

Beginning with the '73 hospitalization, Dr. Wruble told how Elvis was "swollen from the top of his nose to the bottom of his toes" when he arrived at Baptist and about the difficulty we had making a diagnosis. He was toxic from massive cortisone treatments administered by a Los Angeles doctor, who admitted injecting shots of cortisone mixed with Novocain and Demerol into Elvis's body for more than eight weeks. His condition was made even worse by the cortisone sprays he'd used to combat the dry climate in Nevada. These unorthodox treatments left Elvis addicted to both steroids and Demerol.

Dr. Wruble also related how doctors on the West Coast had misdiagnosed Elvis's condition, claiming it was a rare illness due to his inability to digest food, but that "literally a paralyzed and distended colon" had caused an extreme buildup of fluid in his intestines.

Previous testimony by a doctor for the prosecution claimed the use of narcotics had created a situation where the churning motion of the stomach and intestines necessary for digestion was slowed down or stopped, causing his medical problem. That was speculation; it was never determined that the use of narcotics caused Elvis's colon problems. Dr. Wruble told how Elvis's condition was so bad during his '75 hospitalization that the medication he usually gave in such instances did not work. We finally had to call a specialist from the Johns Hopkins University Medical School for advice.

"It was a very, very difficult situation," Dr. Wruble concluded.

There was one last witness before I would take the stand: Dr. Forrest Tennant Jr., our top expert witness, executive director of a UCLA-affiliated laboratory that was reported to be the largest drug abuse center in the western United States. As Dr. Tennant walked up to the witness stand, Neal cut his eyes in my direction, lifting an eyebrow. I took that to mean, "We'll see." There was a reason. We were hoping to ride to freedom in Dr. Tennant's wagon, and his wheels were really wobbly.

Dr. Tennant has "one of the first pain clinics in the U.S. . . . well ahead of everybody in this area of medicine," Neal shared with me after his long trip to meet the doctor who "was mayor of a little town east of Los Angeles."

This morning Neal's view was less enthusiastic. "We had a hard time getting our expert witness, Forrest Tennant, prepared," he'd told me.

I totally understood how difficult it was to learn the process of how to tell the truth without allowing openings for a prosecutor to jump in before you could make your point.

"We worked with him until about ten o'clock [the night before his testimony], and he still wasn't right. I was whipped from being in the courtroom all day. We were sitting in a hotel room, and I turned to Tom [Dunden] and said, 'Keep working with [him] and maybe you can get it out of him. I'm going to bed.' I said that in his [Dr. Tennant's] presence because I was so frustrated.

"After he spent all night with him, Dunden called me up at about six in the morning and said, 'I think he's ready, but it is going to be like walking through a mine field.'"

Dr. Tennant was indeed ready. "I have the greatest respect for those who have the courage to treat an abuser at the risk of their own career," he said.

This statement was preparation, as well, for advancement of his theory of drug maintenance therapy in the international forum that my criminal trial had become.

The prosecution's case rested on their contention that I had merely fed my patients' drug habits over the years, giving drugs for no legitimate reason, and thus violating "acceptable standards of medical practice."

Dr. Tennant had a different take: "Those standards have changed. A body of medical research in the past five years shows that drug maintenance in severe cases is the only realistic treatment for addiction . . . Many people come for treatment and we fully realize we can't get them off drugs; but

Special Collections, University of Memphis Libraries

Dr. Nick, followed by Attorney Tom Dunden, leaves after a good day at his criminal trial, October 1981. Attorney James Neal (far right) watches.

frankly, I don't know what to do about some drug abusers but to control their drugs."

He claimed it was apparent after studying the medical records of the patients who had been cited that I was not negligent in their treatments.

"All script doctors do is write prescriptions," Dr. Tennant said, adding that I had given my patients "comprehensive care," even when they could not pay for it.

Dr. Tennant outlined three ways to treat addiction: detoxification, which physically withdraws the patient from drugs; psychological therapy; and, in severe cases, maintaining the patient on drugs.

There you have it, I thought. *The experts for both the prosecution and the defense agreed on how to treat addiction, and it turned out to be just what I was doing.*

During cross-examination, Miller reviewed Dr. Knott's testimony, stating his opinion that a physician should not give amphetamines to a patient addicted to the drug. The prosecution took each of the other patients in my indictment and had Dr. Tennant render his medical opinion. Dr. Tennant remained steadfast: "The best standard of medical care today is the physician who has the *guts* to say he will maintain his [drug-addicted] patient on drugs."

BY THE TIME I placed my hand upon the Bible, I felt confident that truth would be my salvation. I had seen how testimony that looked so damaging had turned around under cross-examination. I saw that as a clear example of how faith in truth works. When I took the hot seat, I was much calmer than I had expected to be. I felt prepared by the best in the business.

Still, Neal's words kept reminding me: "If a defendant is going to take the stand—ultimately everything rests back on how well he or she does, because what the lawyer can do is prepare the ground . . . if he takes the stand, that is the *critical, critical, critical* moment."

Discussion began with the celebrity patients, as I knew it would. Neal's approach to Elvis Presley was to expound on the testimony of our other witnesses to continue showing I had always had legitimate medical reasons and good intentions for prescribing medications to my patients. He began a dialogue with me, asking what we had done to treat Elvis's condition in 1973.

"He was admitted to the Baptist Hospital in Memphis," I answered, "and we began a slow process of reducing his intake of painkillers and steroids that he had been getting in LA. But the steroids had made the Demerol ten times more potent than normal. It was a tough go."

"When he returned to Graceland, was he entirely drug free?"

"No," I answered. "But his medication was reduced drastically. I put him on a 'limited regimen' of medication designed mainly to cure his insomnia. I sealed off his access by moving a nurse to Graceland, who administered his medications in small packets to keep bottles out of his hands."

"Didn't you use placebos and low-dosage injections?"

"We used syringes to draw much of the chemicals from capsules, refilling them with saline solution—the same way I 'watered down' the injections. So he wasn't getting all the medication he thought he was."

"Did you try that on tour?"

"Yes, in fact, I reduced him at one point to zero when he performed by using placebo injections. And he was sensational. But then I told him about it. And he said, 'I knew it. I knew that's why I was feeling so bad out there.' From then on he was very suspicious."

We went down the list, individually addressing the other patients listed in the indictment. I explained that all of them were using addictive drugs when they came to me.

Neal talked about each patient and then asked, "What was your goal?"

"The goal . . . was to control the drugs they were getting, to try to keep them from getting them off the street, and to eventually wean them off the drugs," I answered, stating that we had been successful in accomplishing that in several cases.

Then Jewett Miller turned to the subject of Elvis Presley, calling me on the quantity of drugs that had gone to Elvis's entourage, asking, "What percentage of the drugs prescribed did you think Mr. Presley actually took?"

"We estimated we discarded better than 75 to 80 percent of this medication during the indictment period," I said of the numbers in question, stating that I guessed between one-third and one-fourth is what we used.

Then Miller focused on the "protocol" or regimen for the dispensing of various amounts of medications used only when Elvis was performing on road dates or concerts in Nevada. Depending on which of those circumstances applied, the protocol might call for about ten different medications when he awoke in the morning up until showtime; one hour before the show, there were five to seven other medications given; immediately before the show, he got a shot of caffeine and eyedrops; after the show there might be up to five medications; before bed—sedatives as needed. As much as was possible, placebos were substituted.

"Does this piece of paper represent the life of Elvis Presley on tour?" Miller asked, holding up a protocol I had scribbled on a piece of paper for my nurse Tish to use as a guide when she was on tour with Elvis in Tahoe.

"No," I answered. "I don't think it describes his life. Tours were his life. They were what turned him on."

I explained that I didn't prescribe amphetamines to Elvis when he was not on tour, except for weight loss, although I did prescribe sleeping medication for him then, as well as blood pressure medication.

I had no problem admitting that the number of drugs I had prescribed exceeded the amounts recommended in the *Physicians' Desk Reference*, the standard handbook for prescribing drugs. The *PDR* guidelines are for people who have never used the listed drugs before. The patients in question had all developed a tolerance to them, which required that they take higher doses than recommended.

At the end of my testimony, the attorneys discussed waiving closing arguments. Since they were unable to agree, Judge Bernie Weinman decided it was not time to cut corners. We all went home to dream about the final outcome.

A few days before my trial came to a close, Judge Weinman directed acquittal of three of the counts against me, after a witness for the prosecution testified while examining my medical records that there could have been a valid medical justification for prescribing the medications for another patient and myself. I silently thanked the prosecution for calling the witness who unintentionally testified on my behalf.

Sixteen days after the trial began, the closing arguments took place. They dealt with the main issue agreed on at the beginning of the trial: whether I acted with criminal intent in prescribing to Elvis Presley, Jerry Lee Lewis, and others.

In the final analysis it came down to two views of Dr. George Constantine Nichopoulos. The prosecution portrayed me as a pill pusher, the defense as a good Samaritan. The prosecution saw me as a physician who had abused my authority in dispensing "dangerous and addictive drugs." They implied that money was my motive—personal gain. They claimed I had prescribed "excessive" drugs "unlawfully, willfully, and feloniously" to Elvis Presley, Jerry Lee Lewis, and seven others, with "almost total disregard" for accepted standards of medical practice. Their witnesses implied I had prescribed "unnecessary" drugs for "no legitimate medical reason."

The defense saw me as a physician who treated drug-dependent patients whom no one else would take. We said I prescribed the medications to control my already-addicted patients' consumption of drugs they had been obtaining from various other sources that could be unsafe or illegal. We contended that my motive was to wean them off drugs. Our expert witness revealed I had by need stumbled on "drug maintenance theory," the newest approach currently in use for treatment of drug abusers at a progressive clinic in California. Others told how I treated patients who had no one else to turn to.

Judge Weinman charged the jury to decide on my guilt or innocence solely from the evidence presented to them by the criminal court. The jury began deliberating my fate at one o'clock in the afternoon, and three hours later there was a decision.

The jury foreman handed the indictment jacket to Judge Weinman.

I was dazed—light enough to float—ears ringing, palms sticky, mouth dry, eyes teary. I was concentrating on my physical self to keep from fainting.

How embarrassing that would be! I thought.

I looked over at my wife and daughters; they were crying. I glanced at Father Vieron; his hands were folded in prayer and his eyes raised to heaven.

Had I spaced out and missed the verdict?

Judge Weinman was polling the jurors individually. The defense team was all smiles.

It was true! Not guilty! I was free!

Friends considerately waited to heap their congratulations on me until after I embraced my family and pastor. The jurors, strangers when we had met less than a month before, seemed as happy for me as my closest friends were.

"Are we going to have a party?" one of the jurors asked, catching us totally off guard.

Edna did not hesitate: "If you want to, come on out to the home."

Her genuine Southern, Greek welcome was quickly taken to heart. By the time we arrived home, the street was lined with vehicles. It took less than a half hour for well-wishers to pack the house. Charles Vergos led the way with a trademark platter from his famous Rendezvous restaurant. That was a great beginning. The Greek cooks in our church had been busy, as well as neighbors we had not known that well before the ordeal began.

Several of the jurors came to the celebration and shared guests-of-honor roles with my stellar legal team and me. They delighted in explaining to our fascinated guests how they had arrived at their decisions.

"It all boiled down to whether he had motivation for overprescribing drugs. It didn't matter how many prescriptions they showed us," one juror said, smiling.

"The big thing we discussed was, did he prescribe drugs for a reason?" another said.

"The easiest counts to decide were the ones about Elvis Presley and Jerry Lee Lewis. We thought he tried his hardest to help them."

That remark came as a surprise to us.

"The most important witness was the drug expert from California. He made me see you were doing your best to reduce the amounts of drugs to your patients, and that was the best thing you could do for them."

The poor gentleman making the remark had no idea why I led him around by the arm so he could repeat his opinion to each member of my legal defense team, one of whom had worked all night to make certain the good doctor was prepared to deliver his forceful testimony.

It was definitely a time to rejoice and give thanks, and Father Vieron arrived to do that very thing.

LATER, A SPOKESPERSON for the Tennessee Board of Medical Examiners told reporters that my acquittal all but closed the door on the possibility that they would take further action against me, since no additional evidence had surfaced during the trial.

Despite my gratitude, there were many issues I would have to work through regarding the past two years. I was still heartsick over the public's perception of me as "the doctor who killed Elvis" portrayed in the 20/20 cover-up story. I felt sorry for the innocent people whose "confidential" patient information had to be drudged up for public perusal. I regretted the focus the spotlight placed on Elvis's weaknesses and his struggle against addictive demons. He had made such great strides in overcoming drug dependency toward the end of his life. I wanted people to understand that progress had been made and not think badly of us that we were not able to fully succeed.

Worst of all, there was a hard knot of anger in the place where I wanted there to be forgiveness. The trial that had caused my loved ones so much pain had been needless. The financial burden levied by my legal expenses and from loss of income was devastating. All I could do was go back to what I loved: treating patients. In helping other people heal, maybe I could heal myself.

I was tremendously grateful for my acquittal, for all who had helped me earn it and for those who had supported me through it. Never did I suspect, even for a moment, that it was not the end of my problems—that the worst was yet to come.

"Not Guilty—All Charges." Attorneys and family leaving courthouse in victory, November 4, 1981. (left to right: Tom Dunden, Elaine Nichopoulos, Dr. Nick, Kissy Nichopoulos, James Neal, and Edna Nichopoulos)

NINE

THE PRICE PAID

12-11-81   Dr George Nichopoulos

Dr. Nick reflects on the outcome of his criminal trial in an exclusive interview held in his home office.

On November 6, 1981, I returned to my beloved profession. Doing business as usual felt really good, at first. I valued my acquittal from a criminal court trial that could just as easily have rendered a different sentence. It was not long, however, before attitudes toward me seemed to change—especially at Baptist Hospital. I might have just been paranoid, but I felt the staff was whispering about me behind my back. A number of situations were making me uneasy.

Since the majority of my new patients came through referrals from my other patients, and other doctors at our clinic were consistently assigning their problem pain patients to me, I was acquiring a disproportionate number of chronic pain sufferers. Given the legal difficulties I had encountered over prescribing pain medications, I was reluctant about treating pain problems. The medical profession had only recently begun to recognize the need for treatment of chronic pain, and controversy over how doctors treated it was leading to heated speculation and frosty judgment. I did not want any part of either. When the city finally opened its first pain clinic, I began doing what I could to refer my chronic pain patients to specialists there.

There was another matter. During my probationary period with the Board of Medical Examiners, the deadly acquired immune deficiency syndrome, known as the AIDS virus, struck the nation. The HIV/AIDS epidemic terrified the general public, as well as the medical profession. There was no information available about the disease in its earliest stages. No one knew what caused it, how it was transmitted, how to treat it—only that it was almost always fatal. Fearing that exposure to AIDS patients would contaminate them, doctors and nurses began leaving the medical profession in droves. It was then I made the decision to learn what I could about the disease and step into the fearful gaps left by the exodus of logic and sensibility.

My goal was always to be a complete doctor, so in 1962 I started taking additional training at least once a year at Johns Hopkins. When the hospital began offering coursework in how to evaluate and treat AIDS, I attended not because I wanted to specialize in the disease, but because I wanted to know how to treat my patients who suffered with it. I knew I had to do all that I could to try and save their lives. Word soon spread, however, that I was treating these disenfranchised individuals, and desperate patients began traveling for help from towns hundreds of miles away. This influx created an extremely heavy patient load.

Adding to my workplace stress, a couple of new books got the public all stirred up about the role drugs could have played in Elvis's death. The rock 'n' roll scenario was a hot topic once again. Attracting the most attention was *Elvis*, a hideously demeaning biography written by Albert Goldman. Penned in collaboration with a member of Elvis's Memphis Mafia, Goldman's book chose to humiliate Elvis and to expand on the unfavorable portrayal of our relationship depicted by *20/20* in "The Elvis Cover-Up."

The controversy was all over TV. Various authors, family, and members of his entourage stumbled over one another giving interviews depicting Elvis as a man obsessed over drugs and lured to his fate by unscrupulous doctors, primarily me.

THERE WAS NO notice for the next upheaval in my life. It began as a routine maneuver: I opened a letter from the Medical Group and read its straightforward contents. I was on my own; I had been practicing too much "free medicine." After twenty years of being part of a co-op, I was booted out. I had no equipment, instruments, nothing.

For a brief time I was able to hook up with a doctor housed in the infamous white marble high-rise next door to the Medical Group on Madison Avenue. Following that was another temporary stint using the offices at the Sutherland Group in the Baptist Hospital East Medical Building.

Photo by Rose Clayton Phillips

The white marble high-rise, owned by the Medical Group, towers above their regular office building. Elvis's vacant parking spot is in the foreground.

Then I made a deal with Dr. David Meyer to practice at his location in the impressive Ridgeway Center. Dr. Meyer, by now one of the top ophthalmologists in the South, needed a doctor to examine patients in his large practice before they underwent eye surgery. It was a convenience for him to have me there, and a wonderful space in which to see my own patients.

As the media's coverage of me continued, however, Dr. Meyer's patients began to complain about lurking photographers. I could tell he was reluctant when he asked me if I could make other arrangements, but I understood and complied with his request as soon as I was able.

AN ACCELERANT FOR my media popularity was the latest Elvis book and the incredible publicity it generated as a result of its connection with "The Elvis Cover-Up." A couple of my patients had been warning me for some time that Charles Thompson and his sidekick, James Cole, were conducting interviews for a book elaborating on their actions behind the scenes during their *20/20* investigation. Their book, *The Death of Elvis: What Really Happened*, published in 1991, was worse than I expected. It literally explained step-by-step how they waged war against me, making their case that drugs caused Elvis's death.

What the authors had wanted all along was a copy of Elvis's autopsy report to give substance to their allegations and suppositions. Now they had it. Their prized acquisition came as a deathbed wish from Dr. Harold Sexton. The former Baptist pathologist had apparently found a loophole, a way to get the confidential autopsy report published without Baptist Hospital breaking its word to Elvis Presley's estate.

Line by line the authors boasted about the case they built against Elvis and me, how they worked with investigators to compel witnesses to share information they could not have obtained without government intervention, and then used that information to influence public opinion—actions they had previously denied. It sickened me to read the show's producer bragging about the role he had played in forcing my medical board hearing and criminal trial. Defending myself against allegations the authors had been unable to prove legally had cost more than three hundred thousand dollars in legal fees and years of lost income, and tarnished Elvis's image, my good name, and any hope for a future in medicine. Now they had the nerve to brag about their "investigative reporting," turning their story into a venture for personal gain.

Fallout from the book was steady for a couple of years. First the publication of the hardback and its national media tour, then publication of the soft cover and another round of publicity, with appearances on *Geraldo*, a talk show hosted by the correspondent from "The Elvis Cover-Up."

After reading *The Death of Elvis*, members of the Shelby County Commission began to wonder if a conspiracy *had* actually taken place. Led by Vasco Smith, the commission drafted a resolution specifying that Elvis Presley's death certificate should be regarded as false and misleading. It requested that the case of Elvis Presley be reopened and the findings reported to them at the earliest possible date, citing irreconcilable differences between the autopsy records published in the book and the death certificate Dr. Francisco signed and submitted to the state Department of Public Health.

In the meantime the pressure on me did not let up. On March 11, 1992, the Division of Health Related Boards delivered its latest Notice of Charges to George C. Nichopoulos, MD. It was about the same as the others before it. An audit had been conducted in Memphis area pharmacies for Schedule II controlled substances prescribed by the respondent. "The quantity of drugs prescribed and dispensed to the patients . . . is in excess of that amount, if any, which was medically appropriate for their treatment."

This time there was an added charge. I was accused of not having "met any of those regulations and was not licensed, certified, or otherwise approved to utilize Methadone in a drug detoxification or maintenance program." Although there were numerous patients listed in the charges, only one name would remain when I eventually faced the medical board.

Meanwhile the commission was still waiting for an answer regarding its request for an investigation into Elvis's death. On April 8, 1992, Charles Burson, the state attorney general and reporter, wrote a short response from the state registrar's office stating that they had "looked into the allegations of irregularities or violations of the law in connection with the death certificate of Elvis Presley . . . there is insufficient reason to conclude that there were any irregularities or violations of the law in the death certificate of Elvis Presley."

That wasn't the end of it. After state officials refused to reopen the case, the commission filed a lawsuit. The Associated Press picked up the local news story, saying the state's decision did not go far enough because *The Death of Elvis* showed that specimens had been sent to private laboratories, which found that Elvis died from a reaction to drugs. To those who had not read the book, the prominence of its publicity was all the proof they needed to believe the alleged Elvis cover-up had at last been exposed. No one reported otherwise.

STATE OF TENNESSEE
Office of the Attorney General

JOHN KNOX WALKUP
SOLICITOR GENERAL

456 JAMES ROBERTSON PARKWAY
ATTORNEY GENERAL & REPORTER
NASHVILLE, TENNESSEE 37243-0485

TELEPHONE (615) 741-3491
FACSIMILE (615) 741-5069

CHARLES W. BURSON
ATTORNEY GENERAL AND REPORTER

JEAN NELSON
CHIEF DEPUTY ATTORNEY GENERAL

DEPUTY ATTORNEYS GENERAL
ANDY D. BENNETT
MICHAEL W. CATALANO
DONALD L. CORLEW
PERRY A. CRAFT
KIMBERLY J. DEAN
KATE EYLER
STEVEN A. HART
DAVID M. HIMMELREICH
CHARLES L. LEWIS
CHRISTINE MODISHER
MICHAEL D. PEARIGEN
JENNIFER H. SMALL
JERRY L. SMITH
GORDON W. SMITH
JIMMY G. CREECY
CHIEF SPECIAL COUNSEL

April 8, 1992

Mr. Brian L. Kuhn
Shelby County Attorney
160 North Mid America Mall
Suite 801
Memphis, Tennessee 38103

RE: Shelby County Resolutions Nos. 39 and 51;
Investigation of Death of Elvis Presley

Dear Mr. Kuhn:

Based upon the Resolutions of the Shelby County Commission, and pursuant to her discretionary authority under T.C.A. § 68-3-105, the State Registrar has requested the appropriate officials to look into the allegations of irregularities or violations of the law in connection with the death certificate of Elvis Presley. We are advised that all relevant documents referenced in the Resolutions have been reviewed and/or re-reviewed by the Chief Medical Examiner of the State of Tennessee. We are further advised that based upon this investigation, there is insufficient reason to conclude that there were any irregularities or violations of the law in connection with the death certificate of Elvis Presley.

We appreciate the Commission's actions in formally bringing this matter to our attention, and we are pleased we were able to resolve it short of litigation. If we can be of further assistance to you and the Commission in the future, please let me know.

Sincerely yours,

CHARLES W. BURSON
Attorney General and Reporter

CWB:JWT/sg

xc: Paula Taylor
State Registrar

EXHIBIT
6

Nichopoulos Collection

A patient of mine, who was Vasco Smith's friend, assured me Smith's search for a cover-up was not a personal indictment against me; it was about Smith's determination to get Dr. Francisco out of office. Could that be it? Since Smith had been unsuccessful in obtaining a copy of the autopsy from Dr. Jerry Francisco, he apparently seized the information revealed in the book as an opportunity to renew his campaign for discovery of any wrongdoing on Dr. Francisco's part. Was it simply a political vendetta against Dr. Francisco that had prompted Smith to encourage the suspicions of *20/20* and put the reputations of Elvis and me on the firing line?

With a proliferation of exposés and news articles in the marketplace continuing to tout Elvis's drug exploits, it was no wonder that twelve months after the Shelby County Commission launched its lawsuit, Paula Taylor, the state registrar of vital records, agreed to "a new probe based on speculations that drugs—and not heart disease—caused Elvis's death." She stated that the new investigation was "solely out of deference to the deep and prolonged concerns formerly acted upon by the Shelby County Commission."

Accordingly, Elvis Presley's body would not be exhumed. The state's investigation would be based on a review of Elvis's "medical records, the actual autopsy report and notes, and slides of body tissues and drug toxicology reports." That included all the information held by Baptist Memorial. *Elvis and I will be exonerated*, I thought. I could only hope it would happen sooner than later.

Just five months after the state's decision for a new Elvis autopsy, my attorney advised me to voluntarily surrender my DEA permit. On September 15, 1992, *The Commercial Appeal* made the announcement: "'Dr. Nick' to give up his drug license."

In the article, reporter Jon Hamilton quoted Alan Foster, the state health department attorney, as saying: "The charges stem from an investigation prompted by a complaint that Nichopoulos was giving injections of addictive drugs to patients unnecessarily." That was confirmation to me that a lone anonymous tip had caused the DEA to start a new file on me. Subsequent hate mail kept the pressure on. The DEA began scrutinizing prescriptions I had written and flagged the one for methadone. That was just the beginning.

It would be years, however, before I learned the full extent of what had gone on behind the scenes while I was treating Jerry Lee Lewis and other chronic pain patients that compelled the DEA's renewed interest in me. It was as bizarre as the plot of a B movie. It involved a clandestine meeting among informants of dubious reputation and a DEA officer from Nashville, and a treacherous hate-mail campaign that solicited letters from all over the world telling the medical board that it would soon have another death on its hands if it did not act immediately regarding my treatment of Jerry Lee Lewis. I thought anyone should have been able to see that the juvenile letter-writing campaign was a malicious setup, but obviously not.

At least I was able to continue treating patients without prescribing Schedule II narcotics while I awaited my day in court. Originally scheduled for eight months earlier, the hearing date was reset for January 13, 1993. There was a lot of work to do in the meantime.

FOR WEEKS I called doctors I knew in town, seeking help in caring for pain patients I could no longer treat effectively. Although I had no luck there, I found a November 1992 issue of the medical journal *Cortlandt Forum* that proved beneficial. It contained an informative article entitled simply "Pain Management" by Dr. Daniel Brookoff, an assistant professor of medicine at the University of Tennessee College of Medicine in Memphis. Grateful for the lead, I decided to call and see if I could convince Dr. Brookoff to treat my chronic pain patients most desperately in need of medication I could no longer prescribe. After several failed attempts to reach him, I was relieved when Dr. Brookoff finally returned my call and agreed to meet with a couple of my patients, whose names I have changed.

"Her name was Lydia Cramer, a very lovely young lady from a good family," Dr. Brookoff remembered later while talking with my attorney and me. "Soon after the birth of their second child, Lydia's husband developed a 'mysterious illness' and eventually died at home. It was assumed AIDS was his cause of death . . . A couple of years later, Lydia was diagnosed with the disease. Immediately afterward, her parents took custody of her children . . . Lydia's parents sold her home and moved her into an isolated little cottage where they would leave food by the door and bring the kids by twice a week, holding them up to the window so she could see them.

"By the time I met Lydia, she could no longer be treated because Dr. Nichopoulos could not write the drugs she needed," Dr. Brookoff continued. "I had asked some other doctors in Memphis for help with her care—being that she had a real illness and came from a good family and all. There were still quite a lot of negative feelings among physicians about caring for patients with AIDS, and it certainly did not help that Dr. Nick had previously cared for her.

"I remember the day Lydia first came down to where I worked in the county hospital. She was covered in herpes lesions and in terrible pain. She had brought pounds of records that documented weekly doctor visits and pretty sophisticated medical treatments. Dr. Nick had enrolled in special coursework to learn how to better care for patients with AIDS. I remember going over all the documents and telling Lydia, 'You must be spending a fortune on medical care.' She told me that Dr. Nick hadn't charged her a penny in years. It was at that point that I decided I had to go help Dr. Nick myself—something I had previously been loath to do and warned against."

There was another patient who had touched his heart, Dr. Brookoff told my attorney as we prepared for his deposition.

"He was an elderly fellow named Emory Williams, who had suffered frostbite and been left for dead at the age of eighteen. Military doctors told him he would never walk again. Somehow he made it through physical therapy and eventually got a job where he was able to support himself and later a family of his own.

"One day an accident at work crushed his back, and Mr. Williams had to be given steady doses of morphine, which he never changed or abused. Mr. Williams somehow recovered and stayed active into his advanced years. He was a good husband and father and eventually a doting grandpa. In the years I took care of Mr. Williams, he walked two or three miles nearly every day and never missed a regular doctor's appointment. He'd had to travel from a bordering state, almost two hundred miles away, to Memphis to be treated by Dr. Nick, because no doctor closer to home would take care of him."

It was an answer to prayer that Dr. Brookoff agreed to administer aid to these patients. We were desperate. The medical board makes no provisions for the care of patients whose doctors have been stripped of their privileges during the long months it takes for a resolution.

TIME CAME FOR the Tennessee Board of Medical Examiners to begin its depositions for the hearings that would again determine whether I had the right to retain my medical license.

By then Dr. Brookoff was valiantly trying to help me with my complex legal issues. I remember his going to the medical schools in Memphis and Nashville pleading with some of the older professors to stick up for me, but none of them would dare. Dr. Brookoff told me they would confide in him: "He's really a good doctor, and he takes good care of his patients, but we just can't get involved in all of that right now."

Finally, due process began. After deposing me, Yarnell Beatty, the attorney for the state medical board, took Dr. Brookoff's deposition. Beatty asked Dr. Brookoff if he had any disagreements about the way I had used narcotic medications to treat some of the patients he was currently seeing on my behalf. Dr. Brookoff answered that he did.

Beatty looked surprised and quickly asked about the nature of that disagreement. He was told that my patients had not been given *enough* medication. Their doses had to be *increased*.

Then Dr. Brookoff went on to relate how I had given Mrs. Cramer codeine for pain, and he felt she needed morphine. After he gave her the morphine, she came back the following week and returned the medication, telling him it was too strong, so he prescribed a weaker painkiller. Dr. Brookoff maintained that Mrs. Cramer was "not a drug abuser by any means."

Eventually it came time for my medical board hearing in Nashville. Dr. Brookoff and my pastor, Father Vieron, went along for support—ready and willing to testify if called upon.

MY LONGTIME FRIEND and attorney Robert Green had encouraged me to hire Dan Warlick to represent me before the medical board in Nashville. I had readily agreed, having always been impressed with Warlick's professionalism. We had met while he was the chief investigator with the Shelby County Medical Examiners Office handling the probe into Elvis's death at Graceland on that tragic day.

Warlick was knowledgeable and decisive and had a congenial personality. In the intervening years since Elvis's death, he had moved to Nashville and become a medical malpractice attorney but still had clients in Memphis. He gladly accepted my case, quickly assembling twenty-five able witnesses and estimating my defense would take six days to present. There were discussions about a potential settlement, but that collapsed when neither the state nor I presented a plan for settling our dispute. We were not naïve enough to think the board would agree to anything I submitted other than a total admission of guilt. That was not doable.

The hearings got under way in a customary manner. Three days of testimony netted three witnesses. On the fourth day there was potential for change. Based on a deposition Green had taken on my behalf and some research Warlick had completed recently, Warlick planned a different approach with the state's expert.

"Things were going pretty routinely that day until we got to the cross-examination of the state's key witness, Dr. Roland W. Gray, MD," Dr. Brookoff recalled later when we were reviewing the ill-fated hearing. "Dr. Gray had a long record of well-paid service to the Tennessee Medical Board. He essentially reviewed cases of patients who had been prescribed narcotic medications. He testified their medicines had been prescribed in 'addictive quantities,' and that alone was invariably enough to win the case for the prosecution, resulting in either an expensive retraining and supervision program, which Dr. Gray also ran, or revocation of the physician's medical license.

"Dr. Gray had been a practicing *pediatrician* [italics added] for more than twenty years and was said to be affiliated with a prestigious treatment center in Nashville for nearly as long," Dr. Brookoff continued. "He had been a longtime volunteer for the Physicians Health Program in Tennessee, helping fellow doctors who had developed addictions to drugs or alcohol."

Warlick and Dr. Gray had tangled many times before in cases involving alleged overprescribing by other physicians. It usually came down to Warlick asking Dr. Gray if he had any knowledge that the patients had been harmed, or if he even knew if they were addicted, and Dr. Gray's replying that he could not form a medical judgment on a patient he had never seen, but one thing he was certain of was that the medications were prescribed in "excessive and addictive quantities." Then the case would essentially be closed.

Dr. Gray squirmed uncomfortably in his chair and cleared his throat as he waited for Warlick to begin his questioning.

Warlick asked if there was any indication in the record Dr. Gray had reviewed that the patient being discussed was taking the medication for any reason other than pain.

Dr. Gray answered negatively.

Then Warlick wanted to know if there was any indication the patient in question was taking the medicine for a euphoric effect.

The doctor again answered no.

Through astute questioning by Warlick, the expert admitted that he simply *assumed* most of the drug notations in the patients' records were *my* prescriptions and not notes of prescriptions written by some three dozen specialists to whom I had referred my patients for their pain. Dr. Gray even agreed that many patients build up tolerance to drugs and often need increasing doses to ease them of pain. Next Warlick closed in on what would literally wake up all the people nodding off in the room.

He asked the doctor to give his current title at the treatment center with which he was identified as having an affiliation.

Dr. Gray admitted that he didn't actually have what one would call "a title."

Warlick pressed on, asking if the expert was currently on the medical staff at the facility.

His answer was negative.

Then Warlick apologized as he continued to press for clarification by asking if the doctor was the medical director for the organization.

Again his answer was no.

This time Warlick got a timid but affirmative answer.

As it turned out, the state's expert witness ruling on whether I was over-prescribing medication to AIDS and chronic pain patients was a pediatrician, and his only affiliation with a treatment center was as a patient, not a doctor or instructor.

Warlick looked up at Dr. Oscar McCallum, the board president, walked silently over to face him head-on, and delivered his line as resolutely as possible: "Dr. McCallum, I move that Dr. Gray be disqualified as an expert witness."

Dr. McCallum stared at the board's attorney, who just shook his head. Dr. McCallum told Warlick that he could just forget his legal tricks. Then he added that Dr. Gray had been a fine expert witness for the board for many years, and they were not about to throw him overboard just on Warlick's say-so.

The administrative judge turned to the board and stated that Mr. Warlick did voice a legitimate concern.

Dr. McCallum told the judge he was ready for him on that one, claiming he had been through that kind of manipulation before. He reminded the judge that the medical board was not just a *jury*, but a board of *experts*, and that they don't *need* any expert testimony in order to make their judgments.

Warlick nearly bowed as he respectfully continued addressing the board. "Then with all due respect, sir, I would like permission to voir dire the board so that we can establish their level of expertise in this field."

Dr. McCallum's face reddened; his nervousness heightened as he blurted out that Warlick couldn't do that. Then he turned to the judge and asked sheepishly if he could.

The hearing judge shook his head, stating that he didn't know if that issue had ever really come up.

Dr. McCallum looked sternly at Warlick, stating that the board was not going to be subject to his interrogations or other shenanigans, and that was just that. He stated emphatically that they were the Medical Board of the State of Tennessee and as such were the experts on the practice of medicine in the state, with full backing from the governor and legislature. He left no doubt that the members of the medical board were the judges on my ruling, and that was final.

"On that point Dr. McCallum was technically right," explained Dr. Brookoff as he continued to recap the hearing. "In regular civil and criminal trials, the jurors are assumed to have no prior expertise or information on the issues at hand, and so they are forced to rely on evidence presented to them by experts in order to form a judgment. In fact, in order to make sure that jurors are not contaminated by any preexisting expertise or experience that would prevent them from making judgments based on the presented evidence alone, they undergo questioning by the opposing attorneys and sometimes even the judge before they can be seated. This process of questioning the jurors is called *voir dire*."

Back to the hearing: the other members of the board nodded their heads in assent to Dr. McCallum's remarks concerning the status of the board.

Warlick humbly replied, "Yes, sir. I meant no disrespect at all, sir."

Dr. McCallum was satisfied with Warlick's answer, and Dr. Gray slumped in his chair, breathing an audible sigh of relief.

"The administrative law judge put his hands over his face," Dr. Brookoff said. "He knew that they had just handed Warlick grounds for appeals that could upset rulings going back years. Dr. McCallum adjourned the hearings, and the board members ran for the doors."

The proceedings against me dragged on for nearly a year. By that time the list of patients in question had been whittled down to one—Jerry Lee Lewis.

"The board found that Dr. Nichopoulos had violated federal law in his treatment of Jerry Lee Lewis and therefore should have his license to practice medicine in the state of Tennessee removed," Dr. Brookoff continued in summary. "The requirement of a specialized license for a physician to undertake methadone maintenance is actually not a law but a Department of Justice regulation, and as such does not carry the power of statute, which is why Dr. Nick was never considered for indictment for his treatment of Jerry Lee Lewis . . . Despite Warlick's forceful protest, the board chose not to recognize that distinction."

Warlick got busy filing an appeal dealing with the state's so-called expert. The only consolation I had in the interim was that I was still able to practice medicine—prescribing Schedule V (low risk of addiction) medications only, of course. As a result, I was constantly working to find other doctors willing to treat my most critical patients. Unfortunately, my patients still had to suffer under the cloud of the Elvis Presley death controversy.

ONE DAY A friend mailed me validation: a copy of "Pathologist Sought for Elvis Autopsy," from the Tennessean August 31, 1993, confirming the search was ongoing. I read: "We've been working on this 17 years," Smith said [probably referring to public criticism of certain Francisco rulings prior to Elvis's death]. "If it took a few more months to find someone of national recognition, who is not or has not been affiliated in any way with Dr. Jerry Francisco, then I think it's worth the wait."

Reporter Jim East went on to say, "Smith, a Memphis dentist, has led a 17-year battle to expose what he views as misconduct by Francisco and have him ousted as the county medical examiner. A 1991 book on Presley's death showed that doctors sent specimens to private laboratories, which concluded the singer died from a reaction to drugs."

Knowing I was right did not ease the aggravation of what the experience had cost.

In 1994, seventeen years after Elvis's death, the state released a statement regarding the "final autopsy" ordered to give the persistent Shelby County Commission a definitive answer regarding a cover-up in the case of Elvis Presley. The State of Tennessee had hired Dr. Joseph Davis from the University of Miami School of Medicine to deliver the ultimate verdict. Davis was the former chief medical examiner for Dade County, Florida, and he claimed to have conducted more than twenty thousand autopsies during his forty-year career. The Baptist Hospital, eager to have their original diagnosis confirmed, shipped to Dr. Davis its trunk of materials: tissue samples, slides, autopsy photos, extensive paperwork, and, of course, the Bio-Science laboratory report.

At that time, pathologists were able to discriminate recently taken psychoactive drugs from those of their psychoinactive metabolites. Active compounds were generally taken within twelve hours of their discovery. Many of the drugs in Elvis's body could be categorized as metabolites. In some particular compounds, the concentrations were quite elevated. Taking this phenomenon into consideration, Elvis's overall drug levels were considerably lower than they were initially interpreted to be at the time of his death.

Dr. Davis's verdict was unequivocal: drugs did not kill Elvis Presley. His conclusion sounded like a wobbling needle caught on a scratched record: "It takes hours to die from drugs. Elvis would have slipped into an increased state of slumber. The scene itself told what happened to Elvis."

Then he added that there was no fluid found in his lungs, which would have been necessary for Elvis to have died of respiratory failure due to chemicals. Dr. Davis believed Elvis's death "was a textbook case of death by heart attack."

That report was also reexamined by a panel of distinguished toxicologists, said to have included Dr. Kevin S. Merigian. By that time he was a medical toxicologist and clinical pharmacologist at the Toxicology Center at the Regional Medical Center at Memphis (the Med), where the Elvis Presley Trauma Center is also located.

Dr. Merigian said he did not serve on that panel, although he was often called for consultation on cases where he was not specifically told the subject in question. He had earlier voiced his opinion to anyone willing to listen: "The death is not the result of multiple drug ingestion."

Dr. Davis's panel scrutinized the Bio-Science Laboratory report, especially the single paragraph that caused all the trouble: ". . . it is *our view* that death in the case of Baptist Memorial Hospital A77-160 resulted from multiple drugs ingestion [commonly known as *polypharmacy*]. Of particular note is the combination of codeine, ethchlorvynol and barbiturates detected in body fluids and tissues. The levels in the body fluids and tissues exceed *some* other known identifiable multiple drug overdose cases where codeine has been implicated" (italics added).

My writer, a patient of mine who was working on another book at the time, consulted Dr. Merigian for his professional opinion regarding the toxicology findings. She shared his interview with me. Dr. Merigian took the time to compare Elvis's drug and metabolite levels, reported by the Bio-Science Laboratory, with the levels in his forensic toxicology references and he used these textbooks to interpret the levels.

"Now, you have codeine here," Dr. Merigian began ". . . at 1.6 mcg/gm in the liver and 2.3 mcg/gm in the kidney . . . An average codeine level in someone who is thought to have had a fatal codeine overdose would be 2.8 mcg/ml and his was 1.08 mcg/ml. So, literally, that's not enough of the drug, to associate his death with a fatal codeine overdose. The liver normally has about 6.8 mcg/gm concentration in a fatal overdose and his liver had 1.6 mcg/gm concentration. So we can see that there is not a huge amount of this drug in his system. Now, he also had morphine 0.03 mcg/ml in the serum, 0.04 mcg/gm in the liver, and 0.04 mcg/gm in the kidney. What that's telling you is that he probably took codeine [in that form], because codeine metabolizes to morphine.

"He also has diazepam. What it [Bio-Science Laboratory report] says is a 'diazepam metabolite.' It doesn't say exactly which one it is, because diazepam is Valium; and a diazepam metabolite could be oxazepam or nordiazepam . . . Those are the two most common. If I knew exactly which one of those metabolites was detected and at what concentration, I could tell you approximately how much parent compound would have been taken. I could project the amount, based on how much metabolite was present. You could probably roughly extrapolate the dose of Valium and about when he took it. The pharmacokinetic profile of a known standard dose of Valium allows us to do that. So, he's got more metabolite than parent compounds; that implies this drug was taken remote to the time when this specimen [used in the BSL report] was donated.

"He may have taken the Valium twelve hours prior to when this was procured," Dr. Merigian continued. "All that's remaining is a metabolite, and there's not a lot of metabolite here actually. That's what's very curious about the findings. Since usually a high concentration of diazepam in their blood is necessary to consider the patient dead from a Valium overdose. When I say *high*, I'm referring to 30 mcg/ml. His is measured at 0.01 mcg/ml; so it's very, very small in comparison. It's like 1/600th of what it should be measured at for an overdose.

"He also has ethchlorvynol, which is a sedative/hypnotic very common in the fifties and the sixties. Again, looking at the averages, the blood concentration in a fatal ethchlorvynol case would roughly be around 84 mcg/ml. He's got 7.5 mcg/ml; so he's not even at 1/10th of what a fatal concentration would be.

"Amobarbital, which is a short-acting barbiturate, again, is usually used as a sedative/hypnotic, or sleeper. Fatal cases, on average, we're looking at blood around probably 100 mcg/ml. He's got 11 mcg/ml. Again, he's got 1/10th of what one would consider to be a *high* dose. Phenobarbital is 5 mcg/ml; that's not even in the therapeutic range. That probably wouldn't make anyone even sleepy.

"Methaqualone—Quaaludes is the common term . . . Again tissue distribution in the blood for perhaps some of the fatal cases can be as low as 6.4 mcg/ml. Well, he has a concentration of 6.0 mcg/ml, so that may be consistent. However, even though his liver was positive and his kidney was positive, no one quantitated the tissues. Like in this case [reading from the toxicology textbook]: This person's blood was 6.4 mcg/ml and their liver was 58 mcg/ml; so the liver [concentration] was ten times higher than the blood. We don't have that data for Elvis. They [BSL] did not quantify Methaqualone. I interpret that finding to mean that he did not have enough in his body to be a cause of death.

"Certainly Demerol was found in the liver and in the kidney, but no concentrations were measured in the blood or in the serum. There are a lot of drugs and metabolites identified in his body fluids and tissues but the reality remains that I don't see anything in these results, with perhaps the exception of the Quaaludes, that could even be implicated with some kind of drug related fatality—that he just overdosed—and stopped breathing.

"None of these drugs are significantly associated with arrhythmias, or causing heart failure—none of these," Dr. Merigian reasoned, after pausing briefly. "The thing you have to realize is the way that someone dies from sedative/hypnotic and/or narcotic drugs [found in the body at death] is that he or she will just go to sleep and stop breathing. That's it . . .

"If this man was alert or awake when this event happened, the cause of death could *not* have been an overdose. And it's just that straightforward . . . The reality is there were a lot of drugs identified as trace amounts or metabolites. None of these drugs *in* and *of* or *by* themselves would have caused a problem.

"I totally disagree with that [Bio-Science Laboratory report] conclusion. His [death] is *not* a result of *multiple* drug ingestion. I think they are trying to put a square peg in a round hole," Dr. Merigian concluded emphatically. "A person would have a better chance of being struck by lightning than succumbing to a cardiac arrhythmia from drugs in these concentrations."

I had originally considered the BSL statement weak in its wording. Years later I read where Dr. Dwight Reed, one of the consultants for the Bio-Science Laboratory report following Elvis's death, made the statement that the "polypharmacy ruling was just an opinion, not a medical certainty . . . a well-educated guess."

The Baptist Memorial pathologists certainly did not read it that way. Neither did the press. None of the new information seemed to matter. The news media had little interest in hearing that Elvis had died of natural causes. No one wanted Elvis to be *normal*. It just did not fit the image of the king of rock 'n' roll. The media had invested too much in their drug overdose theory to back down now. With little fanfare, the state sealed its report after satisfying the Memphis politicians with an impartial analysis of the autopsy findings.

I hoped someone would step forward on Elvis's behalf and insist that the press set the record straight, but it never happened. I felt bad about Elvis's continuing to be labeled as dying of a drug overdose, but I was not even able to help myself. My battle with the medical board was still raging, although I had been able in the interim to set up my own private practice—leased by the month—We Care, Inc. Strangely enough, it would be Jerry Lee Lewis and not Elvis Presley who would prove to be my nemesis.

A LETTER DATED April 11, 1995, contained an offer to settle my case that had been dragging on for four years of preparation, depositions, research, and attorney fees. Marked "confidential," it was sent to my counsel by A. Yarnell Beatty, in his position as associate general counsel for the State of Tennessee. The letter contained six steps of compliance, which upon my agreement would be presented to the medical board. I had a week to reply to these points. I stopped at number 1: "Dr. Nichopoulos must admit to all alleged facts and conclusions of law." Even if I admitted to the charges, there was no guarantee the charges against me would be dropped. I was in essence being asked to confess all and take my chances. No way.

My loyal supporters and I had traveled too far for me to fold my tent at this point. I would not admit to a crime I had not committed just to make my problems go away.

Ironically, in a letter dated July 4, 1995, Beatty issued a ruling on our appeal regarding the board's unqualified expert Dr. Roland Gray: "The statute authorizes the board members to rely on their own expertise in determining which level of care is required and applies a statewide standard of care."

That was just another way of saying the board could make up its mind without any help, and we had no right to question their credentials for making their decision. I knew what would come next.

On August 7, 1995, the letter I dreaded arrived: "The Tennessee Board of Medical Examiners takes this action in order to safeguard the health, safety, and welfare of the citizens of Tennessee having found the Respondent guilty of certain violations of the Medical Practice Act. The medical license of the Respondent is hereby REVOKED by this order . . ."

The five board members who voted to revoke my license were all new appointees. None of the doctors deciding my fate had treated chronic pain patients or drug addiction. It did not matter that they had no evidence proving I had harmed patients, or credentials qualifying them to make that decision. They had the power, and that is all it took to end my career.

The busy board had not finished its long-overdue correspondence. On September 19, 1995, the Tennessee Board of Medical Examiners adopted guidelines as policy for "Management of Prescribing with Emphasis on Addictive or Dependence Producing Drugs" over the signature of Oscar M.

McCallum, M.D., President. The board had not actually written the guide-lines. They acknowledged adopting them from the State of North Carolina and the Minnesota Board of Medical Examiners.

Then, on February 20, 1996, they adopted guidelines as policy for "Principles of Medical Ethics," again over the signature of Dr. McCallum.

They acknowledged that these principles, as well, were adopted from the American Medical Association and were not laws, but standards of conduct. The penalty for breaking them in the eyes of your peers was the same: expulsion from the profession.

At least, after fifteen years in uncharted territory, other doctors could actually read in *print* what I had found to be only in the minds of my accusers. Matters were worse for me now than ever, however. Not only were there legal bills to pay; I had no job and no income.

Luckily I caught a break. Jerry Lee Lewis and I were still friends, and he was looking for a road manager, basically somebody to handle travel arrangements and personal matters for him. Jerry Lee, who by this time was Dr. Brookoff's patient, was concerned because his extensive travel was taking him overseas, where he was not familiar with the doctors who would be

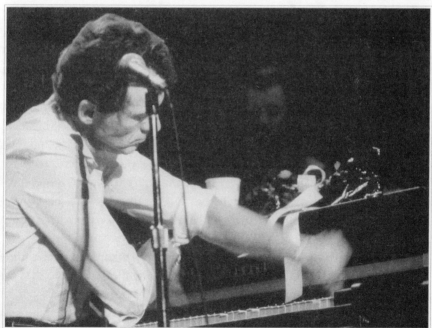

Photo by Rose Clayton Phillips

Jerry Lee Lewis in concert at the Orpheum Theatre, Memphis, 1986.

treating him. He asked if I could come along as sort of a consultant for his medical needs and help him out until he found a road manager. It was not a full-time job, but it gave me some income, as well as allowing me to at least be close to the medical field.

For four eventful years I traveled with Jerry Lee, watching him perform—thrilling fans night after night. There was a great deal of satisfaction in knowing that although almost everyone had given up on him, he had succeeded. Jerry Lee is living proof of what determination and time can do.

NATURALLY, I APPEALED the fatal decision. I had a strong group of supporters—patients, patients' families, as well as doctors—whom I had treated and worked with for decades. They believed in my abilities and encouraged me to fight on. I doubted the board would seriously consider my appeal following the revocation of my license, but I chose to go for it.

David T. Dodd, MD, medical director from the Physician Health Program in Tennessee, had contacted me earlier. The organization helps impaired physicians regain their licenses after losing them primarily because of addiction to drugs or alcohol. I was in such a state of distraction at the time Dr. Dodd approached me that I didn't even know what he was talking about. I hadn't considered myself "impaired."

At Dr. Dodd's suggestion, I underwent a weeklong assessment/psychoanalysis at Abbott Northwestern in Minneapolis at my own expense. The tests revealed that I had codependency tendencies, so Dr. Dodd recommended I complete some coursework that could help me. I attended Vanderbilt University in the spring of '97 for "Current Topics in Substance Abuse: Physician/Patient Relationships," which mainly demonstrated the role of the physician and ways he or she can relate to patients. I began seeing a psychologist on a regular basis for what was termed "my problem" and even tried to find a twelve-step program for people with codependency issues. One of the most difficult things I had to learn was how a doctor can care *too* much about his patient, almost in a pathological way.

Unfortunately, word filtered down to my attorney that it would be futile to keep working at reinstatement; the board's prior ruling would stand. That negative assessment did not deter me.

On February 24, 1998, I received a letter from Frank J. Scanlon, the new attorney hired by a team of businessmen who were working on my behalf to review the procedural position of my case. Since Scanlon had vigorously prosecuted me in "The World's Most Famous Medical Board Hearing" in 1980, I thought it was a strange move. Later I learned a doctor on the board (obviously weary of Warlick's steadfast skill) told one of the gentlemen that he thought Warlick was "too confrontational" and that I might have better luck with Scanlon.

I had last appeared before the board on an "application" for licensure, which was denied. Scanlon recommended that I let the appeal period for that application run out and then file a new one. I complied with Scanlon's advice. While we waited for my new application to be reviewed, I set up a plan where I could see patients at a walk-in clinic for a family practitioner. During the ten hours a day that the clinic was open, I would be supervised by an emergency room physician, who would be available to prescribe pain medication if he decided the situation warranted it.

On March 18, 1999, I received a letter from Frank Scanlon stating that he had attended the meeting of the Tennessee Board of Medical Examiners two days earlier, where three board members reviewed the recommendation of Dr. Godfrey Vaz, the board's medical director, that my new application to practice medicine be denied. Scanlon's letter said he spoke to the board when my application came up for consideration and requested an additional hearing on my behalf.

The board quickly responded that they did not know what I "would say or offer differently" than what I had presented the year before. Scanlon replied that I'd had a year to reflect on the matter, and the board "would hear a very different person." He added that we could provide evidence of a "well supervised and controlled place of employment."

The board member from Chattanooga expressed concern that in an informal setting I would attempt to "manipulate" the board and not be subject to cross-examination. The chairman of the board from Nashville reminded the panel that a contested court hearing would be a "circus," and I had not hesitated in the past to subject the board to days of contested case proceedings. So with not-so-fond memories of the past, the board voted and denied my new application and Scanlon's request for a hearing.

That pretty much summed it up. I felt as though my world had come to an end. My only remaining option was a contested case hearing. My financial resources had been exhausted long ago; I could not afford to begin what would probably be a series of costly encounters. It was time to face reality and see what, if any, other options were available to me. After twenty long years of legal conflict, it was over.

During my appeals process, I had begun researching different ways of treating chronic pain, such as nerve blockage. That field, as well as most areas I investigated, was not open to me without a medical license. The main problem was my inability to get malpractice insurance or to admit a patient to a hospital.

I explored working at a wound and burn unit, and a doctor had agreed to supervise me, but that was also denied. I found it almost incomprehensible, with the need for doctors so great, that no one would even talk to me about a paramedical position. It kept going through my mind that at one point I had been the only doctor performing kidney dialysis in the South, and now there was nothing available to me.

My saving grace came in 2000, when my good and faithful friend Fred Smith offered me a job at his Federal Express International headquarters. It was a godsend—a full-time position with benefits, and it was in the medical field, so to speak. I was hired as a medical advisor to review various treatments FedEx employees received to see if they followed company guidelines. That position allowed me to become current with different procedures and treatments I had only been able to read about. Unfortunately, after six years FedEx outsourced my job, and I was unable to find another place for myself in the medical field I loved so much.

SOME FIFTEEN YEARS after losing my license, I still talk occasionally with Dr. Dan Brookoff about what more I could have done or what I could have done differently to have kept Elvis's image and my medical license from dying in ill repute. There's not a single day that it doesn't cross my mind.

"I guess I should have listened to other doctors early on," I confided to Dr. Brookoff. "They told me, 'You need to treat all your patients' symptoms the same way, regardless of their personal case.' I had to treat each individual's need. I couldn't treat people like a recipe in a cookbook."

"That's the art of being a doctor," Dr. Brookoff told me. "And that's what you were, Dr. Nick—Elvis's doctor. You tried to help your patients live the best life they could. This was Elvis's life—a weird life, but the one he chose, which was extraordinary. And he needed an extraordinary doctor."

Dr. Brookoff's kind words helped, but their sentiment meant even more. I believe I am finally at peace with life and my journey through the unpredictable world of rock 'n' roll with perhaps the greatest entertainer of our time. I no longer obsess, as I once did, about what I might have contributed to my chosen profession if I had been allowed to continue treating patients.

In the blink of an eye, I can envision thousands of cheering faces, my own included, capturing the memory of a lifetime in Elvis's world—the drama, the passion, the music, the love—the precise second when Elvis burst onto the stage—the moment when I knew I was a part of the dream that made his life worth living right up to the end.

That's what I focus on each day: the gift given, not the price paid.

Carese Rice Collection

Final concert, Indianapolis, Indiana, June 26, 1977.

EPILOGUE

THAT'S THE WAY IT IS

Three weeks after my manuscript met its deadline, my ringing cell phone roused me from an afternoon nap. It was my writer. "Are you watching TV?"

I glanced at the blank screen in front of me. "Which channel?"

"Any one will do. "It's breaking news. I'm on CNN."

I quickly responded and we watched in silence along with millions of other viewers as the shocking scenario unfolded before us.

The date: June 25, 2009. I automatically looked at my wristwatch. Time: 2:27 p.m. CST. My body shifted into an eerie space, returning in memory to the worst day of my life.

The current scene: an ambulance leaving the gates of an elite residence and heading to a nearby hospital in a desperate attempt to save a patient said not to be breathing. Some reports placed a doctor in the ambulance with his patient. Paparazzi saw no efforts being made to revive the patient, thus starting rumors that the famous passenger was dead.

Before a press conference made the doleful announcement official, comparisons were already being made to a similar scenario in another place and time. The deceased subjects were, after all, music's two kings: the king of rock 'n' roll and the king of pop.

It was a different world Elvis left in 1977 compared to the world Michael Jackson left thirty-two years later. In 1977 celebrity news was in its infancy; there were no cable channels battling networks for news scoops. There was no Internet spreading the word lightning fast; no "citizen journalists" whose opinions found gullible messengers to unwittingly carry their insight—or lack of it—around the world as gospel truth. The big dilemma after Elvis died had been whether evening newscasts should lead with the announcement of his death. In 2009 instantaneous scenes, some furnished by iReporters, kept viewers witnessing history in real time. By nightfall on Jackson's death day, there were already hour-long talk show discussions examining his unprecedented life, his accomplishments, and his foibles, as well as the manner in which he died.

For weeks I could not answer my home phones. The callers on my voicemail asked "to talk to Elvis's doctor personally." They were eager for my opinion on the similarities in the deaths of perhaps the two most famous entertainers of our lifetime.

"THERE IS NONE. These are two different scenarios, two different situations," Dr. Kevin Merigian confirmed when my writer and I dropped by his office one afternoon and discussed the media's obsession with comparing the megastars' deaths. (When she first interviewed him in 1994, Dr. Merigian was a clinical pharmacologist and toxicologist at the Elvis Presley Trauma Center. Now he is a solo practitioner in a clinic called the Stone Institute, the Center for Medicinal Arts, in Cordova, Tennessee.)

I had a copy of an article from CNN's Web site: "Michael Jackson's death was a homicide, coroner rules." It cited a press release from the Los Angeles County coroner: "The drugs propofol and lorazepam were found to be the primary drugs responsible for Mr. Jackson's death. Other drugs detected were: midazolam, diazepam, lidocaine and ephedrine." The release stated Jackson died from "acute propofol [Diprivan] intoxication" and "other conditions contributing to death: benzodiazepine effect." (A benzodiazepine effect is referring to a combination of midazolam [Versed], diazepam [Valium], and lorazepam [Ativan].)

The press release also stated that the full and final autopsy report and the complete toxicology report "will remain on security hold at the request of the Los Angeles Police Department and the Los Angeles County district attorney." Dr. Murray was reported to have told detectives in a sworn statement that he gave Jackson three anti-anxiety drugs in an effort to induce sleep before administering propofol (the generic name for Diprivan), diluted with the anesthetic lidocaine, via an intravenous drip, while monitoring him on a machine that measured oxygen saturation in the blood.

The doctor was said to have stepped out of the room for two minutes. When he returned, Jackson had stopped breathing and failed to respond to CPR. A call went out to 911. Paramedics were unable to revive the superstar, whose heart had apparently stopped while he was attempting to sleep. The entertainer had been working out earlier in preparation for his upcoming tour.

The CNN article reported that Dr. Murray told detectives he had treated Jackson for insomnia for about six weeks. And, "Worried that Jackson might become addicted to the drug, Murray said he tried to wean Jackson from it, putting together combinations of other drugs that succeeded in helping him sleep during the two nights before his death."

An agency spokesperson said the federal drug administration was conducting an independent investigation into matters the "LAPD's investigation uncovered that may be directly related to the cause of death."

The crux of the matter was that propofol is an anesthetic agent that is considered dangerous if not properly administered. Propofol cannot be legally dispensed for use outside of a hospital or by someone who is not a licensed anesthesiologist. Critics began questioning Dr. Murray's ability and judgment when it became known that he was a cardiologist, not an anesthesiologist. Then rumors began to surface that Dr. Murray might be criminally liable for Jackson's death following his admission in the leaked detectives' report that he administered the drug "after repeated demands/requests from Jackson."

"It's hard to believe he'd take something like that," Dr. Merigian said referring to Jackson, "because I've seen that drug used in the emergency room. I've seen it cause respiratory depression and low blood pressure in people given small doses . . . In very small levels it will cause your brain to shut down. It's an induction agent for general anesthesia . . . That's not like anything that Elvis was on."

I remembered my own futile efforts to help Elvis get a full night's sleep; I had wanted so much to help him conquer his lifelong battle with insomnia, an issue I felt affected his other medical problems. To my knowledge, I had exhausted everything doable.

Dr. Merigian discussed options available today for treating insomnia. "If you're going to use an induction agent, why not give an inhalation anesthesia?" he asked facetiously. You can just knock people down with plain old ether . . . I mean there are inhalation agents that would do what propofol does." Dr. Merigian got more serious. "There is an approved drug called *Xyrem*, which you can use for insomnia, and it's an anesthesia agent [in pill form]. I have some patients on it and it works well . . . It will knock you out, but it lasts for only four hours. Patients wake back up, so you've got to re-dose then. That's how most insomniacs slumber. They get to sleep for three or four hours and then they wake up. Lots of times they re-dose themselves when they use Xyrem and then they go back to sleep."

I recalled how some people around Elvis scoffed when he asked for an additional nightly packet to re-dose for his insomnia. They claimed his actions as "evidence" he was a drug addict. That, of course, was before sleep aids such as Lunesta and Ambien became available.

"Probably at least 35 percent of the people I see have insomnia," Dr. Merigian interjected.

"And not all for the same reason," I remarked, emphasizing that insomnia acute enough to require the care of a physician is found not only in world-class entertainers, but also in nurses, doctors, pilots, veterans, and people simply compelled to work the night shift.

"The more fatigued they get, the more insomnia they have. What causes it? Nobody knows," Dr. Merigian sighed.

Then we discussed Elvis's leaked autopsy report, the case dissenters made regarding what they claimed was death by polypharmacy, and their efforts to hold me responsible. Dr. Merigian referred to the Bio-Science Laboratory toxicology report of drug levels found in Elvis's body that my writer had handed him to see if he still felt the same about his conclusion of years ago. "When I see all of the drug and metabolite levels, there's nothing here to substantiate a drug overdose to any degree of certainty. I mean there's nothing that jumps out and says, 'Oh, my gosh, he's OD'd!'

"Back then there were only a handful of drugs you could use [for helping a patient to sleep], and any patient is going to get tolerant to any medication used nightly. So I understand why there are several [the variety of medications] in the results."

I reminded Dr. Merigian that the Baptist pathologists claimed Elvis's death was polypharmacy because of the combination of drugs and the level of depressants in his system. "They did not take into account that the drugs involved did not affect the brain in the same way."

"That's true. Correct. Each individual drug has a different effect on the brain," Dr. Merigian affirmed. "There was a time in my professional life when all I did was evaluate and treat overdose patients. The idea of synergy or amplification of two separate drugs on the brain while they are in the body at one time, if you will, is not pharmacologic truth. It is more like a pharmacologic theory that has been said so many times that it has become a truism without any scientific bench work proving it. If somebody says to you, 'Well, you can take Valium and morphine together, but when you combine them, each becomes much more toxic to you than if you use each one individually versus another,' it is not true; it's a myth. There is no animal or human experimental data that suggests that this postulate is even remotely truthful.

"Let's look at intoxications people don't get confused about. You take the drug alcohol. How does alcohol depress your brain? Well, it changes your chloride ion movement in certain tissues in the brain. You drink enough of it and it makes you loopy, and it can depress your ability to function. Let's say you add in Valium. How does Valium work? There's benzodiazepine receptors that it attaches to . . . so that Valium will bind to the receptors and affect its changes on brain function through receptor-mediated ion conductance change.

"Alcohol and Valium together—for many years toxicology experts have said, 'Oh, it's a death combination,' but in reality the drugs act very differently," Dr. Merigian explained. "I understand that if you've been naïve to these drugs; that is, if you've never had Valium, never had alcohol [the affect could be deadly]. You're probably better off doing a Valium overdose, because you're probably not going to die. If you are naïve to ethanol and drink an overwhelming amount of alcohol it will kill you. The literature is filled with hundreds of case reports throughout the years."

Dr. Merigian continued: "But Elvis was on those medicines [listed in the report] for some time; he had tolerance to them. Anyone who works in the field of medicine and prescribes any kind of sedative hypnotics in their patients, these physicians soon realize that their patients get tolerant to all these medications. Eventually they will stop working. That's why he had so many drugs in so small amounts [in his body] because none of the medications worked, and he stopped taking them or he probably rotated them. I would suggest that he take drug holidays and do the same thing."

"I kept changing his medicines after a few months to something else thinking I could come back to it at a later date when he's sensitive to it again," I explained. Dr. Merigian understood.

"You can always become resensitized if you get off the medicine during a drug holiday, and then he could resume taking it again," he said. "Clearly those medicines would work again. He'd respond to the medicine just like he was naïve to it. Unfortunately, he'd down regulate very quickly, but he'd still be sensitive in the first few weeks of opportunity. If the physician prescribes barbiturates and then switches within the barbiturate class, the switching won't work. But if the physician switches to a benzodiazepine it will work, and then the doctor can resume the barbiturate at some future date."

"That's what we were doing. That's why he had such small amounts of those drugs in him. We were giving him Phenobarbital, a long-acting barbiturate, to prevent seizures," I explained. "He'd had a serious seizure and was almost dead when we found him alone in his hotel room once in St. Louis."

I shared how people are so astounded when they see certain people taking astronomical amounts of pills and it does not kill them. They just assume that person is a drug addict. They don't understand that when a patient becomes tolerant, the receptors in his brain shut down. Tolerance is like closing the door to the brain, and the medicine can't get to where it needs to go to be effectual. It does not work anymore no matter how much the patient takes. So, it is not making him high; the side effects might make him stupid, or sick (toxic). That's why doctors try to avoid prescribing medication over a longer period of time than necessary, to avoid a patient's getting tolerant to the point that the medication no longer helps him. So people just can't look at the levels of drugs in the body and say a person has OD'd.

"You have to look at everything as a whole in its entirety—the whole body of work, I guess you would say," Dr. Merigian said in agreement, emphasizing that total raw numbers [for the levels of drugs in the body] all have specific meaning in science when you are looking at laboratory precision and accuracy.

"Be that as it may," he added, "it still leaves it up to someone to interpret the data. And you will have measurement variations many fold, depending on the testing techniques and methods used. Interpreting the data is the most important aspect of the testing, especially in this case. It is not necessarily the raw data itself.

"If you sit here, you can fragment the human physiology and all sorts of so-called 'experts' will propose possible death scenarios. Ultimately all roads lead to 'I don't know.' I think the interesting thing is that if ten doctors sat around a table and informally analyzed Elvis's clinical data from the full autopsy report, they would all come up with different scenarios explaining his death.

"In the end, we don't know why Elvis died. We weren't actually with him at the time of death. We have to assume that what we know now is all we are going to know. From whatever data anyone looks at on Elvis Presley, it resoundingly exonerates drug overdose. If he has all this medicine in him and he is symptomatic from it, how does he even get to the bathroom?"

Courtesy of Dick Grob

Memphis City policemen at Graceland preparing for the funeral procession of the king of rock 'n' roll.

I REITERATED MY theory that Valsalva maneuver could have played a part in Elvis's situation to see what Dr. Merigian's reaction would be: How Elvis might had strained, causing his heart rate to slow down. When his heart tried to compensate for the maneuver by speeding up, it possibly overcompensated, causing the arrhythmia and his blood pressure to drop; then causing him to lose consciousness.

"It's possible," Dr. Merigian said, "but if he passed out, he probably would have regained consciousness. I just think he had a heart arrhythmia for whatever reason. Anyone could speculate all day long why he had the arrhythmia. Having worked in the emergency room for seventeen years and having personally witnessed people coming in with arrhythmias and dying, it doesn't strike me as odd. Now why it particularly happened to him at that moment of his world is unknown.

"Here's a guy face down on the floor trying to breathe (with forceful enough breathing to get carpet fibers in his mouth). If he'd had a drug over-dose those findings [carpet fibers] would not have been there. I don't know how many hundreds of patients I have taken care of in my professional career who were significant drug overdoses. They didn't breathe with force . . . So for

Elvis, the way I read the report, his hands were on his chest—he had possibly encountered some chest pain—and he went down. He was struggling. It doesn't appear that he was *without some effort to breathe.* Drug overdoses from sedative hypnotic medication don't struggle to die; they just die. I think Michael Jackson's death proved that to the public."

"What about a seizure?" I asked—referring to a grand mal seizure, caused by a drop in blood pressure.

"He *could* have had a seizure—now that's the other theory—and that would go with the *lack* of or withdrawal from drugs, not an overdose," Dr. Merigian remarked. "He either seized without them or he could have had a generalized seizure and fibrillated in his heart and died. When people seize they don't just die, the heart continues to beat and maintain circulation. Of those people going into barbiturate withdrawal, a quarter of them die if untreated. Without medication they will die. You would be better off saying Elvis probably had a withdrawal syndrome, a withdrawal seizure, or something, than you would an overdose if he'd got into clinical tolerance.

"You can 'cold turkey' narcotics and it won't kill you. You'll wish you were dead, but it won't kill you. That's why law enforcement agents can take a heroin addict and lock him up in jail and he won't die. But if you are a barbiturate or an alcohol addict and you go into barbiturate withdrawal delirium tremens, you can die.

"Any scenario [regarding Elvis] is probably more likely than a drug overdose. There is something sinister about this idea of drug overdose. It's got people captivated. That whole thing is a distracter. I think it's [perpetuated by] a select few people who have an agenda for their own self-gain."

We talked awhile about my situation: how the years had not changed many people's perception of me; how the loss of my medical license had fueled my desire to find what killed Elvis; how Elvis continued to be labeled in an unfair way by people seeking their own redemption from his death.

"Anybody can accuse you of anything in America and bring it to the forefront of the pubic consciousness without having any basis for any of it, and because we have such a vicious media, they'll destroy you," Dr. Merigian said.

Then Dr. Merigian looked at my writer and tilted his head in my direction. "There are many facets of his life that have been affected by this situation. I know that Elvis didn't die from an overdose. I saw the autopsy and the forensic toxicology report. So who really died in this [purported drug] overdose? Did Elvis die? Yes. Did Dr. Nick die? Yes. They both went down. From what I know of Dr. Nick, there was no intention on his part to harm Elvis. Dr. Nick did nothing to harm Elvis with his prescriptive habits or judicious use of the medications. Dr. Nick has been investigated to the max.

"Elvis died but a lot happened to him after his death. All these allegations of drug abuse tarnished his world. He was a good guy . . . All the charities and all of the community activities he participated in, and all the money he gave to the Memphis community. He was always open and friendly to his fans, and he believed in Memphis. Look at these people taking shots at him when he's dead. They would never have said anything if he were still alive. I bet Dr. Nick would still be practicing and would not have missed a beat."

We continued talking into the late afternoon. Then we discussed celebrity: the sacrifice it requires from those rare individuals whose lives are open to the imagination of other people observing isolated pieces of their journey and judging them out of a need to enhance their own self-worth.

"You read about all this, and you just say there is evil out there," Dr. Merigian said. "That's the way it is and it won't go away. People who show up in your life aren't always your friends, and you have to be smart about that . . . There is no question that after he [Elvis] passed, people decided they could make a lot of money off of this [drug overdose concept], and they did ugly things at his expense for their selfish gain."

Dr. Merigian turned to me with words of consolation: "The reality is you do the best you can with what you've got to help people out in life. Sometimes it works. Sometimes it doesn't. But that's the story of life. That's just the way it is."

He's right, I thought. *That's the way it is.*

ACKNOWLEDGMENTS

Sincere thanks to my family—Edna, Dean, Kissy, and Elaine Nichopoulos—for enduring this extensive process that allowed me to achieve a long-time dream. Your encouragement, love, and patience helped me to persevere through all the difficult times in my life that otherwise would have been unbearable. Your good memories of Elvis provided wonderful insight, lifted my spirits, and helped me past the painful moments.

Special thanks to Bill Browder, aka T. G. Sheppard, for believing so passionately that my story with Elvis needed to be told and opening the doors to making this book a reality. Thanks to Jud Phillips for coordinating and managing the project so ably and for his constant willingness to do whatever was necessary to get the job done.

To Pat Levine, my patient of so many years, for her heartfelt introduction to my book and for continuing to bless me with her friendship. There are several writers who gave unselfishly of their time and talent, aiding me in organizing my thoughts and experiences in previous attempts to bring my story with Elvis to print. I appreciate your efforts on my behalf more than you know: Peter Arnett, Stanley Booth, Dr. Daniel Brookoff, Robert Gordon, Joe Russo, Murray Silver.

To those who were fundamental in getting this printed version completed, I thank you: Sally Hill McMillan, my agent; David Dunham, who teamed with T. G. Sheppard to make this book happen; Thomas Nelson: Joel Miller, publisher; Kristen Parrish, editor in chief; Heather Skelton, editor; Kristi Henson, marketing director; Curt Harding, publicist; Kristen Vasgaard, packaging manager; Walter Petrie, designer; Janene MacIvor, copyeditor and project manager; and Virtual Marketing: Ronna Zinn, proofreader.

To the gifted artist John Robinette for sharing his pastel of Elvis and setting the tone so beautifully for the color section in my book. To the talented professional photographers and artists whose work captured and enhanced the story so beautifully and did magic with what I had for them to work with: Mike Chase, William Eggleston, Ronnie McDowell, Steve Roberts, Frederick Toma. For capturing the essence of my experience throughout the years in both my playful and solemn moments or for providing photos that did: Jim Baker, Dennis L. Breo, Jeanne LeMay Dumas, Joe Esposito, Dick Grob, Richard Long, Jud Phillips, Rose Clayton Phillips, Sandi Pichon, Pat Rainer, Carese Rice, Tom Salva, Jimmy Velvet, Terry Quinley, and my children, Kissy, Elaine, and Dean Nichopoulos.

There are many others who contributed in numerous ways to the story of my life with Elvis both during his life and after his death. To them I would like to express my sincere appreciation: members of the Memphis Mafia and Elvis entourage and staff, especially those who were there for me when I most needed them—Joe Esposito, Dick Grob, Joe Guercio, Linda and Lowell Hays, George Klein, Sam Thompson, Nancy Rooks, Al Strada. Also Elvis's TLC ladies: Sheila Ryan Caan, Shirley Dieu, JoCathy Brownlee Elkington, Barbara Klein Bauer.

To my faithful church community: Father Nicholas Vieron, my pastor, advisor, and unfailing ally; Spero Angelakis; the Tashie family; George Touliatos; Charlie Vergos and the entire Vergos family; and numerous other parishioners whose friendships I value.

To loyal supporters who stepped up in various ways and spoke out in my defense: Joe Cooper, Clifford Davis Jr., Dr. Varna Love, the William B. Tanner family.

To members of my legal defense teams who gave of their time to help me recreate the history I had tried so hard to forget: Thomas Dunden, Judge Frank Crawford, Robert L. Green, Darryl Grisham, Ken Masterson, James Neal, Donna Phillips, Frank Scanlon, John S. Thomason, Marie Kay Thurmond, Daniel D. Warlick. Thanks to the jurors and board members who heard my story with an open mind and ruled on my behalf.

To members of the medical community who worked so zealously discovering solutions to Elvis's medical problems and helping me find peace with my efforts to treat him: Dr. Thomas Abell, Dr. David Adams, Betty Carter, John Coleman, Dr. Robert Fink, Tish Henley, Dr. David Knott, Dr. Wiley E. Koon, Dr. Chris Lahr, Pat Levine, Dr. Kevin Merigian, Dr. David Meyer, Dr. Jack Morgan, Dr. Mike Purdue, Dr. Forest Tennant, Dr. Lawrence Wruble. A special thanks to Harry Sinclair of the Medical Group for his deep friendship and his countless efforts to help me keep my medical practice going.

To my great success story, friend, and patient—Jerry Lee Lewis, his daughter, Phoebe, and his son Lee. Thanks to the other patients who stuck with me through thick and thin for their faith and confidence in me. There are so many patients, dear people, that I could not name everyone. I apologize for that deep from my heart. Please know I am grateful to you.

To wonderful friends who provided a great environment, tasty food, and good friendship over the years, and especially during the completion of this project: Pete & Sam's Veta and Sam Bomarito; Randy Smith at Perkins Germantown; Marlowe's Tony and Liz Gilardi, Missy and Mike Coleman.

To numerous others who contributed significant materials, information and/or valuable insight into people and events in the story line that impacted my life: Patsy Andersen, Papni Bhargava, Lynn and Linda Clanton, Debbie Cohen, Winston Eggleston, Paula High, Judy Howell, Renee Noel, Karen and Neil Shea, Robert P. Stefanow, Johnnie Waldrup Wilson, Frank Woodard.

To Sam Phillips Recording Studio for providing a comfortable, nostalgic home for interviews: Knox Phillips, Dean Phillips, Roland Janes, and Jud Phillips.

One of my best and most devoted friends is my writer, Rose Clayton Phillips. Despite often being very sick, she continued to work hard during those difficult times. She had the feel for the story line that no one else could have captured. I can never thank her enough. She has all the respect and love that I'm capable of.

SOURCE DATA

The source material in this memoir comes primarily from the author's and/or writer's recollections of personal experiences, either from firsthand interactions with or observations of the persons and/or scenes discussed or reported. Much of the factual information involved in the medical board hearing and criminal trial were verified by newspaper clippings located in the Mississippi Valley Collection at the University of Memphis (MVC/UMem) through access granted by Dr. Richard R. Ranta, dean of the College of Communications and Fine Arts, with assistance from Edwin G. Frank, curator of special collections, and his staff. Information taken from various other printed materials and alternate interviews have been noted whenever possible and feasible. Some information has simply become a part of the Elvis Presley myth, a large portion of which impacted the life story of the author. Whenever possible, we have attempted to acknowledge sources in the original context of the manuscript, to minimize confusion.

IMAGE CREDITS

Every effort has been make to track copyright holders. If any unintended omissions were made, please notify the publisher for appropriate acknowledgments in future issues. Specific photo references are cited within the text.

BIOGRAPHIES AND MEMOIRS

Brown, Peter Harry and Pat H. Broeske. *Down at the End of Lonely Street: The Life and Death of Elvis Presley*. New York: Dutton, 1997.

Clayton, Rose M. and Richard M. Heard. *Elvis Up Close: In the Words of Those Who Knew Him Best*. Atlanta: Turner Publishing, 1994.

Dundy, Elaine. *Elvis and Gladys*. New York: Macmillan, 1985.

Esposito, Joe, with Elena Oumano. *Good Rockin' Tonight*. New York: Simon and Schuster, 1994.

_____, and Darwin Lamm. *Elvis . . . Intimate & Rare: Memories & Photos from the Personal Collection of Joe Esposito*. USA: Elvis International Forum Books, 1997.

_____, and Joe Russo. *Elvis Straight Up*. CA: Steamroller Publishing, LLC, 2007.

Goldman, Albert. *Elvis*. New York: McGraw-Hill, 1981.

Fortas, Alan. *From Memphis to Hollywood*. Ann Arbor: Popular Culture Ink, 1992.

_____, *Elvis: The Last 24 Hours*. New York: St. Martin's Paperbacks, 1991.

Gregory, Neal and Janice Neal. *When Elvis Died*. New York: Pharos, 1992.

Grob, Dick. *The Elvis Conspiracy?* Las Vegas: Fox Reflections Publishing, 1996.

Guralnick, Peter. *Last Train to Memphis: The Rise of Elvis Presley*. Boston: Little, Brown and Company, 1994.

_____, *Careless Love: The Unmaking of Elvis Presley*. Boston: Little, Brown and Company, 1999.

Hodge, Charlie, with Charles Goodman. *Me 'n Elvis*. Memphis: Castle Books, 1988.

Jenkins, Mary, as told to Beth Pease. *Memories Beyond Graceland Gates*. Buena Park, CA: West Coast Publishing, 1989.

Lacker, Marty, Patsy Lacker, and Leslie S. Smith. *Elvis: Portrait of a Friend*. New York: Bantam, 1980.

Loyd, Harold. *Elvis Presley's Graceland Gates*. Franklin, TN: Jimmy Velvet Publications, 1987.

Nash, Alanna, with Billy Smith, Marty Lacker, and Lamar Fike. *Elvis Aaron Presley: Revelations of the Memphis Mafia*. New York: HarperCollins, 1995.

Marcus, Greil. *Dead Elvis: A Chronicle of a Cultural Obsession*. New York: Doubleday, 1991.

_____, *Mystery Train: Images of America in Rock 'n' Roll History*. New York: Dutton, 1975.

McAdams, Tara. *Elvis Handbook*. London: MQ Publications Ltd., 2004.

Marsh, Dave. *Elvis*. New York: Thunder's Mouth Press, 1982.

Mann, May. *The Private Elvis*. New York: Pocket Books, 1977.

Parker, Ed. *Inside Elvis*. Orange, CA: Rampart House Ltd., 1978.

Presley, Dee, and Billy, Rick, and David Stanley, as told to Martin Torgoff. *Elvis: We Love You Tender*. New York: Delacorte, 1980.

Presley, Priscilla Beaulieu, with Susan Harmon. *Elvis and Me*. New York: Berkley Books, 1985.

Presley, Vester, as told to Deda Bonura. *A Presley Speaks*. Memphis: Wimmer Books, 1994.

Presley-Early, Donna, and Eddie Hand, with Linda Edge. *Elvis: Precious Memories*. Birmingham: The Best of Times, 1997.

Rooks, Nancy. *Inside Graceland: Elvis' Maid Remembers*. Bloomington, IN: Xlibris Corporation, 2005.

Schilling, Jerry, with Chuck Crisafulli. *Me and a Guy Named Elvis*. New York: Gotham Books, 2006.

Smith, Gene. *Elvis's Man Friday*. Nashville: Light of Day Publishing, 1994.

Thompson, Charles C., II and James P. Cole. *The Death of Elvis: What Really Happened*. New York: Delacorte Press, 1991.

Thompson, Sam. *Elvis on Tour: The Last Year*. Memphis: Still Brook, 1992.

West, Red, Sonny West, and Dave Hebler, as told to Steve Dunleavy. *Elvis: What Happened?* New York: Ballantine Books, 1977.

Yancey, Becky and Cliff Linedecker. *My Life with Elvis*. New York: St. martin's Press, 1977.

INTERVIEWS

Abell, Dr. Thomas, and Dr. Chris Lahr. June 2008. Interview by George Nichopoulos, Dean Nichopoulos, and Rose Clayton Phillips. Tape recording. Jackson, MS.

Brookoff, Dr. Dan, and Dr. George Nichopoulos. January 24, 1994. Taped interview by Rose Clayton. Memphis, TN.

_____. 2008 and 2009. Phone conversations with Rose Clayton Phillips.

Carter, Betty. 2009. Telephone conversation. Memphis, TN.

Elkington, JoCathy Brownlee. 2009. Interview by George Nichopoulos, Dean Nichopoulos, and Rose Clayton Phillips. Tape recording. Memphis, TN.

Elliott, Maurice. January 15, 1980. Interview by Rose Clayton. Memphis, TN.

Esposito, Joe. 2008–2009. Numerous telephone conversations.

Francisco, Dr. Jerry. 1993. Interview by Rose Clayton. Tape recording. Memphis, TN.

Foster, Alan. 1993. Interview by Rose Clayton. Tape recording. Nashville, TN.

_____. 2008. Telephone conversation with Dr. George Nichopoulos.

Grob, Dick. 2009. E-mail and telephone conversations with Dr. George Nichopoulos and Rose Clayton Phillips.

Henley, Tish, and Dr. George Nichopoulos. May 19, 2009. Interview by Rose Clayton Phillips. Tape recording. Memphis, TN.

Howell, Judy. 2009. Telephone interview by Rose Clayton Phillips.

Bauer, Barbara Little Klein. 2009. Interview by Dr. George Nichopoulos, Dean Nichopoulos, and Rose Clayton Phillips. Tape recording. Memphis, TN.

McMahon, Mike. 2009. Telephone interviews by Dr. George Nichopoulos and Jud Phillips. Tape recording.

Merigian, Dr. Kevin. 1993. Interview by Rose Clayton. Tape recording. Memphis, TN.

_____. 2009. Interview by Dr. George Nichopoulos and Rose Clayton Phillips. Tape recording. Cordova, TN.

Meyer, Dr. David. 2001. Interview by Rose Clayton Phillips.

Morris, William. 2009. Telephone interview by Rose Clayton Phillips. Memphis, TN.

Neal, James F. 1981. Interview by Rose Clayton.

_____. January 22, 2009. Interview by George Nichopoulos, Dean Nichopoulos, Rose Clayton Phillips, and Jud Phillips. Tape interview. Nashville, TN.

Nichopoulos, Edna, Kissy Nichopoulos, Elaine Nichopoulos, and Dean Nichopoulos. 2008 and 2009. Numerous interviews by Dr. George Nichopoulos and Rose Clayton Phillips.

Rooks, Nancy. March 2009. Interview by Dr. George Nichopoulos, Dean Nichopoulos, and Rose Clayton Phillips. Tape recording. Memphis, TN.

Strada, Al. Spring 2009. Telephone interview by Dr. George Nichopoulos, Dean Nichopoulos, and Rose Clayton.

Sugarman, Russell, Judge. 2004. Personal conversation with Dr. George Nichopoulos. Memphis, TN.

Thompson, Sam. 2009. Telephone conversations with Dr. George Nichopoulos. Memphis, TN.

Vieron, Father Nicholas. June 2009. Phone and e-mail interviews by Rose Clayton Phillips. Memphis, TN.

Warlick, Dan. January 21, 2009. Interview by George Nichopoulos, Dean Nichopoulos, Rose Clayton Phillips, and Jud Phillips. Tape recording. Nashville, TN.

_____. February 11, 2009. Interview by Dr. George Nichopoulos and Rose Clayton Phillips. Tape recording. Memphis, TN.

INTERVIEW NOTES FROM VARIOUS CONTRIBUTORS

Arnett, Peter. May 26, 1983. Notes from six hours of raw interviews with Dr. George Nichopoulos for CNN broadcast.

Booth, Stanley. "The King Is Dead! Hang the Doctor" (article in *The Elvis Reader*).

Brookoff, Dr. Dan. "JOB in Memphis" (proposal).

Gordon, Robert. September 5, 1995. Notes from interview with Dr. George Nichopoulos.

Hopkins, Jerry. Notes and interviews for *Elvis: The Final Years*. MVC/UMem.

Turner's Archive. January 24, 1990. Interview with Dr. George Nichopoulos re: Jerry Lee Lewis.

LETTERS

Adams, David B., PhD (Atlanta Medical & Neurological Psychology). November 8, 1990. Letter to author re: death and psychopathology.

Beatty, A. Yarnell (associate gen. counsel, Office of General Counsel, Department of Health, State of Tennessee). Letter to Daniel D. Warlick re: expert testimony.

_____. October 30, 1997. Letter to author re: application review.

Borod, Ronald S. May 11, 1981. Letter to James F. Neal re: payment on statement for legal services.

SOURCE DATA

Burchfield, Terri Miller (legislative director, Migraine Awareness Group). June 30, 1999. Letter to author re: Elvis Presley's migraine history.

Burson, Charles W. (attorney general and reporter). April 8, 1992. Letter to Brian L. Kuhn re: Shelby County Resolutions Nos. 39 and 51; Investigation of Death of Elvis Presley.

Coleman, John J. (assistant administrator of operations, Drug Enforcement Administration, U.S. Department of Justice). July 2, 1993. Letter to Daniel Brookoff, MD, PhD.

Cooper, Joe (of Tanner Companies). January 22, 1998. Letter to author re: verification of doctor who will be "boss" in the Emergency Room Clinic.

_____. (for William B. Tanner Enterprises). January 31, 1998. Letter to author re: meeting with Dr. Daniel Starnes re: reinstatement of medical license.

_____. (for William B. Tanner Jr.) February 8, 1998. Letter to author re: game plan to reinstate medical license of Dr. Nick.

Davis, Clifford Y., Jr. January 10, 1998. letter to Daniel Starnes, MD, re: testimony for Dr. George Nichopoulos.

Dodd, David T., MD (medical director, Tennessee Medical Foundation, Physicians Health Program). April 9, 1997. Letter to author re: Reinstatement of Medical License.

_____. August 5, 1997. Letter to Linda Hudgins, Administrator, Tennessee Board of Medical Examiners, re: Verification of Dr. George Nichopoulos's participation in the course "Current Topics in Substance Abuse: Physician/Patient Relationships" held at Vanderbilt University.

Drug Enforcement Administration, U.S. Department of Justice. July 23, 1993. Letter to author re: Confirmation of DEA Registration Number to prescribe Schedule 5 controlled substances.

Hendrix, Roy W., Jr. January 27, 1977. Letter to Frank J. Glankler Jr.

Koon, Wiley, MD. October 30, 1979. Letter to author re: detoxification information to use in defense.

Lewis, Jerry Lee. Letter "To Whom It May Concern" (for Tennessee Board of Medical Examiners).

Neal, James F. January 27, 1981. Letter to author re: confirmation of legal counsel in *State of Tennessee v. George C. Nichopoulos*.

_____. January 30, 1981. Letter to author re: legal agreement.

_____. March 13, 1981. Letter to author re: bill for legal services.

_____. November 9, 1981. Letter to author re: statement of expenses and services rendered.

_____. November 17, 1981. Letter to author re: final bill.

_____. January 18, 1982. Letter to author re: copy of witness expenses.

Nichopoulos, George, MD. October 19, 1976. Letter to R. Wendell Ward, MD, Medical Director, American Life Insurance Company, re: Elvis Presley medical history and complete physical.

_____. September 26, 1979. Letter to Kenneth Masterson re: legal representation.

Scanlon, Frank J. February 24, 1998. Letter to author.

_____. March 18, 1999. Letter to author.

Warlick, Daniel D. July 6, 1995. Letter to A. Yarnell Beatty re: Motion of Declaratory Ruling and Motion of Continuance.

We Care, Inc. September 4, 1989. Check to the Drug Enforcement Administration for DEA Registration Number.

LEGAL DOCUMENTS

Audiotapes of the Medical Board Hearing. January 1980.

Deposition of George Nichopoulos, MD. September 7, 1992.

Deposition of Roland William Gray, MD. September 4, 1992.

Nichopoulos, George, MD. January 2, 1980. Deposition for the Board of Medical Examiners State of Tennessee, by Frank J. Scanlon, Sr. Asst. Attorney General.

Results of assessment/psychoanalysis at Abbott Northwestern in Minnesota.

State of Tennessee Department of Health In the Matter of George Nichopoulos, MD, respondent Before the Board of Medical Examiners, Docket No. 17.16-12-0713 A.

Sworn affidavit: August 13, 2007. Robert F. Stefanow to Tennessee Board of Medical Examiners.

COURT RECORDS

Center Courts, Inc., a Tennessee Corporation, Plaintiff vs. Elvis Presley, Defendant: Complaint, March 12, 1976.

Chancery Court of Davidson County, Tennessee, No. 93-1490-1, May 21, 1993.

County Chancery Court No. 94-1511-I, May 18, 1994: Petition for Temporary Restraining Order and Temporary Injunction.

George Nichopoulos, MD, before the Board of Medical Examiners State of Tennessee, Department of Health, Docket No. 17.18-12-0713A, Notice of Charges, March 11, 1992.

George Nichopoulos, MD, before the Board of Medical Examiners State of Tennessee, Department of Health, Docket No. 17.18-12-0713A, Final Order, August 9, 1995.

George Nichopoulos, MD, v. State of Tennessee Board of Medical Examiners, Davidson County Chancery Court, April 2, 1993.

George Nichopoulos, MD, v. State of Tennessee Board of Medical Examiners, Davidson County Chancery Court No. 93-975-I, June 23, 1993: Brief of Petitioner. (Includes Motion To Voir Dire Board Members)

George Nichopoulos, MD, v. State of Tennessee Board of Medical Examiners, Davidson County Chancery Court No. 93-975-I, Aug. 12, 1993: Reply Brief of Petitioner.

George Nichopoulos, MD, v. State of Tennessee Board of Medical Examiners, Davidson County Chancery Court No. 94-1511, May 18, 1994: Petition For Temporary Restraining Order And Temporary Injunction.

George Nichopoulos, MD, v. State of Tennessee Board of Medical Examiners, Davidson.

Joe C. Davis and L. C. Anderson, Jr., individually and d/b/a D-A Enterprises Plaintiffs vs. Vernon E. Presley, Executor of the Estate of Elvis A. Presley, George C. Nichopoulos, Joseph Esposito, T. Michael McMahon and Center Courts, Inc., a Tennessee corporation, No. 78-263-III., November 1977.

Petition for Writ of Mandamus: *Board of County Commissioners of Shelby County, Tennessee, vs. Paula Taylor, State of Tennessee Registrar of Vital Records*, in the *State of Tennessee v. George C. Nichopoulos, MD*, Criminal Court, 16th Judicial Circuit, indictment, proceedings and investigative interviews.

Tennessee Board of Medical Examiners v. George C, Nichopoulos, MD, complaint, September 4, 1979.

ARTICLES

Associated Press (Chicago). "Former Bodyguard Says Elvis Had Drug Problem." *Memphis Press-Scimitar*. August 17, 1977. Page 8.

Associated Press (Memphis, TN). "Doctor Says Elvis Was Given Placebos, Not Drugs." *Anniston Star*. August 25, 1977.

Boffey, Philip M. "A Question of Treatment; New Analysis." Special to the *New York Times*. November 6, 1981.

Burk, Bill E. "Shock Envelops Presley's Family, Close Friends." *Memphis Press-Scimitar*, August 17, 1977. Page 8.

The Commercial Appeal, Scripps-Howard Publishing, 1977–1998.

Duke, Alan. "Michael Jackson's death was a homicide, coroner rules." CNN.com. September 8, 2009.

"Elvis' Body in State at Graceland; Funeral Is Scheduled Tomorrow." *Memphis Press-Scimitar*. August 17, 1977. Page 1.

"Examiner Is Firm: Heart Disease Fatal to Presley," *American Medical News*. October 12, 1979.

Goodman, Charles, and Henry Bailey. "Mourners in Waiting for Last Homecoming." *Memphis Press-Scimitar*. August 17, 1977. Page 1.

Harris, Ron and Tim Schick. "Elvis Dies Quickly at Graceland After Suffering Heart Failure." *Memphis Press-Scimitar*. August 17, 1977. Page 8.

"Investigation Clouded." *Memphis Press Scimitar*. May 3, 1980.

McLellan, Iain. "Drug Scandals Rock Our Top Country Stars." *Examiner*. April 21, 1981. Page 11.

Mehr, Bob. "Parallels in Lives, Deaths of Michael Jackson, and Elvis." Commercialappeal.com. June 28, 2009.

Memphis Press-Scimitar. 1977, 1979, 1980, 1981. Clipping re: Dr. George C. Nichopoulos medical board hearing and criminal trial (MVC/UMem).

Moore, Solomon. "Doctor Reveals Details of Michael Jackson's Autopsy Report." NYTimes.com. October 1, 2009.

SOURCE DATA

Porteous, Clark. "A Lonely Life Ends on Elvis Presley Boulevard." *Memphis Press-Scimitar*. August 17, 1977. Page 1.

"Presley's MD Struggles for a New Life." *American Medical News*. December 11, 1981.

"Schlitz to Laud Man Who Made Memphis Famous." *The Commercial Appeal*. August 21, 1977. Section A, Page 1.

Smith, Bob. "The Elvis File: Why He Had To Die." *Star*. July 15, 1997.

Stuart, Reginald. "Disclosures on Presley Drugs at Doctor's Trial Shake Fans." Special to the *New York Times*. October 25, 1981.

Thomas, William. "Presley's Death Writes New Chapter in History. *The Commercial Appeal* (Memphis, TN). August 21, 1977. Section A, Page 1.

United Press International (UPI). "Presley's Doctor on Trial over Prescriptions." *New York Times*. September 30, 1981.

DOCUMENTARIES

Elvis on Tour. Los Angeles: MGM, 1972.

Elvis: That's the Way It Is. Los Angeles: MGM, 1970.

TELEVISION SPECIALS

"Elvis." Burbank, CA: NBC. Aired December 3, 1968.

"Elvis: Aloha from Hawaii." Honolulu: Honolulu International Center Arena. Taped January 14, 1973. Broadcast live by satellite around the world.

"The Elvis Cover-Up." *20/20*. ABC News. Aired September 13, 1979, and December 27, 1979.

"Elvis in Concert." CBS. Taped in June 1977; aired October 3, 1977.

OTHER RESOURCES

Charter of Racquet Ball of Memphis, Inc.

Cotten, Lee. *All Shook Up: Elvis Day-By-Day, 1954–1977*. Ann Arbor: Popular Culture, Ink, 1992.

Lahr, Dr. Christopher J., MD. *Why Can't I Go?* Charleston: Sunburst Press, 2004.

The Physicians' Desk Reference, 1976, ed. Oradell, NJ: Medical Economics Co., 1976.

Policy Statement, Tennessee State Board of Medical Examiners, "Management of Prescribing with Emphasis on Addictive or Dependence-Producing Drugs."

Quain, Kevin, ed. *The Elvis Reader: Texts and Sources on the King of Rock 'n' Roll*. New York: St. Martin's Press, 1992.

Rules of Tennessee Board of Medical Examiners, Division of Health Related Boards, General Rules and Regulations Governing the Practice of Medicine.

Rules of Tennessee Board of Medical Examiners, Division of Health Related Boards, Rules of Procedure for Hearing Contested Cases.

Tunzi, Joseph A. *Elvis Sessions: The Recorded Music of Elvis Aaron Presley 1953–1977*. Chicago: JAT Productions, 1993.

Worth, Fred L., and Steve D. Tamerius. *Elvis: His Life from A to Z*. New York: Wings Books, 1992.

ABOUT THE AUTHOR

Photo by Kissy Nichopoulos

The George Constantine Nichopoulos family in their Memphis home in 2009. (seated: Edna; standing left to right: Dean, Kissy, Elaine, and Dr. Nick)

George Constantine Nichopoulos, the son of Greek immigrants, was born in Ridgeway, Pennsylvania, on October 29, 1927, and grew up in Anniston, Alabama. He served in the Army Medical Corps in Germany from 1946 to 1948, before enrolling at the University of the South, Sewanee, Tennessee, where he gained his BS degree in 1951.

He entered Vanderbilt University Medical School, Nashville, Tennessee, and spent a year doing research in the departments of pharmacology and anatomy there, before moving to the University of Tennessee, Memphis, to study for a doctorate in Clinical Physiology from 1953 to 1956. While there Nichopoulos developed the first artificial kidney in the South and introduced dialysis for the treatment of renal failure. At that time UT, Memphis, was the only hospital with kidney dialysis in the South, so Nichopoulos traveled through the southern states performing dialysis. He reentered Vanderbilt University Medical School in 1956 and received his MD in 1959. Following his graduation from med school he did four years of postgraduate schooling, which included three years training in internal medicine and a year training in endocrinology and neurology. During this four-year period he was in charge of the renal program at Vanderbilt and St. Thomas hospitals in Nashville.

His internship was at St. Thomas Hospital, Nashville, and his residencies were a joint venture with St. Thomas, Vanderbilt, and Nashville City Hospital from 1959 to 1963. He returned to Memphis, becoming an instructor of clinical medicine at the University of Tennessee College of Medicine from 1965 to 1968, when he was promoted to Clinical Assistant Professor, Department of Medicine. Dr. Nichopoulos served on the staff of the Baptist Memorial Hospital and Doctors Hospital in Memphis, Tennessee, and had membership at five other local hospitals.

In 1967, Dr. Nichopoulos gained entertainer Elvis Presley as a patient. After Elvis resumed his career in live entertaining, Dr. Nichopoulos accompanied him on many of his tours.

Dr Nichopoulos was a practicing partner with the Medical Group in Memphis from 1963 to 1986. He maintained a solo private medical practice until 1995, when his license was rescinded amid continued accusations of overprescribing controlled substances. Appeals for his reinstatement were denied, forcing him to find employment in the business sector as a medical consultant. Dr. Nichopoulos and his wife Edna reside in Memphis, where their daughters Kissy and Elaine and son Dean also live. Dr. Nick and Edna have four grandchildren and two great-grandchildren.

ABOUT THE WRITER

Photo by Steve Roberts ©

Author George Nichopoulos, MD, with his long-time friend and
writer Rose Clayton Phillips.

Rose Clayton Phillips is a native Memphian, who first met Elvis Presley
when he was just a teenager. Her father, Bill McAfee, was a pioneer newsreel
cameraman, whose work helped chronicle Elvis's rise to fame. She witnessed

firsthand many of the pivotal events in Elvis's career—even traveling on his final tour. As a correspondent for *Billboard* and *Rolling Stone* magazines and a freelance research/booker for ABC News, she reported on lawsuits involving the Elvis Presley Estate and Colonel Tom Parker, as well as Dr. George Nichopoulos. While working as an independent field producer, she helped develop numerous stories on both the king and Dr. Nick for *Entertainment Tonight.* She is coauthor of *Elvis Up Close: In the Words of Those Who Knew Him Best* and writer / producer of the Grammy-award-winning Best Spoken Word album: *Interviews From The Recording Sessions Of The Class Of '55*, about the Sun Records artists. Rose and her husband, Jud, live in Memphis, Tennessee.

Photo by Claudia Knos

Elvis Presley's music note on world famous Beale Street, Memphis, Tennessee.